D1432774

Courtesy of Mrs. Frank S. Stevens. From the original portrait.

JAMES E. BIRCH

"THE MAN WHO PUT AN EMPIRE ON WHEELS."

SIX HORSES

By

Captain William Banning
and George Hugh Banning

✶✶

WITH A FOREWORD BY

Major Frederick Russell Burnham, D.S.O.

CHIEF OF SCOUTS UNDER

LORD ROBERTS

✶✶

New York · THE CENTURY CO. *· London*

11852

DEDICATED TO THE MEMORY OF

PHINEAS BANNING

A PIONEER STAGEMAN OF CALIFORNIA

FOREWORD

As a small boy, when I used to ride as a mounted messenger for the Western Union, I saw one of General Phineas Banning's drivers—the eminent reinsman, John Reynolds—having an argument without words with his off leader. Watching him intently for a moment, I asked:

"How does the horse know what you want him to do?"

"I talk to him through the ribbons, sonny," he answered.

And now I have just climbed down from the box of a coach belonging to that same old stage line, a line passing through its seventy-seventh year of operation. The vehicle, itself more than a half century old, was driven by a son of the original proprietor, by a pupil of the same John Reynolds. It was one of the old "Concords," but so perfectly preserved that it typified immaculately the period of its colorful reign, the days when it might have carried Barnum and his songbird, Jenny Lind, or the tragic Booth, besides many long-forgotten patriots, together with sweethearts that later became our grandparents.

Captain William Banning, the driver, as he tooled me along behind "six of the best," sending his invisible and silent commands along the ribbons, carried me back, not to the Wild West of fancy and myth, but to an old West that I recognized for the first time in many years. No other vehicle could have done it—no other could have come rolling down from those times and found itself still in such excellent trim that it could swing about, as it were, and roll back.

So we talked of the days long ago. We talked of the Argonauts, with their creaking ox-driven wheels, or their billowing sails, impelled by the power of gold to cross the deserts and mountains, or to brave the stormy seas of Cape Horn, to overwhelm the dons in their Arcadia. We thought of those hardy adventurers in their trials and disappointments; for they soon found that nature was still making it difficult to exploit her golden hoard. A few fortunes were made along the edges of the broad valley that could be reached by the huge ox-wagons, but the great wealth lay far up in the rugged hills and cañons. Means of rapid transportation thence, and dependable communication, became then a problem so imperative that, unless the exigency could be filled, this vast, new land might easily slip away from political and social contact with the older States of the Atlantic seaboard. Even the gold, the great lure, might lie in reef and bar unmined unless some means of intercourse, swift and sure, could be provided at once.

Here, then, was the opportunity for youth to "do the impossible"; and these pages tell how it was done—

how a group of young men, headed by the immortal
Birch, provided the romantic institution by which this
country could be served (if not saved) while awaiting
the arrival of the Iron Horse.

These young men combined in their unusual per-
sonalities the power to apply the Arab's knowledge of
the horse to the mechanical perfection of wheel as
developed by the craftsmen of Concord; for theirs
was the American Coach known not only to the vast
West that it was destined to conquer, but to the wil-
dernesses of the world, including those even of the
colonies of coach-loving England. I have traveled
many thousands of miles through South Africa in
these splendid vehicles. Drawn by ten mules, whose
Boer driver used a whip so long that he could easily
reach the distant leaders, they carried as many as
twenty-two passengers to the load, and endured a
stress and strain from climate as well as country which
would have shrunk and shaken any other stage-coach
to pieces. It is no wonder that, long before these Concords made their way across the "American Desert,"
California found it necessary to import them by sail
around Cape Horn. And in view of their inimitable
qualities of excellence, great indeed was the heritage of
these young pioneers and of the empire that so depended upon them.

High in the list of the adventuresome group mentioned in these pages let me stress the name of General
Phineas Banning, to whose memory this book has been

dedicated. He had many of the qualities of the great Cecil John Rhodes of Africa—a massive frame, dynamic in action, a keen brain, violent passions, and an abundant heart. So expansive was his vision that he could see without jealousy the end of his brain child, the coach and six. He could see the passing of power from the ribbons of leather to the ribbons of steel, the prancing thoroughbreds driven from the roads by the snorting steam-engine. All of us in California are reaping the benefit of his having lived among us; for during the years of our blindness it was he who kept alive the vision of things yet to be. Captain Banning, the son, is the last of the great drivers. One wonders if the silent message that passes from and to his beloved six is not that of the Roman gladiators—"We who are about to die salute you."

These are not sad thoughts; for each generation does its bit and passes down to the rest, and in this instance should do so without a pang. For close by stands a slender youth, a scion of the old general, the writer of these pages, an interpreter for him who "talks through the ribbons"; and, while not building the empire with thundering hoofs and wheels, he rises from it and its mother institutions to soar on man-made wings and look out upon it from the domain of the eagle, to view it in panorama, to sketch and recall it as it was.

F. R. Burnham

Los Angeles, California

ACKNOWLEDGMENT

For all the bare points of history involved—such chronicles of old record, for example, as any one might have assembled—I as the compiler and the writer alone am amenable, leaving to my collaborator, my uncle, William Banning, other responsibilities more vital to this work and more to the purpose of our undertaking.

It is not enough to say: without his life's experience as a stageman, without his power to re-create an old environment by means of his living models in stages and teams, without his spirit, patience, and careful technical direction, this book could not have been attempted; for, indeed, many scribes, unattended by any named partner in authorship, have made similar admissions in justice to some indispensable keystone which has chanced merely to be in a position to support their labors. But in this case, as it happens, there is to acknowledge a great deal more than such indispensable support.

In fact, to whatever extent we may have approached our chief aims—portrayed the singular *personality* of the stage-coach world—just so far have I been able to grasp his conceptions, hold to his sense of direction, survey our field through his eyes, and, as it were, express him rather than myself. In a word, with the sincerity of all else at stake, his and not mine is the picture, if I have painted one. His, too, *in totum*, is the Afterword—"Commentaries of a Stage Driver."

With respect to the historical matter of old record through these pages, a general omission of source notes was agreed upon only after an experiment had proved that any consistent method of documentation would demand an average of at least five lines of notes to the page, these notes exceptionally useless, being referable for the main part only to a few libraries of the country. (See Bibliography.) Thousands of old newspaper extracts, one balanced against another, all weighed against time and otherwise verified or listed for amendment through as many other records as seemed warranted or available, would scarcely lend themselves to the purpose—would, as a documentary prop, amount to no more than an academic swagger-stick. With a few apologies, therefore, we have foregone the scholarly gesture.

In further acknowledgment, a lasting indebtedness toward Mrs. Frank S. Stevens of Massachusetts is expressed with what gratitude may be readily understood, her contributions, through correspondence and interview, representing by all odds the most precious results of this research—old letter files devoted to the writings of California Stage Company officials, old relics of the Pony Express and of the *Central America* disaster, photographs of old portraits, paintings and daguerreotypes, to include, above all, those treasures shedding more light upon the historic figure of Birch.

But it is fairly certain that no such bounteous friend as Mrs. Stevens would have been known to these chronicles but for the good work of Howard M. Chapin of the Rhode Island Historical Society and W. S. Ball and W. E. Stone of the "Providence Journal" in their successful attempts to pick up a lost trail. To them, moreover, through Mrs. Stevens, I am further indebted for my subsequent acquaintance and profitable interviews in California with Mrs. H. J. Maginnity of the old staging family of Kelton (into which Birch married)—indebted, too, for my chats with Israel Brayton of Massachusetts and the members of his genial family, who have likewise shown an active interest in the lives of these important Forty-niners.

For free access to the rich diggings of the Bancroft Collection in the University of California Library a word of the deepest appreciation is extended to the hard workers therein, particularly to Dr. Herbert E. Bolton and to Dr. H. I. Priestly for their suggestions and generous regard, tolerating as they did my many months of book-ferreting, file-perusing, desk-taking ubiquity as cheerfully almost as they did that of my wife. (For she was wherever I was not.) But what other sweet and dusty environment could have held us so long, whetting one appetite as it partially satisfied another, I know not, and doubt its existence.

To the distinguished scout of three continents, Major Frederick R. Burnham, gratitude is not merely expressed but dwelt upon in memory, not alone for that contribution closest to this page but for others more difficult to find. We are also grateful to his son, Roderick Burnham, for pleasant associations as well as for some splendid photography by him in Stagedom.

And to my sister, Mrs. John C. Macfarland, I am indebted even more than usual; but that is such a private affair that I race on, thinking of the Pony Express and the son of one of its proprietors—the Hon. Greene Majors of California, whose interest in the subject, as manifested through our discussions and arguments, has been prized along with the splendid photograph of his father and other things of great value to this writing. I wish also to thank Mrs. Martha Vance Kimball not only for several photographs of historic worth but for graphic descriptions of her life as the young mistress of an overland stage station. Nor can I pass on without hearing the old voice of Mark Regan, telling stories of his life as a driver in the Overland days.

For other profitable contacts through correspondence, interview or association I am obliged to Captain Robert Howe Fletcher, Professor George Barron, Frank Cliff, Frank Morrison, Chester Lee White, Captain L. Robinson, William E. Connelley, Dr. Robert Glass Cleland, Thomas C. Mayhew, Sarah Bixby Smith, Mrs. J. J. Mellus, Mrs. William Hood, Frank

H. Stevens, Joseph Henry Jackson, Paul Augsberg, A. M. Harbinson, Mr. and Mrs. John Bruce, Harold Lamb, L. D. Clark, Captain A. M. Turner, John McGann, William Gael, William Foeurr, W. B. Gibson, Jacabo Chavez, Miss Mary Corcoran, E. G. Bangs, Alexander Horn, John C. Macfarland, and many more whose names have slipped my mind but whose contributions pass before me in taunting review. Also, for various courtesies the obligation is extended to "The Argonaut" and the M. H. De Young Museum of San Francisco, and to the Rhode Island Historical Society, "The Sunset Magazine," the Wells Fargo Bank and Trust Company, "Touring Topics," the Kansas State Historical Society, the Los Angeles and the Carmell libraries, and to the Bartlett Collection (library) of Vermejo, New Mexico.

All this not to mention again one who is still in my mind—my wife.

G. H. B.

New York, November 1929

CONTENTS

PART ONE

THE WHIP OF BIRCH

PART TWO

THE WHIP OF BUTTERFIELD

PART THREE

THE WHIP OF MAJORS AND RUSSELL

xvii

CONTENTS

ILLUSTRATIONS

xix

PART ONE

THE WHIP OF BIRCH

SIX HORSES

Chapter I

THE MAN WHO WOULD BE KING

STAGES, with their teams of six, are backed up in long rows, sweating porters and baggage-masters in front and behind. John Chinaman, with long tail wound at the back of his head, is running distractedly through the crowd in search of a lost bundle; anxious women, prolific in crinoline and gorgeous in silks and satins, are fretting and scolding over crushed bandboxes; and stern-looking men of an official cast are shouting fiercely:

"This way, gents! Over here with your baggage! Bring it along if you want it weighed; if you don't, it won't go—that's all!"

And there is the machine that weighs; and there stands the inexorable gentleman that marks off the weights—ten, forty, sixty, ninety pounds per passenger—thirty pounds allowed; all extra baggage twenty-five cents per pound.

"Fifteen dollars for you, sir." "Twenty-five for you, sir." "Forty-six for you, madam." "Seventy-five for you, miss—heavy trunk that, miss."

3

"Oh, dear! Oh, goodness gracious! Must I pay seventy-five dollars for my trunk?"

"Yes, miss—sorry for it—no getting over it."

"Oh!"

"Quick, if you please, ladies and gents! Stages behind time—won't get to Placerville before dark!"

"All aboard!" and off goes stage No. 1.

"Pile in, gents. Get down from that front seat, you, sir—place engaged. All aboard!" and off goes stage No. 2.

"Pitch in, Cap—all set!" and stage No. 3 follows through the dusty clouds that cover the road and the hillsides. And so on till we are all fairly in and off, looking back with fervent thanks that we are clear at last. . . .

It was as J. Ross Browne found and described it on a lively day in the middle sixties when there existed a daily stage-coach service across the plains—a distance of nearly two thousand miles, coursed within seventeen days.

It is certain [he writes] there is no such a country in the world for feats of horse-flesh. . . . The length of our stage routes, the rapidity with which we travel upon them, and the facilities afforded by the expresses, are matters of astonishment to the people of Europe, who have not the faintest idea of the real difficulties to be overcome in carrying enterprises into effect in a wild country like ours.

During my sojourn in Germany, I received a letter

From a modern photograph by Keystone.

THE OLD TYPICAL

CONCORD COACH AND TEAM, DIRECTLY DESCENDANT FROM A LINE OF THE EARLY FIFTIES WHOSE EQUIPMENTS HAVE BEEN CAREFULLY MAINTAINED TO REPRESENT ACCURATELY THE OLD PIONEER INSTITUTION.

from California by Pony Express in less than four weeks after it was written; and it was not until I showed the date and express stamp and carefully explained the whole matter that I was enabled to overcome the incredulity of my Teutonic friends. The idea of such a feat being accomplished by horse-flesh was something they could not comprehend. Nor could they quite reconcile their notions of the practicable that we had spanned the continent with our stages—crossing deserts and mountains, from San Francisco to Missouri, as they would cross the cultivated plains and well-graded hills of their native country.[1]

Such enterprise was, moreover, unparalleled in the world's annals; for the world had never, perhaps, made such demands. It was a natural development, and a naturally rapid development with, not unlikely, the continued unity of the very nation at stake.

The prodigious gold rush of forty-nine was followed by a period of some thirteen years before any Pacific Railroad measure became a law, not to mention the seven additional years required for the law to become a railroad. It was in spite of the fact that the earliest floods of westward emigration had put the project rather clearly in the light of an exigency. As early as 1850, with California's admission into statehood, alarmists were not alone in their misgivings that the retention of perhaps half the new Western empire might depend upon the immediate driving of

[1] "Adventures in the Apache Country," 308–315.

spikes and the clenching of iron bands across the continent.

Stage lines, real stage lines with regular and frequent relays over the wilderness to fill the temporary need, might have been vaguely suggested by the crude night-camping mule wagons that trekked with the mail and occasional passengers from the Missouri frontiers to Santa Fé or to the Mormon city at Salt Lake; but for all that any system of horse transportation might have meant toward the preservation of national ties, there was to choose, it seemed, between the utterly inadequate and the utterly fantastic or impossible. The delay of the railroad was not to be taken lightly.

The very wilderness, with its unconquered nations of Indians, its deserts, its Continental Divide, its coastal barriers—the vast, vague map of the future —presented such uncertainties that it was not difficult to fancy as many national boundaries as those over the Continent of Europe. The virtual principality of Mormons, which often appeared to be waiting for the day—*der Tag*—when Uncle Sam might see fit to take issue with its attitude of independence—here was a slight manifestation of possibilities. But the youthful State of California, with her appalling increase of population, with her heavy infusion of foreign blood, young blood, and with her national barriers and resources—here were real potentialities; and they could not be overlooked.

Ties with the new State of the Pacific were more sound, no doubt, than all of the East was prepared to believe; but they were based to a considerable extent upon the promise of benefits which were being everlastingly withheld. The bond, though perhaps stanchly elastic, was stretching; and it was a stretch more like that of a hopeful imagination than of any pervading sense of national allegiance.

But this situation was not the most ominous one. The extended delay of rail legislation was a far lesser menace in itself than the circumstances causing the delay. For the same conditions of broadly divided national interests, leading rapidly and surely toward civil war, were likewise throwing one political faction against the other on the question of what overland route should be favored by Federal appropriations. Any feasible line of communication which happened to pass through Northern territories was sure to be condemned by the South and *vice versa*.

Thus, at a critical time when the ties between the North and the South were being tensed toward their point of breaking, those between the East and the West were being put to an unwonted test. Something had to be done; and suffice it to say that *perhaps* the stage-coach did it, idle though it may be to speculate on what might have been the history and geography of any country had worse come to worst. But considering the tremendous rôle that the old vehicle assumed, and the visionary aspect which that rôle first presented, one is apt to look for a genius among the pioneers—some one who perceived the opportunity, asked for no precedent but simply drove in to fill the breach.

There was such a genius—a man, broadly, whom nobody knows. Not as many as two consecutive pages of history or biography have heretofore been devoted to his memory; but he died as the emperor of the whole West-American stage-coach institution; and it may be said of him fairly that he put an empire on wheels. He was Jim Birch, a Yankee. He is James E. Birch, with middle name lost even to his surviving kin, although some of them dwell in the mansion which he built from the gold-dust that swirled up from the fast wheels of his pioneer stage.

It was with the creaking of ox-yokes and the slogging of cloven hoofs that he made his first journey to the Pacific Coast. And from the big muddy Missouri, along the green of the Platte, over the passes of the Rocky Mountains, and across deserts beyond, there were moving the fleets of young men like himself, the Argonauts of forty-nine—one white, monotonous, almost endless file. It was contracting and expanding, stopping here and starting there, yet in the grip, it would seem, of but one irresistible power, winding in such fiber as the maps of empires are made of, such stuff as romance is spun from—material like

Birch, and also like Frank Shaw Stevens, who was fairly a part of Birch.

Now, in the course of their four months' journey from Providence, Rhode Island, to Sacramento, California, they were rocking in their saddles, side by side, relaying the cries from other horsemen in advance, and inhaling the dust of an interminable caravan. Dust and more dust, but they enjoyed it; they were dusty by trade—they were, or had been, stage drivers.

Whether or not they would ever "drive stage" again they could not have predicted with much certainty. But once a man had learned to hold the whip, to wield it and to handle the multiple lines; once he had trained his foot to the delicate manipulation of the brake and gloried in the sight of four or six horses pattering along before him, responding by shades of movement to his every whim, he was married to an art and could not hope to abandon it without surrendering much of himself. There was an infinite glamour to his calling. His whip had been his scepter and his box a throne. He had held the sway of the road and all that fringed it, from the little boys that tossed their caps as he passed, or the guests of the tavern who hung on his words, or the farmer's wife who urged him to sample her biscuits and cider, to the eyes that peeped at him from upstairs windows and the small handkerchief that sometimes waved.

Knight of the Reins! Here he comes! There he goes! He knew what it was to be king.

Young Birch and Stevens were not, therefore, of any very humble origin, although now they were learning what it was to be looked upon simply as any mere Tom, Dick, or Harry. What was a driver, or even a reinsman, a master out here in this wilderness where the need of him as yet was wholly nil?

It was true—not a coach wheel turned in any land from the Missouri River to the Pacific shores. Some day, perhaps, some one would lay on the whip; but now travelers shifted for themselves and cared not so long as they "got there." The whole affair seemed only as a temporary fling. The New West, the new waste, was to be shorn of its gold; then . . . home again!

Thus Birch may have been thinking in rather broad transcontinental terms even at this early date; and if already his visionary travels involved a stage route of his own across this wild expanse, perhaps he was not alone in his fancies. There were rumors, for one thing, of a firm in St. Louis, bent on establishing a wagon service of a kind to ply between the Missouri frontiers and California, carrying some hundred and twenty passengers to the trip at $200 a head. It was an enterprise which, like several others of the kind, was destined to die in the embryo; and Birch was too practical a stageman to think of operating a mere passenger mule train with any hope of success.

But there were many other stagemen bumping

along somewhere or other in the line—Charles Mc-
Laughlin, perhaps, and Warren F. Hall, J. B. Crandall, John Dillon, other whips not incapable of
driving between the lines of history. In short, here in
this caravan were embodied all the potentialities—the
modes and methods, the habits and traditions—the
best blood of New England's old stage-coach order.
It was flowing toward a fertile field, the richest soil
for which it could possibly have hoped. It was moving
toward a land where it was bound to flourish independent of mail contracts—of government, politics
—and to flourish to such an extent that a line extended eastward across the continent would appear
not only as practicable but as a natural growth. The
transplanted Yankee system was to know an eastward rather than a westward progression. From California, as more than a predominating influence, an
improved New England school was to become the
school of the plains.

All this could scarcely have been foreseen by the
many whips now on their way to the new El Dorado.
But dreams were at large, and there were probably
few more glittering than those which accompanied
the train of Birch and Stevens. Twenty-one years
being the age of them both, they were apt to have had
great expectations; yet Stevens appeared as sophis-
ticated and deliberate as the typical driver of New
England, openly suspicious of anything that glit-
tered, to say nothing of the yarns from El Dorado.

Birch was different—electrical, his eyes burning and sparkling as from a runaway dynamo within him. But he had himself well in control; and his mastery cannot be more clearly demonstrated than by his actions upon reaching the Gold Coast with the wild men of forty-nine.

Here, amid the carnival whirl of what-not in big boots and scraggly or braided beards, in sombreros and flaming serapes, in raven coats and craven stovepipes, in pig-tails and silken jackets—amid all that gyrated between Sacramento and Hangtown, between gambling-houses and churches, between temporary distraction and permanent dementia—Birch, by his equanimity, must have appeared madder than them all. He began doing only what he had done at home. He commenced "driving stage."

Stevens seemed also to be underestimating possibilities. He had invested in a wooden shack, a hotel in the center of Sacramento City—the center, that was, so long as two merchant vessels, retailing wares from their decks, remained in their present berths along the river bank. There were other rival establishments. "Eating is Done Here" was the sign on one; "Tip-Top Accommodations for Men and Beasts" was the boast of another; "Rest for the Weary and Storage for Trunks" was the appeal of the building of Stevens.

Here James Birch may have stored a saddle roll and wished his old friend well; but he, just now at

From an old lithograph.

SAN FRANCISCO IN THE WINTER OF FORTY-NINE

ORIGINAL ILLUSTRATION FROM "MOUNTAINS AND MOLEHILLS,"
BY FRANK MARRYAT.

Courtesy of the Bancroft Library. From an old lithograph.

SACRAMENTO CITY, 1849

ORIGINAL ILLUSTRATION FROM JOHN M. LETTS'S "CALIFORNIA
ILLUSTRATED."

least, was not seeking rest. There were relay stations to organize and stock to buy; and, while his route was to be only about thirty miles in extent, the investment and responsibilities were considerable. Several sporadic attempts at the staging business by rancheros and others (who knew nothing about it) had already resulted in so many failures. There was that to consider. Still, there was reason to believe that he, Birch, an experienced driver, was not taking quite their chances.

There was, moreover, a certain Alexander Todd, pioneering in the Western express business, just as Birch was pioneering along stage lines. Todd, too, could point back to premature efforts and failures of others; but having invested in a rowboat on the Rio San Joaquin, now he was prospering. If Todd could deliver mail to Stockton at a rate of four dollars per letter, carry gold-dust back in butter kegs at other such rates of profit, tax his oarsmen (his power plant) sixteen dollars a head, going and coming, and divide sometimes as much as a thousand dollars a day with his partner, surely the prospects were bright enough in the business of transportation. And thirty dollars a passenger would be no presumptuous rate of fare for a thirty-mile drive by stage.

In any event, Birch appeared one morning in September with an old rancho wagon. He was perched upon it in as stately a manner as though on the box of a Concord coach fresh from the shops of Abbot-

Downing. Holding some bull-whacker's lash as a true linesman would hold a stage-whip, he humored four nervous mustangs, four Mexican broncos that were apparently stage-struck before the gathering throngs. But it was:

"All aboard for Mormon Island! Forks of the American River! All aboard!"

It was all aboard for the maiden trip; all aboard, incidentally, for the very inception of everything which was to be regarded in days to come as West-American staging. He had conceived the embryo of a colossus; it was to become a giant even under his patronage, and stand prepared to meet a national crisis before passing from his control.

Blanket rolls, guns, and boots; picks and shovels and tin pans; hairy faces and war-whoops; wild horses but master reins. . . .

"All aboard!"

Chapter II

THE EARLY STAGES

THERE was to be established in the following year (1850), over an old mail route between Independence, Missouri, and Santa Fé, an isolated and rather forlorn mule-wagon concern which, even after more than a decade of operation, would boast only several relay stations over a distance of about 850 miles! A few other similar but still more primitive systems for the carriage of mail in various parts of the plains region were forthcoming shortly; but they were to be purely trekking institutions. And at present these camping-out lines could no more suggest a solution to the overland problem than did Birch's line of stock in California. The railroad was the project. One heard nothing but railroad.

There were arguments on the subject of routes for the laying of tracks, and of negotiable passes through the high Sierra Nevadas, as though the locomotive were just outside, whistling for some one to open a gate. During 1849, and a brief several years thereafter, there was a locomotive attached to the general train of thought from the Atlantic Coast to California.

We want the railroad [cried the "New York Tribune" while the year was yet 1850] and cannot have it an hour too soon. If it were done to-morrow the difficulty would not be to find business enough, but to do all that would offer. California is a State of this Union, but is 40 days' journey from the seat of government. She should not be above ten days; she must not be if we would have our Republican Empire hold together and realize in the future all the greatness we so fondly imagine.[1]

The South had recently made another of her periodic gestures toward secession. As for California—"each year, and she grows more powerful, populous and wealthy," the "Tribune" concluded; "the tie that binds her to the confederation will become weaker unless it be strengthened by iron bands."

Roaring steam of this nature was being let off with equal force in Washington, St. Louis, New Orleans, and elsewhere, not to mention the volumes of it that were generated in the various meetings, conventions, newspaper offices, and all spheres of common converse on the Pacific Coast.

Albeit, nearly two decades were to pass before the advent of rails across the continent. There was strife ahead, and enough of it without a civil war—more than enough arising from the railroad itself. Coveted by the South to serve Southern territory and by the North to serve its own, the project was soon to become so involved in sectional wrangling as to be

---

[1] Quoted by the "California Courier," November 6, 1850.

classed with hopes deferred. If visible ties of union were required to meet the pending crisis, there was meaning to the crack of a pioneer's whip, to his cry of "All aboard!"

To Birch himself, it seems, there was a far-reaching significance involved; but it was of a rather personal and private nature. It had to do with a young girl in New England, Julia Chase, stepdaughter of his former employer, Otis Kelton of Providence. It had to do with ways and means of returning to her with what fortune in gold would be needed to support a wife.

Thus Birch was bound to the country he had left by a wisp of hair. California, as the "New York Tribune" might well have considered along with its fears of disunion, was likewise bound to the nation that claimed it by myriads of similar wisps—dark ones, light ones, red, white, and all but blue ones; but of all these, there was one to warrant some special regard.

The romance involved in the life of Birch (which was also the romance of Stevens) was to have a peculiar but positive bearing upon his public career and hence, providentially, even upon the development of overland transportation throughout the West.

Frank Stevens did not join his friend Birch at once in the business of staging; and in fact his national significance as a stageman is of a rather singular nature.

It is true that his biography might accord him a conspicuous place among the earlier and later proprietors of important lines; that it might recall him, for instance, as having formed apparently the first and most perfect link in one of the later great overland chains, or as having served many years as an active vice-president, and later as a mainstay, of what was at one time the largest stage-coach firm in the world, or as having been a financial power behind one early overland line. All this was a part of his career; but it was the least of it. Alone, it would have placed him in a class of splendid pioneer whips who, though they served to put an empire on wheels, are all too numerous to name. And his other—his greater enterprises—unfortunately are not to be found in Stagedom. But this fact remains:

Frank Stevens was a friend of Birch; his life is inextricable from the romantic saga of Birch; and to Birch—first and last—belongs the story of a very noteworthy pioneer phase.

Now, however, Stevens was merely saving a few generous pinches of "dust," trying to content himself, perhaps, with "Rest for the Weary and Storage for Trunks," while stages went clattering off to the mines and back with a share of their gold. Birch, having led off in the race, had been joined by others. The rumble of his wheels had been accompanied by a prospering jingle and attracted men of his calling from many parts of the country. Never before, in the world of hoofs and wheels, had there appeared such unbounded opportunities.

Travel—it was the impulse and the act and the life. There were fairly no moorings: neither home nor bonnet nor bib. There were restless young men in droves; there was the atmosphere of adventure with prospects everywhere. Be it slump or boom here or there in the gold-fields, the stages packed them coming and going. They sheared the gold fleece from their will-o'-the-wisps at a rate as high as a dollar to the mile. Soon there was scarcely a place in the whole mining region where four and six horse teams were not leaving their tracks.

Down the craggy mountains, loaded with passengers and express, came the stage, the driver with one foot, two arms, both shoulders, and all fingers working, his body swaying like a sailor's to the motion of a ship, his leaders dancing at the brink of damnation, wheels striking sparks out of granite, flicking chips into space, while passengers stared out over the blue tops of pines, chewing their cigars to a pulp. It was a common spectacle; miles by the hundreds were being rolled out every day.

The precocious nature of the yearling institution is suggested in part through the "Recollections" of California's first American governor, Peter Burnett. News of "the Department's" leap into statehood during the fall of 1850 had already thrown San Francisco into happy riot, but had yet to be despatched to the capitol at San José. The governor himself joined the race among bearers, his vehicle a stage-coach, his driver one J. B. Crandall,[1] a new part-owner with Warren Hall of the line.

"He was one of the celebrated stagemen," observes Burnett, who might have added, by the way, that Crandall, after a very enviable career among the pioneers of his kind, was to be the first to span the Sierra Nevadas with a stage route. But at this early juncture he was regarded only as "a most excellent man . . . a cool, kind but determined and skillful driver."

"There were two rival lines to San José," Burnett goes on. And their quaint advertisements, to interrupt the late governor again, may be appropriately reprinted here so that we may select our own vehicle or driver in the race to San José. These notices appeared in the "Pacific News" during the latter months of 1850.

This was a time [says Peter Burnett] to test their speed.

After passing over the sandy road to the mission, there was some of the most rapid driving that I have ever witnessed. . . . The people flocked to the road to see what caused our fast driving and loud shouting, and without slackening our speed in the slightest

---

[1] In some of the advertisements of the day this name was spelled Crandal, and is so printed in the accompanying reproduction.

degree, we took off our hats, waved them around our heads, and shouted at the top of our voices:

"California is admitted to the Union!"

Thus flew Crandall's team over the dry, hard prairie lands, and onward, through lightning relays, toward the capitol of the State. And there was Crandall himself, known as "the prince of drivers," with the governor beside him, racing on through the dust, through the yellow, whisking grasses and glades of oaks, neck and neck at times with a rattling rival, yet calmly watching his horses with a knowledge of their separate capacities, calling them by name, holding them in, telling each what to do, signaling with the most precise movements of individual or multiple lines, urging them at last, forging ahead. . . .

Ackley & Maurison's opposition advertised "60 miles, in about Six hours," but Ackley & Maurison were to taste the dust of "Berford"—of Hall & Crandall. Crandall had passed. It was fitting that he should have. It was fitting that the governor should be the first to bring the news to his seat of government. But it was perhaps more fitting that it should have been driven home thus to the heart of the new State aboard a stage-coach, and with such a splendid reinsman, and future blazer of overland roads, upon the box.

They had stretched on into San José. California admitted to the Union! Steamer news! California admitted!

Almost literally she had come in on wheels. And

it may have been aboard the typical American coach from Concord, New Hampshire; for the first of an endless succession of them to be imported by clipper around Cape Horn had already appeared, drawn by six splendid bays, in San Francisco (June 24, 1850) several months before Crandall's race.

Upon that occasion—the advent, it appears, of the first real coach of all Trans-Mississippi Stagedom [1]— large crowds had turned out to marvel and to reminisce, to be carried, as one editor was already able to imagine, "several thousand miles over the hills and far away" to The States.

Long since recognized there as the only perfect passenger vehicle in the world, it was an epoch-making Yankee creation whose excellence, in the light of its purpose, had never been, and was never to be, duplicated by other manufacturers. Abbot, Downing & Company alone knew how to make them. With a record (now mostly lost) dating back to 1813, it is not surprising that by 1858 this historic firm, covering four acres of ground in Concord, New Hampshire, was to boast "the largest factory in the United States," [2] with buyers in Mexico, South America, and the colonies even of coach-building England, including Australia and South Africa, one

---

[1] See (San Francisco) "Alta California," June 25, 1850—a date exactly five days before a coach, probably of the Troy or Concord make, is said to have pulled out on a maiden trip from Independence, Missouri, for Santa Fé.

[2] "Sacramento Union," July 31, 1858.

fourth of the yearly output being marked for export. There were reasons for this popularity.

The conveyance itself, as one cannot be reminded too often, was not the worn, torn, dead thing of our museums, much less the grotesque rattletrap of our fiction, drama, and other oft-profaning arts, but a resplendent and proud thing—a heavy but apparently a light thing of beauty and dignity and life. It was as tidy and graceful as a lady, as inspiring to the stagefaring man as a ship to a sailor, and had, incidentally, like the lady and the ship, scarcely a straight line in its body.

With trim decking and panels of the clearest poplar, and with stout frame of well-seasoned ash, this body, in all of its tri-dimensional curves, fairly held itself together by sheer virtue of scientific design and master joinery, for very little iron was used; and this, where needed, was iron only of the best Norway stock.

It was a body design evolved as a pleasing modification from the early nineteenth-century types, shaped somewhat like an egg, but surviving in this period only as "cuts" for advertisements. The newer type, the typical, was, among other things, far more commodious, having ample and well-upholstered space inside for nine passengers. Outside there was room for at least a dozen more, while the "boots" —the cargo holds of the front and rear—devoured mail bags, express boxes, and baggage, if not an oc-

From a modern photograph.

CONCORD MAIL COACH

BUILT BY ABBOT, DOWNING & COMPANY OF CONCORD, NEW
HAMPSHIRE, 1875; IN USE TO-DAY AS A PLEASURE VEHICLE.

Courtesy of Sarah Bixby Smith.

CONCORD STAGE WAGON

GENUINE ABBOT-DOWNING "MUD-WAGON," ONCE OPERATED
BY FLINT, BIXBY & COMPANY ON THE (CALIFORNIA) COAST
LINE; MAINTAINED AS A RELIC TO-DAY BY THE BIXBY FAMILY.

casional stowaway or some passenger desiring to curl up for a little nap.

"Thorough-braces"—two lengths of manifold leather straps of the thickest steer hide—suspended this heavy structure, allowed it to rock fore and aft, and, incidentally, to perform a vital duty beyond the province of any steel springs. It was a function of such importance to the Western staging world that we may hazard the contention that an empire, as well as the body of its coach, once rocked and perhaps depended upon thorough-braces.

Without them, at least, there could have been no staging to meet a crying need. Without them over the rugged wilderness, any vehicle carrying the loads that had to be carried, maintaining such speed as the edicts of staging demanded, would have been efficient only as a killer of horses. For thorough-braces, while they served the purpose of springs to a very adequate extent, had the prime function of acting as shock-absorbers for the benefit of the team. By them violent jerks upon the traces, due to any obstruction in the road, were automatically assuaged and generally eliminated. It was the force of inertia—the forward lunge and the upward lurch of the rocking body—that freed the wheels promptly from impediment, and thus averted each shock before it came upon the animals. Passengers could tolerate a little buffeting, while the coach itself had been made to withstand any shock that any road could impose, and to survive this punishment through a lifetime at least, given the usual care.

Each spoke of the Concord wheel, hand-hewn from the clearest ash, was the result of a series of painstaking selections, carefully weighed and balanced in the hand, and fitted to rim and hub (where eyes could not stray) as snugly as any surface joint in the best of joinery. So well seasoned was the whole that it was practically insensible to the climatic changes in any part of the world. Africa proved the fact for Major Frederick R. Burnham, who saw the wheels of many wagons shrink, warp, and go to pieces, the Concord wheel standing alone and holding its shape. Such qualities of durability in a coach weighing about 2,500 pounds may not appear at once to be the soundest boast, but when it is added that no other vehicle of equal capacity, and few enough of any capacity, ran as easily over the average road, there is little more to be said.

It is no wonder that California, with the rugged mining zones of her mountains to face, began importing Concords before the year of 1850 was half done, and no wonder that scores of them were to follow, though it were by the route of Cape Horn. The growing demand was everywhere apparent. Fifteen months of existence, and the local system could count at least fifteen busy stage firms and a mileage sufficient to extend suggestively well-nigh to the Rocky Mountains.

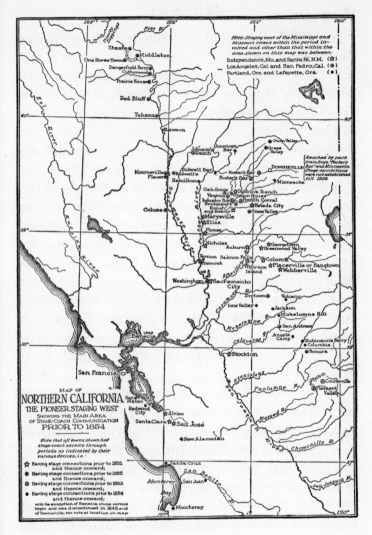

NOTE: Staging west of the Mississippi and
Missouri rivers within the period involved and other than that within the
area shown on this map was between:

Independence, Mo., and Santa Fé, N.M. (☆)
Los Angeles, Cal. and San Pedro, Cal. (◉)
Portland, Ore. and Lafayette, Ore. (•)

North Yreka Spgs
Pitt R.
Shasta
One Horse Town
Middletor.
Dangerfield Ferry
Cottonwood
Prairie House
Red Bluff
Tehama
Lawson
Honey L.

40°   40°

American Bar
Johnson's Ranch
Onion Valley
Grass Valley
Reached by pack
train from "Forbes'y
Bar" and Minnesota.
Stage connections
were not established
till 1859.
DOWNIEVILLE
Monroeville
Didwell Bar
Placerville
Bidwell's
Hamiltons
Foster's Bar
Foster's Bar
Minnesota
Oak Grove
Dobbin's Ranch
Virginia
Oregon House
Industry Bar
French Corral
Bridgeport
Nevada City
Rough
and Ready
Grass Valley
Colusa
Marysville
Eliza
Phums
Nicholas
Georgetown
Auburn
Greenwood Valley
Vernon
Salmon Falls
Coloma
Fremont
Mormon
Placerville or Hangtown
Island
Webberville
Washington
Sacramento
City
Drytown
Volcano
Ione Valley
Jackson
Mokelumne Hill
San Andreas
Angels
Camp
Robinson's Ferry
Columbia
Stockton
Sonora

39°   39°

38°   38°

1849
Benecia
San Francisco
Hill's Cr.
Coulterville
Pleasant
Valley

MAP OF
NORTHERN CALIFORNIA
THE PIONEER STAGING WEST
SHOWING THE MAIN AREA
OF STAGE-COACH COMMUNICATION
PRIOR TO 1854

San
Mateo
Redwood
City
Alviso
Santa Clara
San José
New Alameda

Note that all towns shown had
stage-coach service through
periods as indicated by their
various devices, i. e.:

☆ Having stage connections prior to 1851
and thence onward;
● Having stage connections prior to 1852
and thence onward;
◉ Having stage connections prior to 1853
and thence onward;
• Having stage connections prior to 1854
and thence onward;
with the exception of Benecia whose service
began and was discontinued in 1849, and
of Downieville, see note at location on map

Santa Cruz
Monterey
San Juan
Bay
Monterey

Compiled by the authors

It was in fifty-one when Frank Stevens sprang into the race and founded the "Pioneer Line" from Sacramento to Hangtown or Placerville—the same line which later old Crandall was to project beyond the Sierra Nevada to a point not six hundred miles from Salt Lake City.

Birch had extended his route considerably and was adding two more. He was out to conquer along with a dozen other rising firms in whose dusty tracks opposition rose and fell. The traveler of fifty-one had only to visit one of the larger staging centers—Marysville, Stockton, or, above all, Sacramento—in order to appreciate their numbers and the competition involved.

In Sacramento, for example, he might have stopped at the Crescent City Hotel—a new establishment of seventy-five rooms, extra bunk space, and with coffee, beans, and venison for breakfast by candle-light at five in the morning. But even at this early hour, there was always consolation in the fact that some hundred other travelers had also been routed from their blankets. By disposing hurriedly of breakfast, moreover, he could spend time to advantage at the bar.

This room, before the stages pulled away, was crowded with red or blue shirted miners in boots, with their guns and various accouterments, with their patchwork trousers and fiery complexions, all bound for various diggings; and what a tremendous circus parade of vehicles was required to take them there!

Outside this morning, as every morning, the congestion was a hub-rubbing and swearing affair. Stages stood four abreast, occupying the whole wide street for a distance of some sixty-five yards. And despite this very early date, though the four-horse ranch wagon still prevailed, there were many real Concord coaches among them, and teams—to quote J. D. Borthwick, an Englishman who viewed the scene— "as good as ever galloped with her Majesty's mail." [1]

The animals were pawing and snorting, grooms at the leaders' heads trying to quiet them. Drivers were humoring them and calling out the towns of their devious routes. Runners were living up to their names, hustling here and there, yelping and shouting:

"This way, sir! Nevada City! Over here for Nevada! Over there for Stockton and Sonora! Birch stages connect for Sonora and the Southern Mines!"

"Shasta! Here! Shasta, sir, and Tehama! Baxter & Munroe stages for Tehama and Shasta! . . . One-Horsetown, you say!"

"No. Georgetown!"

"Horsetown! You bet! That's us! One-Horsetown!"

And the Georgetown aspirant, carpet-bag and all,

[1] "American horses" from Ohio, Kentucky, and elsewhere, driven in from over the plains, were rapidly supplanting the native mustangs in the staging world. Borthwick says that at this time dray horses were being imported from Sydney; cab horses were the finest—worth from $1,000 to $1,500 each; that a three-minute horse was the "slowest worth driving," that a two-forty horse was not considered fast, and that stage-coaches sometimes covered "60 miles in about five hours" (which of course *was* considered fast). See Borthwick, "Three Years in California."

was fairly boosted into the Horsetown and Shasta
coach, while the runner went leaping off to catch another and ship him to parts unknown.

Then with a firing-off of whips in the lead, the
great mass of stages began to move. There were the
sounds of cavorting hoofs and the shouting of miners.
Hostlers cleared away as best they could. The rolling mass gained speed, such speed at last that it appeared unable to remain any longer intact. Off flew
the many component parts over the arc of an open
fan, and in nearly as many directions as a fan has
ribs. There was a waving of "wide-awake" hats—
Good-by! *Au revoir! Adiós!* and the same perhaps in
Chinese, Norwegian, Hawaiian, German, Portuguese,
and half the languages of the civilized world; for
these stages were loaded to the utmost with nearly
everything. Away they went over a vast sea of green
sprayed over with wild flowers on a straight course
for the still-invisible mountains. Roadless, fenceless,
postless, hedgeless, houseless—it was, says Mr. Borthwick, like going to sea with a fleet of small vessels.
They spread rapidly away from one another, and
farther away till they were all hull-down on the
horizon.

Then it was:

Creeping through the valley, crawling o'er the hill,
Splashing through the branches, rumbling o'er the
        mill;

Putting nervous gentlemen in a towering rage.
What is so provoking as riding in a stage?

Spinsters fair and forty, maids in youthful charms,
Suddenly are cast into their neighbors' arms;
Children shoot like squirrels darting through a cage—
Isn't it delightful, riding in a stage?

Feet are interlacing, heads severely bumped,
Friend and foe together get their noses thumped;
Dresses act as carpets—listen to the sage:
"Life is but a journey taken in a stage."

It was the impression, at least, of some local bard
of the day whose inspiration, to judge from its domes-
tic flavor, must have sprung from the old Spanish
Camino to San José. Otherwise it might have come
from any or all roads in the State. They were all
rather bumpy. A driver did well to avoid them whenever it was possible, and for this reason they often appeared to be hundreds of feet in width. But in the
mountains the way was so narrow that only at certain
known points could two vehicles pass. A Mrs. D. B.
Bates, telling of the trying conditions to be encountered by women on the Gold Coast in the early fifties,
calls staging in the mountains "perfectly awful":

One night about eleven o'clock [she writes] a lady
came into the hotel [at Marysville] looking more
dead than alive. She was leading a little girl of about
seven years of age, who was in the same plight as

her mother. They were both covered with bruises, scratches and blood, with their garments soiled and torn. They were coming back from Bidwell's Bar, a place about forty miles from Marysville, in a stage-coach in which were nine Chinamen. The coach was all closed, as it was rather cool in the mountains in the evening. All at once they found themselves turning sommersets.

The coach was overturned down a steep bank. All the Chinamen with their long cues reaching to their heels, were rolling and tumbling about in the most ungraceful manner imaginable. They were vociferating at the tops of their voices in a language which, if spoken calmly . . . is harsh and disagreeable in extreme. "And," said she, "such a horrid din of voices as raged in my ears, it was scarcely possible to conceive of; which, together with the fright, was almost sufficient to deprive me of my reason." The driver was seriously hurt, and so were some of the horses; but the inside passengers escaped without having any of their limbs broken, but their cues were awfully disarranged.[1]

Stage-coach accidents, according to all sound experience as well as careful statistics, were, however, extremely rare;[2] but there is no doubt that riding was rough, generally, over the whole staging West.

[1] Mrs. Bates. "Four Years on the Pacific Coast."

[2] Early California daily journals seldom failed to note even the slightest of stage-coach mishaps. One deliberate count of them all covered a period of five years—1855–60—and indicated that, certainly, there was not an average of one accident per month—forty of them over a period of sixty months being the actual findings. All these entailed about twenty-five mentionable injuries and but one consequent death.

Courtesy of Mrs. Frank S. Stevens. From the original portrait.
JULIA (CHASE) BIRCH

In certain regions at certain times, where and when nature granted, this was not the case; and it is true that the building and maintenance of a few highways in later days might have done credit to the work of Sir James and Mr. John Louden McAdam as happily known to the wheels of the old British mail; but it would scarcely do for a Western stageman to boast of his roads—especially in the presence of some coaching enthusiast from England.

He might better confine his boasting to the fact that his roads, however scientifically graded, were terrible, his country rough enough to shake passengers out of their wits, hills steep enough to frighten them into distraction, turns of such a nature that six horses and coach might cover, all at one time, the essential curvatures of the letter S; and so on. Then, not only would he be rather close to the truth, but at the business end of the stage-coach horn. He would be in the position of the seaman from around Cape Horn confronting the mariner from Lake Lucerne: "You've never seen nasty weather, m'lad, and you'll never be a sailor till you do."

In short, there is no warranted comparison between the old British and the later American institutions. The vastness of the latter's country, and the brevity of its life therein, put the problem of good roads almost beyond consideration. It became necessary for the Yankee to develop his equipments, his methods, his men in a manner to surmount obstacles

which neither the British coach, the British methods,
nor the British coachman was ever obliged to contemplate. The Englishman was happily able to make his
ways suit his means; the Yankee was forced to do
the opposite. Two very different systems naturally
evolved.

One Western driver of the early fifties may be recalled from Horace Bell's "Reminiscences" as having
driven a six-horse coach, for certain reasons, over
"a precipice"—it was, no doubt, a very steep grade.
"Down! down! down! Rickety clatter bang! Sometimes the horses ahead of the stage, sometimes the
stage ahead of the horses, all, however, going down!
down with a crash!"

The driver, it seems, was simply proving to an un-
believing world that a stage-coach and team could
traverse this particular mountain; that the pass was
worthy of improvement. The hope was to stimulate
popular subscription for the construction of a road;
and in this light, as it proved, the demonstration was
"a complete success."

The enterprising linesman, having extricated himself and animals from the wreckage, promptly despatched riders with news that the coach had successfully gone over—gone over, in fact, with flying
colors. Appropriations from merchants and business
houses were forthwith advanced. A small army of
men, armed with shovels and picks, were soon on
hand "to repair parts of the road" which the coach

in its descent had "knocked out of joint." Overland trade—freighting and staging—followed between two parts of California which had formerly depended on the sea for all such intercourse; and it was by the route thus blazed that there later passed the first transcontinental stages into northern California as a precursor of the Southern Pacific Railroad.

Thus pathfinding of a kind was sometimes an important part of the Western stageman's business; and, as it may be seen, similar feats to promote the construction of negotiable mountain transits belong with far-reaching significance to the annals of these pioneers. Their ways, in one sense, were rough; but on the whole they were rough in one sense only. There are apparently many misconceived notions with regard to the old order as it ranged in its prime through the West.

Chapter III

SIX-HORSE CALIFORNIA

WITHIN memory to-day some first-class stage routes remain as glowing impressions, something to recall all the brilliance of earlier days; for there were lines of stock in the seventies and eighties —even later—that did not appear to cringe before the "menace of steam"; some teams, vehicles, and trappings continued to carry a sparkling pride and the show of prosperity that had been so pervasive with the pioneers; but such happy recollections have long since ceased to prevail. The general impression of the old Concord coach seems to have become as much of a ruin as the dilapidated salvage in our museums, or the desecrating effigies that totter in our street parades.

"Look, child! See what your great-grandfather traveled in when he came across the plains. Think of riding in that!"

And some poor child's great-grandfather rolls in his grave. Yes, think of traveling in that. . . . What is it?

One old "Concord," having been shipped from the East around Cape Horn, having served long in the

Sierra Nevadas over one of the most historic and immaculate routes in the West (The Pioneer), having been tossed by the Black Hills of South Dakota through the romance of old Deadwood days, ended its adventurous career in a circus, William Cody on the box. Of all those remaining splinters and rags, "Buffalo Bill" was justly proud; for it seems he had helped to rescue what was left of the coach from the Indians. In view of his purpose, and also in view of the man, it was well; but now, unfortunately, there is another Concord to be rescued from another breed of savages before it has been torn to pieces.

If it had been left, as in the case of its story, to suffer only the consequences of slight or neglect—if the casual writer and the casual artist, having no acquaintance with the nature of his subject, had simply left it alone—then the task of rescue would carry more hope, or seem perhaps less presumptuous. Worshipers at the shrine of a West that never was may not like to have the wreck that they call a coach, or the dray animals that they call a stage team, or the teamster that they call a driver, supplanted by anything better. But since it is true that one old California stage line of the early fifties has been carefully preserved in all of its essentials and attributes, to include the pride and love that have kept it in continual operation for more than three quarters of a century, it has been possible to photograph for these pages a living model to demonstrate what once prevailed.

And it seems to be the case that there are few things more comparable to the old-time seafaring pride, as it obtained especially in the handling and maintenance of the clipper ship, than the scrupulous stagefaring attitude of all stagemen toward the arts and crafts of their calling.

So far, of course, these pioneers had been obliged to make the best of what equipage was available. To import stage-coaches and trappings around the continent of South America, and fine animals from across the plains, was costly, and considerable time was involved. Yet it was the very cream of New England's stagemen that had come. They were not apt to content themselves long with makeshifts—this especially as they began to realize that they were transplanting their old institution into the most promising fields that the world had ever before offered; and more especially, perhaps, since James Birch was the man with the whip-handle. He was the coming magnate. If any doubts on this score had existed prior to 1854, now a new phase arose to dispel it.

It came on with a grand merging of at least five sixths of all lines in the State—virtually all lines in the new West, for that matter, there being on the plains as yet no staging worthy of the name. Under the style of "California Stage Company," there sprang into action on New Year's Day, 1854, an unprecedented giant. It was a corporation which, at the outset operated more stock than was later to be known to the Southern Overland Mail, the three-thousand-mile bi-weekly transcontinental stage line; and it was nearly to double its capacity within the succeeding eighteen months, carrying passengers daily over a distance of some fifteen hundred miles, all within the State of California. Indeed, not until the Ben Holladay control of nearly all staging over the central and northwestern plains would there exist a stage-coach firm of greater magnitude than this early company as it ranged in the middle fifties; nor yet can there be found a similar institution, large or small, more perfectly equipped and managed.

Its officials, unlike Ben Holladay and a few other great magnates of later time, were stagefaring. They were men, that is, who understood thoroughly every detail involved in their business, from the care of animals, the setting up of thorough-braces, the adjustment of an axle, the reining of a six-horse team, and so on, to the stocking of a line and the general office administration. They were men born with whips in their hands, and were the prospering survivors of a rattling competition among hundreds.

Birch and Stevens had come out of the boiling to find themselves at the top. Having been prominent among the organizers, Stevens was elected vice-president and Birch the president of the new monopoly. Thus under the thumbs of these twenty-five-year-old whips from Providence was the largest stage-coach firm in the world, its stock being assessed at a million dollars. Combining, as it did, practically all lines radiating out of Sacramento, Marysville, San Francisco, and elsewhere, it afforded a sight for the eyes of history.

There was to behold in Sacramento alone, on any day of the week, a crowd of between two and three hundred prospective passengers all togged out as though about to take any number of parts in the wildest extravaganzas—the conventional chorus of stovepipers, a coolie chorus, a procession of haberdashing Israelites, and the usual big Pikers' mining parade. Although their distribution from this particular center involved only sixteen separate routes, there were generally required twenty or more full-fledged Concord coaches to accommodate the crowd, most of them with six-horse teams.

The bodies of the vehicles, with their graceful hull-like sheering and flaring, were gay with intricate scrollwork, highlight, and color. There were flashes from silver ferules along the whip-stocks, from harness buckles and ivory rings. There were more than a hundred fine horses, champing their bits, swishing their long glossy tails, and thumping the ground. Then, to see them jump at the signal to pull out, to hear the cracking of a score of whips while the gay procession went bounding forth over the plains of the Sacramento Valley—it was a sight for kings, but more to the satisfaction, perhaps, of these young staging princes who could look upon their handiwork. Here was the very acme of perfection in equipage made possible by a prosperity such as few stagemen could possibly have enjoyed before.

During the year preceding this grand merger, nearly all the inadequate spring contraptions on wheels had made way for the thorough-braced product. Demands for the best had come with a sudden vengeance, so that now all things in general were prodigies of flawlessness; virtually everything was new. Like a hundred gay dragons just rid of their last-year's skins, these excellent creations from New Hampshire with their long spanking teams were rampant throughout the gold-fields. In the nature of the circumstances, it would appear incredible that so many of them in such absolute pink of condition could ever have been so concentrated in action at any other time or place in the annals of American staging.

There was also a showing of speed. It was not quite that of the old British Mail at the height of its macadamized career, but in view of the roads or the lack of them, of the grades and multiple turns encountered as these stages came swerving down the Sierra Nevadas, of the precipices they skirted, the banks they shaved, the freighters they passed on the way, in view especially of the crowds they carried along with the heavy express, baggage, and mail, it was speed

Courtesy of the Bancroft Library

Courtesy of the Bancroft Library

enough and generally more than enough for the traveler. Over roads that were often well graded but seldom free of chuck-holes, rocks, and gullies, ten miles an hour was frequently made, six being an exceptionally good average rate for the whole West in later days.

During a heavy competition between Hall & Crandall and Baxter & Company on the run between Sacramento and Shasta, one of the Baxter drivers in the summer of fifty-three is recorded as having come down the valley from Shasta to Colusa, a distance roughly of 160 miles, all stops included, at a rate of more than thirteen miles an hour. A record was made going the other way on a section of the same road in the same year when a stretch of sixty miles was coursed in six hours and fifteen minutes, which included a half-hour's stop for breakfast and, necessarily, twenty-five minutes for the changes of animals. "Through in six hours" over a sixty-five mile run had been the boast of Slocumb & Morse; and the sixty-mile route between San Francisco and San José was often covered in as short a time.

It is likely that the California Stage Company, in the absence of competition, could better afford to spare its teams; but, by the same token, there was now, as never before in California, an economic incentive for stagemen to improve their own roads and thus make fast staging possible without imposing heavily upon endurance of animals, or the nerves, incidentally, of the passengers. It was one case of monoply by which the public not only benefited but appeared to appreciate the benefits.

The great prevalence of the six-horse team was another feature of this singular phase. Not only was there the usual desire for a grand display at the various centers of staging, but often two dozen passengers or more were carried as a single load, and with these heavy cargoes there was required despatch through a rugged and mountainous country, all of which justly compelled a full complement of the finest American stage stock—teams valued at from two to four thousand dollars apiece. The animals had been driven in from Ohio, Pennsylvania, Kentucky, and Virginia, generally by the emigrants but sometimes by special agents of the company itself.

Stagemen now had money to invest, and there was no menace of rails to curb them. Of the California Stage Company's original million-dollar stock valuation, Birch had contributed about seventy-five thousand in animals and vehicles alone. All this he had earned in the business within four years, and had, several years since, put aside enough more to establish himself and bride, the former Julia Chase, in a great mansion which still stands in the village of Swansea, Massachusetts.

Thus bound to California by his stage lines, and to New England more than ever before, he was continuing to think in very expansive terms. His travels between the two places had once been purely visionary, but now he was virtually a commuter by sea between his home in New England and his business on the Pacific Coast! If he had ever before felt the need of better communication between the two places, now he was all but obsessed with the subject; and eyes were already on him as the practical hand to undertake the first coach mail line across the "Great American Desert."

In the Far West he was recognized as a champion of the project. No longer did there appear anything fantastic about the undertaking. Birch was at the head of an organization whose stock, if distributed from Sacramento to St. Louis, would have sufficed for more than adequate service between those termini. Even in Washington, D. C., he was being called upon to discuss the enterprise, to give his estimates of costs and all that might be entailed in the stocking and operating of so vast a system.

A generous government subsidy for the carrying of mail was, of course, the prime necessity. It was also the stumbling-block. It involved the same barrier of politics that had held up the Pacific Railroad. Was the route to lead through Southern or Northern territory?

It was a vital question. The fact that both sections of the country realized that iron rails might materialize in the tracks of Concord wheels made it so much the more difficult to answer. Congressional measures promoted by either faction were blocked or side-tracked by the other, although both, at last, were strong in the opinion that the project was a practical one. Behold the local developments on the Pacific Coast and the man at the reins. But the wheels in Washington were slow. The career of James Birch was therefore to be confined for some time longer to the limits of California.

The pioneer institution, however, after its long stride ahead in fifty-four, did not cease to grow. Indeed, its growth was so rapid that a continued monopoly over all sections became impossible. By 1856, although the corporation had increased its rolling-stock from 111 to 195 coaches and stage wagons (mud wagons, as they were known in later years), there had grown up at least fourteen hundred miles of additional route in the control of independent firms, many of them having been surrendered by the company to its own trustees—Charles McLaughlin, Charles Green, C. S. Coover, and other capable men of long standing. In short, there were about 3,000 miles of line, concentrated within the new State, roughly a year before a single stage, going or coming, had ever crossed her eastern boundary. The overland mail was still being carried in from Salt Lake and beyond on the backs of mules and men; and there remained the whole so-called Wild West without its typifying stage-coach.

In California there was the stage-coach without its

"Wild West." Strangely enough, not until this year, 1856, was the old vehicle any better acquainted with an Indian's war-whoop or a bandit's threat than it was with any other wild attributes that have since been foisted upon it. The month of August, however, was to provide the baptism of fire, a full initiation into the environment of the coming era.

Indians, of course, were generally of little concern to the stagemen of the Pacific Coast. Nearly all transportation in Oregon and Washington, where the natives were apt to be hostile, was confined to navigable streams. But now the California Stage Company was expanding northward toward trouble. With its eyes fastened upon Portland in the adjacent territory, it intended an immediate connection with Jacksonville, just beyond the California border.

Toward this end it had recently stocked a trail that had never known stage wheels before. The route joined Yreka, in the extreme northern region of the State, with Red Bluffs on the Shasta and Sacramento road. The journey involved two days and three nights of continual travel through a country so desolate, in part, as to be more fantastic than real. There were beetling precipices like walls of masonry, rocks of cathedral spires, naked mountains like castles or fortresses, and long vistas through gnarled, scrubby woods revealing all manner of weird forms that were all too suggestive of the very devils known to infest

Courtesy of Mrs. Frank S. Stevens. From the original painting now hanging in the former home of Birch.

"CALIFORNIA STAGE COMPANY . . . DECEMBER 1853"

them. Stages that plied over this section crossed a waterless waste. From the ferry on the Pitt River southward over a distance of twenty miles to a station called Hot Creek, Indians were the only inhabitants.

It was near the last of August. The down stage, driven by one Jared Robbins, or "Curly Jerry" as he was better known, had proceeded southward only several miles from the Pitt River station. He was alone; but he had become accustomed to that. This was no popular route, for about as many reasons as there were Indians in the chaparral. On this occasion Jerry was warned of their proximity only when a shower of arrows announced it. Some grazed and splintered upon the wagon, some pierced his clothes, and others lodged themselves firmly in his body; yet he remained on the box and continued his driving.

There was no chance to double back for the river station. It was a seventeen-mile stretch that he confronted, and other ambuscades as well. No sooner had he cracked his teams into their smartest action, coursing the rocky trail, than another flight flanked him with no less effect than the first. Of course, the Pitt River men were after his animals, yet even some of these had been struck. But they beat on. Wheels bumped over rocks and boulders, or crushed over scrubby snags. Several times the vehicle all but capsized, and more often than this there arose the question of how long it would hold together.

It did hold together a little longer, but not long

enough. Half-way across an open plain, and something snapped. There was a jolt and a heavy listing. One thorough-brace, the multiple straps upon which half the weight of the vehicle depended, had parted, shifting its burden to the brake beam. Another jolt, and this too carried away. Jerry went plunging into the midst of a half-dazed and befuddled team.

Fortunately, the animals held their ground. Their driver, though bleeding from his many wounds whence splintered sticks protruded, was able to quiet them as he pulled himself from the tangle. But there was no time to squander. The Pitt River devils were swarming down—a dusty mass.

Jerry had done well enough, perhaps, to cut away a good horse and show them his heels, but there was that in him, besides broken arrows, to identify him with his race. He had no intention of rewarding the scoundrels with his employers' stock; and before the dust was wholly settled about him, before the Indians could be certain that another flight of arrows might be needed, they beheld their prize, a small cavalcade, making off, the white man riding.

The story is a short one after this, although in length of road it extended over many a painful mile, with here and there another burst from the gauntlet. But there was a still living rider at the end of the trail to slide into the arms of station attendants; and unless the old records here employed spoke a little too soon,

Mr. Jared Robbins, with wounds from sixteen arrows in his body, survived.

The Wild West, it seems, was eager to claim its own. The stage-coach was already entering its world of hazardous romance; and this year of 1856, this month of August, had come on not only with war-whoops but with bandits and bullets as well.

Chapter IV

THE COMING OF THE HOLD-UP MEN

THERE is a story, substantially true, of a very young boy who "took to the road" just for fun. Perhaps the sound of distant coach wheels had prompted him, or it may have been a prank casually planned. In any event, he masked himself with a large bandanna, armed himself with a stick that suggested a pistol, pulled a slouch hat down over his eyes, partially concealed himself in some brush at a bend of the road, and waited.

It was growing rapidly dark. A blackness crept up the canyon like a rising tide. The twilight, taking hold of his shadow, had stretched it out to the proportions of a giant. He felt very big. He stood up on a rock and felt bigger. Now, he thought, he'd give that old stage driver the scare of his life. "Stop!" he'd yell out. "Put up yer hands!" he'd say to the passengers. "Throw down that there express box!" Then they'd all have a good laugh, maybe.

But things didn't turn out that way.

The stage-coach stopped promptly enough—so promptly, in fact, that the command to halt got no farther than the young brigand's throat, where all other peremptory orders were hopelessly jammed. Everything inside him whirled round in a panic. Before he could make himself laugh, or let himself cry, down came the box of Wells-Fargo treasure with a deadening thud to the ground. And down came the heart of the desperado with no less of a thud into his boots. A whip cracked, there was a clamoring of hoofs. A puff of cold air rushed back through the pine-trees, and the dying echoes of Concord wheels sounded faintly like a bag of bones. Stop! But the deed was done. A mere boy, without half trying, had robbed a stage.

There is also an instance of a one-armed man who held up and successfully looted not only one coach but a pair of them. And there is another—a record of all records, the responsibility for which must be shifted to John C. Shay, author of "Thirty Years in California," Mr. Shay having given in convincing detail what must here be dispelled at a breath.

It appeared that a single "road-agent" had held up three coaches in a line. By means of a hat sent the rounds, he was compelling the contributions of all hands, when suddenly there hauled upon the scene five freight wagons! He smiled. So much the better. And, having held them up very casually, he went on with his business—a growing business it might seem; for now, with a clanking of arms and a beating of hoofs, came the crowning feature of the event: about a hundred and fifty mounted soldiers.

The lone robber, surveying them as though they had just drawn up for inspection, made no move to escape. Neither did he alter the angle of his firing-piece. With far more method than madness he kept it trained as before upon the non-combatants. So much for the soldiers! He had brought them to a halt, put them "at ease," and was now proceeding to wind up his affairs. He was a trifle hungry. And it 'peared to him as how one of the teamsters might have a lunch-box to spare.

Mr. Shay is able to lighten the tax upon credulity by explaining that the guns of these troopers were not loaded. But the fact remains: one man was able to hold up a procession of three stage-coaches, five freighters, and several troops of American cavalry! Not only that, but his exploits, from start to finish, proved a thorough success.

All this took place when staging was about to stop; and, surely, if the stopping of stages had come to this; if it were now a game for children and one-armed men, it was perhaps about time that the old institution should have gone to a happier hunting ground. Yet, again, how often did the robbers of earlier times meet real resistance in a stage-coach? Certainly the glamour now attached to our Wild Western road-agent can scarcely be attributed to the hazards of his trade. His risk was generally far less than a burglar's. Of the fire he faced and exchanged in fictional romance, records can show but a spark. Cheap, indeed, has been the price of his chivalric glory—he accepted it with a bonus in cash; and, to insure greater safety in his pursuit of crime, he could even afford to affect or maintain a conscience.

"Sir," says one of his victims, "you've taken my last cent; and there is my unfortunate mother. . . ."

"Oh, well, give her this with my compliments."

"You're not going to take that watch, are you? It's one my grandfather gave me as he lay on his dying bed, saying . . ."

"Hell, keep it!" And to the driver: "Keep yours too. I wouldn't rob a hard-working man." Or to a woman: "Never mind anything from you, miss. I respect a lady."

Sometimes he seemed so considerate and gallant that they invited him to join them in a drink. As a general habit, he would not molest passengers at all. The express box was all he wanted. No one could deny him that. Who but a fool in the average case would see fit to risk his life against such odds even to protect his own purse?

Yet there was a day when, in this light, most men must have been fools. They were apparently such unmitigated madmen that you could not possibly hold up a stage without being considered the fool preëminent. This day belongs to the fifties, the Western pioneer phase. And from forty-nine until well along into the year of fifty-six, there were no open attacks upon a stage-coach. There were several instances of theft from the vehicle; but it was never held up in the accepted sense of the expression.

Common bandits, too, were quite numerous enough. There had been Joaquin Murietta, for one, with his organized packs of road-wolves. He had been active in the California mining belt during a part of 1853—a year of record production throughout the diggings. Considerably more than fifty-seven millions of dollars in dust and bars may be accredited to that year as having come down from the mountains by stage. Through the cluttered little mining towns, through wild and lonely forests and gorges, from station to station, night and day the vehicles ran by the hundreds. Only in very rare instances was there provided an escort other than the occasional express agent or casual passenger. Single cargoes were very apt to range from twenty-five to a hundred thousand dollars; and very often these enormous sums were carried, not, as in later times, in an iron box, bolted down under the driver's seat, but they were packed loosely in a wooden case which more often than not was carelessly strapped in with the baggage in the after-boot!

What richer field of endeavor could have been offered the notorious Joaquin? Yet during his sojourn in these tempting regions, there was not a single stage stopped by him or by any one. There were none held up within these precincts either in 1853 or at any time prior thereto; nor were there to be any for several years to follow. The reason for this need scarcely be explained to any one acquainted with the Pacific Commonwealth as it was in its adolescent years; but the answer may be suggested well enough perhaps through the events of a certain initial exploit.

It was in fifty-six that a bold devil tried it—a man with the alias of "Tom Bell"; for it was Bell who blazed the crooked trail that stage-coach robbers of later times were to follow, improve, and make generally safe for crime, little realizing the perils that had shadowed its pioneer!

Bell was, broadly, of the gentleman type; and, like some of the old buccaneers, his thirst was more for the dramatic than for blood or even for gold. He swaggered under the proscenium arch of his ego, affecting all the bravado and dashing qualities that had immortalized his predecessor, Joaquin. He might, for example, at a time when the world sought his scalp, drop carelessly into a tavern for relaxation. If suspected, or recognized, he would simply wait for action. If none came, he might announce himself, then laugh and vanish.

Like Joaquin, again, he often appeared in two different places at once. It seems he had been shrewd enough to assume the name of a bandit contemporary. The latter was known here and there as an ordinary leader of sneak-thieves, just as the other was elsewhere identified with the bloodiest of desperadoes. Reliable reports as to the appearance and nature of "the man" were thus very often contradictory. They led to so many blind trails and so much more confusion that "Tom Bell," in the minds of many, was neither this nor that—he was purely a mythical character.

He was, none the less, fully six feet of flesh and blood, plus two heavy revolvers, a bowie knife, a jacket of mail, and with some forty-eight followers at his beck and call. His eyes were pale blue, flashing under sandy eyebrows; his hair long and auburn—he might have been very handsome but for an unsightly disfigurement. His nose had been broken, flattened through some accident of childhood.

From Rome, Tennessee, he had come to California with the gold rush, and evidently with a few good intentions, a sound education, and substantial experience for a young man of twenty-five years. He was Dr. Thomas J. Hodges then, a practising physician who had done service through the Mexican War. On the Gold Coast he continued his practice, but it didn't pay. He tried mining with no better success, gambling with no better, grand larceny with still worse; so that he may be said to have started at the bottom in 1855 when he found himself a state prisoner on Angel Island.

His career moved rapidly after this. Through his knowledge of human ailments he was able to develop very plausible symptoms of a trouble which could not be treated on the island. Consequently he was shipped to the county jail in San Francisco; but here, in spite of special treatment, he became convincingly worse—so feeble, it appeared, that he warranted but little watching. Soon he'd be gone, the warden predicted; and soon, indeed, he was. He had vanished completely.

It happened, too, that other prisoners were about to pass away in a similar manner from the State's control. They were too great a burden on the prison budget. They had been gobbling up all the profits of the mess-room contractor. It became necessary for some to escape, and many did.

Alias "Bill White" was among those favored by the hoax, although White was as bloodthirsty and cunning a demon as Angel Island had ever shielded from the noose of the Vigilantes. A wild-eyed German, with a crucifix tattooed on one arm, who called himself Jim Smith, was another thus honorably discharged for the good of the service. Alias "Ned Connor" was a third. There were more, but these three most interested Dr. Hodges.

The doctor, having already borrowed the name of Tom Bell, had identified it most intimately with the highway; and it was a privilege that he conferred upon these late renegades when he enlisted them in his fold. His higher intelligence and more obvious daring helped to uphold him as the leader he presumed to be; but his knowledge of surgery was no small asset in itself. Even one of his victims, wounded by White in a gun battle, was to benefit by Tom Bell's early training—receive professional attention at his hands and be sent off in a wagon held up for that special purpose, the teamster being obliged to pay the doctor's fee.

Tom Bell was no killer. There are no records to indicate positively that he ever killed; yet few nights passed during the spring and summer of fifty-six without word of some lonely traveler's encounter with Bell or with men of his colors. He had already increased his number to some four dozen banditti, with headquarters in the mountain recesses of such wild expanse that they might have concealed a fair-sized army.

But the various members often met in small groups at certain ranch houses, stage stations, and taverns of the mining belt. There was the Mountaineer House on the Auburn and Folsom road, where coaches of the California Stage Company changed their teams, yet where all the inmates from proprietor to hostler were secret agents in the employ of Bell. There was also the Western Exchange, or Hog Ranch House, where another rendezvous was afforded the gang by a gross, red-haired woman, Elizabeth Hood, one of whose several daughters was the mistress of the bandit chief. Of the most immediate importance, however, was

"The California House," about twenty-eight miles from the great staging center at Marysville on the Camptonville road.

It was a narrow highway, cut through an almost impenetrable, and certainly an interminable, forest of pines that reached up to make daylight dark. Along this route the down stage came thundering. When the breeze was low and favoring, one could hear the rattle for miles—the great Concord wheels that supported treasure from some of the richest diggings in the land. It was here for several weeks during the summer that Bell, White, and five more of his boldest followers, planned what was unprecedented in the annals of the new Western empire.

On the twelfth of August there was action.

Down from Camptonville, hell-bound if a coach ever was, Langton's Express came rolling up to the California House. A man dressed as a miner climbed down and the coach drove on. This fellow, Smith Sutton, well known at the rendezvous, was one of Tom Bell's intelligence men. He reported everything as favorable. Although, as usual, there were many passengers aboard, it happened that four were Chinamen and another was a negress. There was no trouble to be expected from them. The rest might fight, but Langton's box was rather worth fighting for. It contained $100,000 in gold.

Tom Bell, Bill White, Jim Smith, Ned Connor,

Monte Jack, English Bob, and a Mexican, Juan Fernandez, were soon in the saddle. They overtook and passed the coach by another route, then, from a junction, doubled back a short distance toward it, where they drew up under cover of a shrubby ravine and waited.

Chapter V

PLUNDERERS OF THE GOLD EXPRESS

THE stage-coach had already finished a down-grade clatter and started on a short climb toward the forks. The Chinamen were gabbling, but all at once, like a wary family of blackbirds, they hushed. The express agent, William Dobson, armed only with two navy revolvers, was glowering through the dust at several mounted men. They were masked and heavily armed. One advanced and ordered a halt.

John Gear, the Langton driver, whose first duty was in behalf of his passengers, obeyed the command; but Dobson, Langton's messenger, whose first duty was in behalf of the treasure, listened only an instant to the threats, then drew and fired, unhorsing the spokesman with the initial shot.

Slight confusion fell upon the bandit ranks along with Dobson's bullets; but the attacking number had suddenly increased. Fire was returned for fire. Four Chinamen and a white man leaped from the stage and fled. The unfortunate woman had been shot dead. Two other passengers had received painful wounds, but they and the remainder joined Dobson in his defense of the coach.

63

It lasted only a short time—an indiscriminate and wild shooting from both sides; but the marauders were obviously on the retreat. Tom Bell, though wounded, and Bill White, both unrecognized at this time, covered the withdrawal and were the last to vanish through the brush of the adjacent ravine.

The stage proceeded slowly, Dobson, in his excitement, threatening to shoot the driver unless he snapped some life into his team. In the heat of the moment he did not know that one of Gear's hands was completely disabled; and before he could discover the fact, the attack had been renewed from another quarter by a mounted Mexican. Bullets flew again. The Mexican was bowled from his saddle by the expressman's fire. He crashed into the thicket. This ended the affray, some forty shots having been exchanged in all; the coach, with its dead and wounded, rocked on into Marysville.

The treasure had been saved at the cost of a disinterested woman's life; but it is noteworthy that no blame for rash proceedings was attached by popular opinion to either Dobson or his employer. In so far as the journals of the time may reflect a public attitude, quite the reverse was the case. For the express agent's bravery a liberal reward, to include a dinner in his honor, was greeted by the press with applause. As for the life that had been lost in the affair and the injuries sustained by passengers and driver—

that was another matter entirely. These misfortunes, of course, would be avenged.

And no one, even at this advanced phase in the development of the Commonwealth, was picturing a mere sheriff and a few half-hearted deputies "on the trail" or as "investigating." No one was worrying about fraudulency in court—judges and jurors who, in exchange for "a little commission," a share in the loot, might be glad to take orders from the defendant, as later in Nevada's silver days. This offense, it seemed, was everybody's business. It was a public affront, a kick at the very props of society. Already more mining communities than one had put down their shovels and taken up their guns. They, least of all, could countenance an attack upon a stage, the vehicle upon whose welfare they were largely dependent.

The offenders, however, had not remained long in the neighborhood; but neither had the authorities and the parties of citizens in pursuit. It was a campaign of several months; but it was one of many when the best citizens of the country—men like Frank Stevens, for example, who carried scars of Vigilante action— were determined, as members of the well-known "Committee," upon a round-up. They were not apt to fail. The capture, in this case, of six accomplices and of White and Fernandez was a long step in the right direction. Any suspect carrying a certain talisman, a bullet curiously marked with several dots and a cross, could be readily identified as a member of the band; and there were other telltales as well. White, having chanced to fall into the hands of the law, had turned state's evidence.

Ned Connor had no such opportunity. Having already been several times wounded during the battle on the Camptonville road, now he engaged a small party of citizens and fell with a bullet through his heart. Few men, if any, of the entire gang escaped altogether. Tom Bell's career ended on October 4, or about six weeks after the hold-up of the Langton stage.

It appears that Elizabeth Hood of the Hog Ranch House, who with her three daughters had been apprehended in the Tulare regions—the central part of the State—had pointed out the trail to a certain deputy sheriff. Then a small body of volunteers did the rest.

It was in the upper reaches of the Merced River that they came upon "the doctor." He sat unsuspecting—a leg tossed carelessly over the saddle of an exhausted mustang. He had mistaken the men for elk hunters. But with his unsightly disfiguration, there had been no mistaking him.

There was no resistance, no attempt to escape. Bell was granted exactly four hours in which to write letters to his family in Tennessee, while his captors waited and dangled a rope from a sycamore. The

deputy sheriff arrived, accommodatingly and tact-
fully, only after this time had elapsed and when there
remained only the letters and the scalp of Tom Bell
to carry back with him to Sacramento.

It was unfortunate, some newspapers believed it a
duty to state, that the deputy had been too tardy to
prevent such lawlessness in the execution of a crimi-
nal. But so it had been; and so it was that the earliest
Western stage-coaches, with their immense cargoes
of gold, had ranged as free and protected as though
under the surveillance of an army. There was the
deterring spirit of a social organization as well as
the ready gun of the passenger.

Even as late as 1859, when some dozen attacks
upon the vehicle by road-agents could be counted
in all, the successful plundering of one was attributed
to the fact that there had not been "any passengers
in the stage to protect it." Then, too, there had been
only $1,500 to protect.

Progress in the business after Bell's pioneering was
slow. But in the following year a second attempt was
made while a coach of A. N. Fisher Company was on
its way to Stockton with an accumulation of express
from three mining camps. Wells-Fargo and Pacific
Express treasure amounted to $37,600; but there were
no special agents in charge, and only one passenger
aboard. The time was about an hour before daylight
on August 17. The stage-coach, in almost total darkness, two miles out of Angel's Camp, was winding

through its most desolate stretch of road, when the monotony was suddenly relieved by the quick, shadowy forms of two men at the heads of the leading team. Three others, mounted, and flourishing their arms, sprang up beside the stage.

There was little that a driver could do under such circumstances. Not only were both his hands very full, but there was the safety of his passengers to consider, however little they were expected to consider him. Yet in this case there was no action whatever. The odds of five to one might have explained it; but, for the "Sacramento Union" it would appear that such odds were not sufficient. The editor believed that, since the lone passenger had been aroused from a sound sleep only to blink down the bore of a double-barreled gun, he must have been "overawed."

In any event, the robbers were allowed their own way for a time. They made off with the box of gold and might have reaped the benefits, had it not been for the prompt action of several mining towns. All the loot was recovered, however, and all the looters were captured before that day was done.

May 3, 1858, was the next stop. By this time travelers were more accustomed to go about unarmed. There was a coach loaded with them on this occasion. Only one occupant carried a weapon—I. N. Dawley of Nevada City, a banker's agent in charge of a large quantity of dust, which he carried on his person. The stage-coach was near the town of Nevada on

From an old lithograph.

WHERE GOLD-DUST WAS LIQUEFIED

ORIGINAL ILLUSTRATION FROM "MOUNTAINS AND MOLEHILLS" BY FRANK MARRYAT.

the Auburn and Folsom road when halted by five men with pistols and double-barreled guns. They told Dawley, among others, what to do with his hands; but this gentleman had a will of his own. He drew!

He might well have drawn his last rattling breath in addition but for one bandit's sense of humor. He told Dawley to be careful. No, no! Somebody might have to kill him.

There was some logic in that. Mr. Dawley replied that he fancied, after all, it *would* be foolish to fight when, really, there was nothing to fight for. The coach just behind, he explained, carried all the express. Nor did a search through the boots and elsewhere belie the statement; and the driver was ordered to drive on.

He did so; but the intrepid Dawley was very uneasy. In order to save the dust of Marks & Company he had parried an attack in the direction of Wells-Fargo. He felt obliged to adjust matters, to rally all hands to the rescue of the other stage, and in open battle if necessary. But it was only to learn of the defenseless condition of his fellows. The robbers, meanwhile, had pounced upon the other victim.

It was to be a rich haul this time, and it might very well have been richer. This second coach happened to be one which certain buyers of dust in Forest City had missed some distance back on the road; and now, on horseback and with $16,000 among them, they were racing to overtake it. They were headed directly for the highwaymen. But the latter, at the ominous sound of hurrying hoofs in their direction, turned and fled with what plunder they had already collected. A moment later and two horsemen, having discharged a third with their mounts, climbed breathlessly with their bags of gold aboard a stage which had just been rifled of $21,000.

Here, with nearly a decade of staging about to close, was the first successful stage hold-up, and the only one of three "successes" during all the fifties worthy of mention. In September, 1858, a woman tried it. She was the notorious "Dutch Kate" of Marysville—wore men's clothes, smoked, gambled, drank whisky along with the best of drinkers; and if it were true that she could swear to do justice to any occasion, there was offered an opportunity on her first stagefaring exploit.

She had just lost $2,000 at cards. There was news of considerable treasure on the road from Camptonville, and Dutch Kate, with two men to show her how, set out on the late Tom Bell's preserves to recover her losses. The work seemed very simple, once she had started it. She beheld ten passengers submitting quietly, perhaps smilingly, to her demands. She wanted only the express box, and it was dropped to her without any ado. When she told the driver to "get up and get," he got—that was all there was to it. When she opened the box . . . that was all there was to that. It was empty, and, worse still, among the passengers whom she had not searched, one, according to the papers of the following morning, had carried a purse worth $15,000.

Other coaches were held up during the year and a considerable number the year after. Express companies were more and more able to stand their losses; and, accordingly, the public was becoming less and less responsible in its attitude, and stage passengers more discreet. Times were changing. No doubt they were changing for the better; but there was something unique about the Fighting Fifties before Tom Bell had blazed the crooked trail.

Then society as an avenging jade had been glad to sit on the lid, as it were, of all treasure boxes transported from the mines. In her hand she held a ready noose. She was not law-abiding, did not intend to be just yet. She was a kind of in-law of the outlaw Judge Lynch, yet differed from him in at least one commendable respect: she was so dispassionate and impersonal in her determination to punish; she was so matter-of-fact, so terrifyingly cool and relentless. Her sparkling display of gold was a lasting temptation; but she was a warning in her very allurement, and withal the most respected creature in the mines.

Some men did not trust her wholly. One man is known to have placed three rattlesnakes in his trunk to guard his dust upon shipment. Other men did not understand her at once; but if they lived through their lessons they were apt to learn. She encouraged them, for instance, to go heavily armed as a means of protecting her; but let any one make a half-threatening slip for his weapon, and see if she cared who shot him.

Order, not of appearance but of fact, and not for to-morrow but now—this was her will above all; and as she looked anxiously toward the stage-coach for her continued prosperity, the stage-coach was a thing tabooed. Some liberties with the vehicle were taken during the fifties, it is true, but no such liberties as are taken by our modern romancers.

Chapter VI

FORCED ACTION

THE stage-coach's baptism of fire by Tom Bell's band and the Pitt River Indians had happened as an appropriate, however unwelcome, ceremony; for the year 1856 was fraught with other action looking toward the advent of a staging era whose most conventional background would belong largely to outlaws and savages.

In view of the hopeless political situation involving the Pacific Railroad, the whole nation was now fairly united in the opinion that, by one route or another, no time should be lost in establishing a fast coach mail across the plains. James Birch, meanwhile, was rapidly gaining influence among the many agitators for the enterprise. He had wisely refrained from any partizan stand, but, as a mail contractor and stageman of substantial resources, was prepared to enter a bid for the desired service over any route that the powers might see fit to ordain.

California, by now, had virtually lost him. Having intrusted his large holdings in her transportation business to friends of the California Stage Company and resigned his position as president (in favor of James

Haworth, one of the trustees), he had withdrawn from all but his affairs at the national capital to a gay life in Massachusetts. Here, in the village of Swansea, with an estate of many acres laid out in broad lawns, terraces, lakes, and sylvan vistas, extending from the old state road to the sea, he found recreation in a hobby which had been his business as a boy! He played stage driver with "toys" that were the envy of Massachusetts.

Besides his new colonial mansion, replete from basement to cupola with such rare treasures as his taste could conceive, there were huge and elaborate stables, filled with blooded horses, various types of coaches and sleighs, together with the finest carriages for Mrs. Birch. Little wonder that the West could not hold him—this year especially; for in October of 1856 a new member was added to his family, a son to be christened "Frank" in honor of Stevens in California.

It was, however, scarcely in the nature of Birch to retire from business on any account at the age of barely twenty-nine years. Yet there remained nothing on the Atlantic Coast to hold his professional interest. Old stage-coach days in the East were clearly on the decline; and California, though it had become a stageman's paradise, was too far from a happy home. For the sake of a continued career, in short, Birch had been compelled to confine his whole energy to the promotion of a transcontinental coach mail.

The project was now being threshed out with real intention at Washington, D. C., but there were still many stumbling-blocks in its path. Steamship interests, threatened by the move, were blamed for pulling all the political strings within reach to prevent the birth of so formidable a rival; and the hopeless wrangling on the eternal question of feasible routes continued to play into their hands.

Five railroad surveys, commenced in 1853, had been completed and reported upon by Secretary of War Jefferson Davis. This report professed to demonstrate, in part, the utter impracticability of the popular emigrant trail to California—a route leading through northern territories by way of the Mormon capital. Deep snows, especially of the Sierra Nevadas, were represented as prohibitive obstacles. Of the remaining routes surveyed, there was only one, it appeared, that was worthy of consideration. It was acknowledged to be hundreds of miles longer than any other. In the shape of a rainbow, it swept as far south as the Mexican border. It entered California at a point as far removed from the populated region as Salt Lake City was distant from Sacramento, and most of the country through which it passed was an untraveled waste. But for a railroad, or for the coach mail line to precede the railroad, no route surveyed but this one through the southern domains had been reported as practicable or negotiable through all seasons of the year.

All this, from the cotton-grower "Jeff" Davis and the cabinet of President Pierce, was likely to be regarded with suspicion. It was perhaps a move toward the development of Territories to become slave States.

In view especially of emigrant needs on the long-neglected Salt Lake trail, it was a move contemplated apparently with an almost brazen disregard for a crying need, the need of the nation at large.

California, naturally inclined to favor the shortest and most popular route not only for the sake of a more rapid and frequent mail service, but to facilitate the emigrant travel as well, joined the loud cry of repudiation. There was a resentful popular opinion on one side and a very powerful administration on the other, either one of which was prepared to block any pertinent measure of the opposing force.

But it was obvious, none the less, to the whole Southern faction that immediate action was necessary. If the mail stage line were to lead the way for a railroad through the new territories of the South, there remained no time to squander. California and Missouri were at the bitter ends of their patience. California was already struggling to raise funds for a highway of her own across her wintry Sierras, across the very backbone of political contention. By way of a pass called Johnson's, which the Federal surveyors had not deemed fit to survey, she was about to build a road and establish a regular line of stages across her eastern frontiers into western Utah (later

From an old lithograph.

IN THE DIGGIN'S

ORIGINAL ILLUSTRATION FROM "MOUNTAINS AND MOLEHILLS"
BY FRANK MARRYAT.

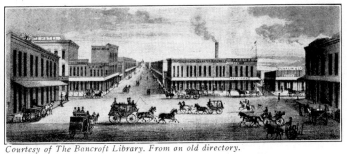

Courtesy of The Bancroft Library. From an old directory.

MARYSVILLE—STAGING CENTER—IN THE FIFTIES

Nevada Territory). She was about to prove, once and forever, that all of her northern gateways were not, after all, beyond further consideration.

And she was otherwise active. Through the energy of a few of her citizens, a colossal petition, begging the immediate construction of a military wagon road to course the Salt Lake emigrant trail, had been circulated throughout the State. It had been presented to the national Senate in the early spring—several huge volumes containing the signatures of 75,000 Californians. As the most gigantic memorial ever brought before that body, and with the strong support of merchants and bankers of New York, Congress was bound to act, and did.

It was in February of the following year—1857. While a very likely overland mail bill (which purposely deferred all question of route) was still pending, a great wagon-road measure was approved by President Pierce. In view of the political difficulties, the appropriation was for the construction of more highways than one, $200,000 being provided for the further improvement of the Southern or Border route, and, among other provisions, a very agreeable $300,000 for the Salt Lake or Central route. The latter appropriation, however, happened to contain an ironical little joker with sharp teeth.

Federal road construction by way of Salt Lake was to terminate at a certain region at the eastern boundary of California; and this "certain region" had been fixed, unaccommodatingly to say the least, at a snowy point well north of California's own selected Sierra Nevada transit—that which she, as a State, had recently surveyed over Johnson's Pass. The state survey had already stimulated private subscription contemplating a trans-Sierra stage road to connect with the government highway. The result was as might have been expected.

Local enthusiasm devoted to this truly strategic development was damped; and that rather cold far-northern section of the State which had been favored by the Federal measure became suddenly very animated and strong in its opposition to the Johnson Pass champions. California, like the nation she had condemned for the same human failing, was divided heatedly against herself. The staging project over her mountains was delayed accordingly. The Southern partizans in Washington, about to make hay while the sun shone, took up the whip with a vengeance, intending this time to drive through and to force the coach mail into action along the circuitous Border route.

The time had come, at any rate, for hopeful mail contractors to stand by. Directly in the wake of the Federal road appropriation was a measure authorizing the Postmaster-General to contract for the long-delayed service. It was news universally welcomed, and especially to those naïve souls who could credit the fact that the selection of the route would be left, according to law, to the mail contractor himself. But the fact that all bidders were to include, with their bids, proposals of route; the fact that the Postmaster-General was to choose whatever bidder most suited him; the fact that he hailed from Memphis, Tennessee, and that Memphis was among the candidates for a position at the eastern terminus of the line—all this and more could not be overlooked. It was something, as history would prove, for all eligible contractors to bear strictly in mind.

James Birch, at any rate, was on hand—a man still in his twenties about to match his experience, capital, and national prestige against the combined forces of John Butterfield, William B. Dinsmore, William G. Fargo, James Gardner, Marcus L. Kenyon, Hamilton Spencer, and Alexander Holland—seven joint bidders representing the most powerful express companies on the Atlantic Coast. But in spite of them, and everything behind them, it appeared at first to most of the world that the rails were not bent in their direction. No bidder but Birch had created and controlled an organization comparable in its magnitude, efficiency, and splendor to the California Stage Company; few men had handled more mail contracts; and no man could combine more capital with experience than he. If he were to be defeated, as even his opponents did not believe he could be, numbers indeed would be required.

Chapter VII

THE WHIP THAT CRACKED THE SIERRAS

MEANWHILE there were certain optimistic Californians who presumed that it might be still within their power to thwart the national administration in what seemed an extravagant intrigue. They were practical men who did not believe it quite necessary to travel all the way down to Mexico in order to reach San Francisco from the Eastern States' frontiers! They were the promoters of the highway over Johnson's Pass, champions of the short main emigrant trail that led in by way of Salt Lake. And if their supporting counties of Sacramento and El Dorado would vote each $25,000 during the September (1857) election, a fair road for stage-coaches could be built over Johnson's Pass into the Carson Valley, where a national highway should, but would not, connect.

But no matter. There was already money subscribed to begin the work. The connection beyond would take care of itself. But to maintain public courage in the face of all obvious national intentions relating to the overland mail was a problem entailing much doubt. Furthermore, the California Stage Company

Courtesy of Mrs. Frank S. Stevens. From an original daguerreotype.

FRANK SHAW STEVENS AND STEPSON, FRANK S. BIRCH

was no longer interested in Johnson's Pass. Due in part to the establishment of a little railroad from Sacramento to Folsom, the firm had moved its headquarters northward to Marysville, where other mountain passes were favored. The one hope seemed to be, dramatically, with an inveterate and typical pioneer stage driver, and none less than J. B. Crandall.

It was the same Crandall who, in 1850, had driven the governor from San Francisco to San José, racing the stage of Ackley & Maurison and bearing the news of California's admittance into the Union. He had been a proprietor of Hall & Crandall's various staging systems from that time until the incorporation of the monopoly. Now as a member of the firm Crandall & Sunderland, operating between Folsom and Placerville (old Hangtown), he was about to extend that line thence eastward to a definite place in history.

Crandall's present system was the same which Frank Stevens, in 1851, had christened "The Pioneer." The name then had not been inappropriate; but now, with Crandall himself at the reins and driving, there was to be no resting upon past laurels—not so far as the line was concerned, nor as the name of Crandall connoted "the prince of drivers." Their goal lay in the white clouds beyond the Sierras where no man had ever driven a stage before.

Enough of all this talk about routes and roads! Enough of all theories and surveys made to order by politicians! If a roadway over these mountains as mapped would not lend itself to staging on paper, he, Crandall, would drive a real stage over the mountains themselves—stock the old emigrant trail and extend his line on to Genoa in the Territory of Utah for regular service! Let them argue then as to whether or not such a thing could be done. It seemed to him that it could be; and, what was more, he would have the line in full operation within ten days.

Thus Crandall had volunteered before certain practical though very optimistic men—a certain board of directors that had been raising funds for the Sacramento and Carson Valley wagon road to cross Johnson's and Luther's passes. The interested counties would vote bonds in September; this was the month of June; but there being enough money on hand for some slight improvements along the trail, Crandall's new venture provided reason enough to let several grading contracts immediately. To determine what sections of the route most needed grading became an object of the expedition; for Crandall had offered to take, on his first trip over the Sierras, as many directors as cared to pile aboard his stage.

Then one morning—June 11, 1857—the famous reinsman, having strung good horses at intervals along the route, aroused himself at an hour which would have been called early even by the most relentless drivers of his school. The smoky lights of Placerville had digested little more than their midnight oil and had guided or supported, perhaps, the last homeward-bounders from the gambling halls only an hour before. Some of the directors, routed shortly after from their dreams, continued thence in various states of consciousness and torment through periods which were cut from eternity. But Crandall's stage had borne them out of town promptly at a quarter past three.

The vague flicker of his candle lamps went rippling along over the cobblestones, went writhing over the washed boulders of a demolished country-side, while pathfinders for a future era jerked and nodded their sleepy heads in the shadows of the Nevada mountains.

They were J. G. McCallum, T. Foster, H. Cheatum, W. M. Cary, C. Stump, a Mr. Randolph, and a newspaper man who was to leave all records but the trace of his own worthy name. They were mostly the directors from Sacramento. Those representing the interests of El Dorado had put out some time before, proceeding for the main part on horseback under the leadership of J. H. Nevitt and C. P. Huntington, Nevitt being the president of the board.

Fortunately for the members of the staging party who could not overcome their sleep, the first stretch of the journey was rather smooth driving. Pleasure-bent coaches had traversed it occasionally on excursions to a place called Sportsman Hall, about twenty

miles east of Placerville; but beyond this point the
first tracks to be left by stage and team were those
of the Crandall expedition.

The adventurers found themselves in better spirits
on leaving the Hall. A six-o'clock breakfast, with
hot coffee included, enabled them to respond to cheers
from an encampment of apostate Mormons near
Bartlett's Springs farther on. These renouncers of
the faith, it seemed, had been "fleeced" by their saintly
chieftains; and they would have no more of it. They
waved farewell with the towels and wash-pans of
their morning ablutions as the stage pulled on toward Brockless Crossing on the South Fork of the
American River.

Considering what significance may be attached to
their journey, it seems a pity that the stage of Crandall was not to be quite the first one over the Sierras.
In so far as its passengers could be certain at the time,
there was a chance that they would be. But it happened that a gay party, whose greatest concern had
been vested in what liquid refreshments remained in
the casks, had been granted the use of a stage by the
California Stage Company and had made a trip from
the town of Oroville northwestward by way of
Chaparral Hill and Roop's Ranch to Honey Lake—
the proposed fixed terminus for the Federal wagon
road across the plains by the Salt Lake route. Having
made, between the dates of May 29 and June 11, a
successful round trip, the California Stage Company

was to win the honors of having despatched the first stage-coach over the eastern boundary of the State.

However, since the Honey Lake expedition led to the establishment of no stage line, and appears to have stimulated no action toward road construction; since, in short, it was utterly without material issue, Crandall and his party may still be regarded as the practical pathfinders. They proved the worth of a route for staging over these barrier ranges—a route which was to be put to immediate service by Crandall himself; the same route which was to make Hank Monk famous (for reasons unknown) in driving Horace Greeley very rapidly into Placerville, and which was to become a section of the Central Overland Mail, without question one of the most exemplary stage roads in the West. Now it was Crandall's extension of Stevens's "Pioneer"—the first line to penetrate the Great Salt Lake basin from the shores of the Pacific Ocean, a definite eastward progression with a future.

The expeditioners themselves were able to foresee a vital import in their possible success. It must have seemed that the halls of the national capital vibrated a little as down the grade to Brockless Bridge the Pioneer stage went thundering. Thence up the other side it merged into a country as wild as the primal creation.

The great pines were already running up to the heavens for their light. Rocky slopes from a mere trail on the mountainside were so cleft away to the bed of Silver Creek that the sight was better left unwatched by those who could pin no faith in the performance of miracles by a reinsman. Aspens all about were trembling their proverbial worst, and there were few complaints, if any, at times when all hands were requested to change from the Crandall line to another very popularly known in the mountains as "Foot & Walker."

Courtesy of the Bancroft Library

THE WELL-KNOWN LINE OF "FOOT & WALKER"
Taken from "Pen-Knife Sketches," by Alonzo Delano (Sacramento, 1853)

The exercise was pleasant and the scenery delightful. Rapid streams gushed out here and there from banks of ferns. Upward, on the hill called Peavine, was a tangled verdure in undergrowth, swinging prickly pods and wildflowers in profusion. Rich green and yellow mosses, and fungus like powdered gold, clung to the shaggy trunks of white oaks and pines. Long festoons of parasite stuff dangled between the branches, or hung wavering among the shadows like gossamer. It was a long climb to the Peavine summit, but it passed with a sigh for a past ordeal. At Foster's Halt, near Strawberry Valley, thirty-five miles from Placerville, cold ham and coffee did for supper, yet sufficed for a spirit of celebration. Then there was sleep under trees whose moss-bearded branches appeared to have tangled in the stars.

Slippery Ford! That was the next ordeal. Some of the party must have dreamed of Slippery Ford.

"You can get past Peavine . . . *maybe;* and you may get on a little farther. But you're at the end of the Pioneer Line, sir, when you run in to Slippery Ford." Warnings to this effect had been proffered by many who believed they knew. It was a subject for conversation at four o'clock the next morning when old Crandall saluted daylight with a crack of his whip.

The team leaped forth toward the impassable ford as though all animals were confident that their hoofs, like the feet of flies, could take a straight wall of rock at a canter. They attempted to prove it at their first opportunity, plunging down into a racing stream and on up a slope of naked granite. Several chip-

munks jumped and fled for their impertinent lives.
There were clatterings and splashings, deep rushing
and gurgling sounds; there was the sight of four
sleek and struggling animals, their sinews tensed in
long ridges and ripples from their craning necks to
their haunches. Crandall spoke to them calmly, his
keen eyes glancing at each of their separate moves.
But it was past in a trice. Some one ventured:

"If you can do that, you can bet your boots you'll
do as well at Slippery."

"It's the end of stage travel, they tell me," mused
the driver; "but I don't see how it can be worse than
what we just hit."

Several passengers who had been smiling now began
to frown; but Crandall went on: "It couldn't be
much worse'n what it actually was. Coming back'll
be easier going. . . ."

Thus the final ordeal in passing fell to ridicule,
real ceremonies being reserved for a point just ahead.
It was reached simultaneously with the first view
of Lake Bigler (Tahoe), seen at a distance through
forest vistas and over the tops of pines as though it
were two separate ponds—great mirrors bearing the
images of peaks and pointed firs, many still white
with snow. The horses were slushing through long
drifts here and there which had tumbled from over-
hanging boughs; for here were the heights of Johnson's Pass about to be christened in honor of the
president of the board.

His name rang out as a bottle of old wine fell and crashed beside the hoofs of the leaders. "Nevitt! Nevitt's Summit!"

Echoes returned the compliment from a valley beyond where Nevitt himself was to meet them. Surely a return compliment had been due—this trip had been an achievement.

The route onward through Lake Valley and Luther's Pass to Cary's Mill and the Mormon station of Genoa was to amount to little more than a continuation of ceremonies—these mostly from the throats of natives who on sight of the stage would find it difficult to believe their senses. Welcoming cheers and the firing of guns were to greet them later upon their return to Placerville; and it was an enthusiasm destined to grow, to materialize in county appropriations to the amount of $50,000 for the bettering of a practicable road—a road, incidentally, which stands for the main part to-day as a California and Nevada boulevard for motorists.

But at the time when Crandall, with his panting team, sat resting on the top of the world, it was all too late to check the wheels of politics. Though ten days be added to the overland journey and nearly a thousand miles to the stage line, the route for mail coaches from Memphis to San Francisco by way of the Mexican border was as good as stocked.

For Crandall, however, there may have been some satisfaction in the thought that here lay a section of the Central route which would advertise a national blunder so long as that blunder obtained. Here lay the impassable bugaboo in the path of the Pioneer Line, being subdued and tamed under the hoofs of his horses, the thong of his whip, and the wheels of his Concord stage.

For seven years this bugaboo had reigned over the Sierra Nevadas, isolating a populated State as though it had been an island colony in some remote zone of the sea. From the Missouri River by way of Salt Lake and along the dreary Humboldt there were long wagon trains, leaving the graves of their drivers and the bones of their oxen to mark the trail, still plodding their way to the Pacific Coast in the manner of the days of forty-nine. A seven years' campaign for something better had only now come to a head—now that the deep basin of California had become a caldron and commenced to boil over.

It had bubbled up to the brim at Honey Lake with a coach of the California Stage Company. Then up and over the brim at Johnson's had popped the stage of Crandall to serve an immediate demand and eventually a lasting benefit. The stages of Birch would be the next ones out, and this time with an impetus to carry on across the plains. The stagemen of the coming era were to tend an empire, following many trails thus blazed by the daring of pioneers.

Chapter VIII

THE END OF A PIONEER'S TRAIL

ON the first day of August in fifty-seven it might have been difficult to transact any serious business with certain officials of the California Stage Company. Not only had the steamer *Golden Age* arrived from Panama bringing news of keen interest to all stagemen, but she had also brought the long-absent Birch, the very man to whom most of the news related.

Vice-President Stevens's offices, at least, could not have been very accessible. Much more than water had flowed under the bridge since he and his old friend had last held conference; but besides their private affairs and their mutual business interests, there were many questions on the subject of the Overland Mail which until now could not have been answered.

It had already been learned that the necessary congressional appropriations had been made; that the Postmaster-General had been vested with the power to choose a contractor, and to favor whatever party most suited him regardless of bids; that the stage route between San Francisco and the Mississippi, which, according to law, the contractor was empowered to select, would none the less be dictated by the Postmaster, and that service over the extended Southern route would probably commence in the fall of the following year. Beyond these facts there were several yet to be learned, one being of a rather startling nature.

That Birch had lost his Great Overland Mail contract was surprising enough in the light of general expectancy; but that his stages were, nevertheless, on the road at that very moment, carrying the United States mail across the deserts on their journey to California, was news indeed. It seemed that he had become the proprietor, not of the great line which he had helped to promote and for which Congress had made special appropriations, but of the Postmaster-General's own unaccountable and very sudden creation. It was the San Antonio & San Diego Mail, to run on a thirty-day schedule twice a month between the Texas and California termini at a rate of compensation from the general postal fund of nearly $150,000 a year.

There being various combinations of stage, rail, and steamer connections between San Antonio and the ports of Indianola and New Orleans, Birch, under Federal patronage, had opened the first overland mail and passenger stage line joining the two oceans. There being a branch reaching off from his route at El Paso northward to Santa Fé, whence another route, extending eastward, communicated with Independence,

Missouri, he had likewise completed the first wheeled transit between the great rivers and the Pacific shores.

He had taken over the contract and made arrangements to stock the road for immediate service shortly before sailing from New York. Not to wait for the inauguration of the main transcontinental line, the Post-Office Department had ordained that there be staging at once over the Border route to California. A route more desolate would have been difficult to find, and terminal points more remote from the populated regions than San Antonio and San Diego could scarcely have been named by a sober man; but the Postmaster-General, as the world would soon learn, was a man of his own convictions. Birch had undertaken the project only on a reasonable assumption that the major contract would be his as well. He had regarded the San Antonio & San Diego line only as a subsidiary part of his future system. But the unexpected had happened.

It was fairly as though he had stood with fingers about to close on a six-hundred-thousand-dollar-per-year, six-year mail contract which the Postmaster-General was extending, when, suddenly, along had come President Buchanan, patting John Butterfield on the back with one hand and staying the hand of the Postmaster-General with the other! The "New York Times," naturally favoring New York interests, and with no unsound arguments on its side in behalf of the New York or Butterfield bidders, had been very agreeably surprised at this abrupt turn of events. Its issue of July 7, which had come on the same steamer with Birch to California, explained in part:

We charged no corruption when we expressed our belief that despite bidding, it had been decided to award the contract to Mr. Birch. Nor did we intimate that any venal motives had prompted the determination. Mr. Birch is a gentleman of large capital and much experience, and more competent, perhaps, than any other single man in the United States to execute this great mail contract. He has influential friends, too, who urged him on the Postmaster General; and we repeat today—and Mr. Birch will not deny it—that he had reason to believe three months ago that he would certainly get the contract—that it was all settled in his favor almost as though the cabinet had formally decided it. We repeat that it was the Postmaster General's determination to give it to him down to a very recent period. . . . So much for our position. The President has overruled the determination to give the contract to Mr. Birch.[1]

"The Times" did not mention the fact that Butterfield and Buchanan were intimate friends of long standing; but certainly this circumstance alone promised a security in favor of the Great Overland Mail which Birch could not have offered. Since the President knew John Butterfield, moreover, he must likewise have known, more than any one else, his capabilities, and the immense joint power behind him. Thus,

[1] See also "The New York Times" of June 25, 1857, and approximate dates.

at any rate, before the onslaught of Butterfield, Dinsmore, Fargo, and all the others, had the lone pioneer been defeated. In fact, near the last he had had reason to expect defeat. He had been urged by his advocates as well as his adversaries to combine his bid with that of the New York expressmen and so settle any difference extant in the President's cabinet. But he had decided on "all or nothing." As it was, he had neither—he was the proprietor of the San Antonio & San Diego Mail, and destined, as such, to take up once more his old rôle of pioneer.

It was the end of a long campaign. Already there were strong and capable hands reaching out for the whip of Birch; but evidently he had no intention of resigning it. He was trail-blazing in a new era, just as he had done in forty-nine, and there appeared prospects now, as before, to win the race he had started. Although bound, for the time being, to the Border route, there were other routes, little though it appeared that the South would ever admit it. And there were certain hopeful champions of the Central short line who, with renewed emphasis, were naming him as the man to take up the reins.

Toward the end, hats were off to old Crandall, quietly driving his stages twice a week on a regular schedule over the tops of the Sierra Nevadas and into the adjacent Territory of Utah (now Nevada). The winter snows might block him for a few weeks this year; but, given more traffic, which would come with more funds for road improvements, and Crandall would be blocked no more. There, then, would be the Great Salt Lake trail, which was nearly a thousand miles shorter than that through the South, wide open and demanding service, a service to knock about seven days off the journey by stage across the plains, if not at least seven bells out of the whole Southern system.

Yet it appears that these prospects were not intended for Birch. The fates were leading him elsewhere. He was not yet thirty years old, but his life ran only into one more page of the calendar. September gave him thirteen days to live.

It was August 20 when he bade Frank Stevens good-by. Then, with a dozen or so messages to carry with him to the Atlantic Coast, with trinkets for his wife and, more significantly, a silver baby's cup from a stagefaring friend for little Frank, he climbed aboard the steamer bound for Panama.

His affairs in the East had called him away a little too soon—he was never to learn of the safe arrival in California of the first San Antonio mail. He was far at sea on the last day of the month when the pueblo of San Diego was all of an uproar. An old cannon in the plaza was booming away, bells and "a hundred anvils" were ringing, there was cheering from an ecstatic crowd. Mail through from San Antonio! Thirty-eight days! Thirty-four days' traveling time! And there was positive assurance that it could

Courtesy of "The Providence Journal." From a modern photograph.

OLD BIRCH-STEVENS HOME, SWANSEA, MASSACHUSETTS

be done in less than thirty, given only a few weeks to improve the organization along the road.

The next arrivals at both ends of the line proved the case. It was while Birch was still on his homeward voyage. It was while a storm on the Atlantic was presaging the fact that he had reached his journey's end.

On the twelfth night of September the end was clearly in view. The palatial side-wheeler *Central America*,[1] some four hundred miles south of Cape Hatteras, had spread her seams and was on her way to the bottom. Women and children had been safely transferred to a sailing vessel, whose crippled condition had left her helpless to render any further assistance. She had been swept, struggling, far to leeward, where she could only await the inevitable sea which would smother the distant lights of the steamer for the last time and bear her down.

Aboard the ill-fated liner, Birch stood on deck among hundreds of men of his own adventuresome cast. If there had been so much as a gesture toward panic, there was not a thought of it now. The young stageman had been seen to refuse the offer of a life-belt. "No, Gabe; it's no use," had been his words as he strode away, smoking a cigar whose glow he fully intended should be extinguished with the breath of his life.

The master, too, had resigned the ship and all hands

[1] Formerly the *George Law*.

to the conquering elements. Everything that could have been done had been done. Standing on the bridge with the mate beside him, he had removed the storm cover from his cap to reveal the gold braid of his office.[1] Now, braced by the rail, he uncovered. A rocket soared aloft. And down into a smothering froth and blackness, from which there was no recovering, plunged the hulk, white seas boiling over. More than two million dollars in gold and some four hundred men followed her to her grave.

Mrs. Birch, with the little boy, was awaiting the arrival of her husband at the old Metropolitan Hotel in New York; but they returned alone to the house in Swansea.

It was strange what followed them there.

It was a large silver cup which a certain John Andrews, agent for the California Stage Company, had put into the hands of Birch on the day of his sailing. "From John to Frank" was the inscription upon it; and from John to Frank it had come . . . through adventures more harrowing than could have been related by any but three of the survivors.

Many men, and some bodies of men, had been recovered from the sea by a second chancing vessel with the dawn that followed the disaster; but the silver cup had been no part of her salvage. It had been carried by Birch himself from the foundering steamer to a crowded mass of wreckage; but as the hours passed,

[1] Captain William H. Herndon, detailed by the United States navy.

many hands let go; and as the days passed, many men succumbed. The cup had then passed into the care of a certain George Dawson, a mulatto. From his hands Mrs. Birch received it.

For it happened that a life-boat, carrying only one survivor, had closed in eventually upon the raft, there to be joined by Dawson and only one more. The three men in an open boat had drifted thence for hundreds of miles. With the cup they had bailed the small craft; they had also used it as a means—an only means—of capturing sufficient rain water to maintain life. Some 478 miles from where the *Central America* had sunk, and fully nine days after the sinking, these men had been picked up and carried into New York Harbor. Birch, as Dawson related, had been swept from the raft and carried away by the sea.

To visit Swansea to-day, and to make casual inquiries among its inhabitants regarding James Birch, is to meet very likely with no response but a frowning shake of the head. There, as elsewhere, strangely, the name is all but forgot. One might be standing at the time of inquiry within sight of his very estate. One might be leaning on an old iron fence, admiring a vast parklike garden of lawn, ivy, gravel walks, maples, and elms, with perhaps a glimpse through the foliage of a broad stretch of water covered with lily pads. There would be the old stables, and there a large yellow dwelling, with green shutters, ornate cupola, columns, and balustrades. But Birch? No. The villager has never heard of him. He might nod, however, toward the big colonial dwelling—

"Ask there. If anybody can tell you about the old-timers of this town, it would be Mrs. Stevens."

To be thinking of Birch and to hear "Stevens"! *What* Stevens! But it seems there is only one of that name in Swansea. Everybody from Fall River to Providence has heard of her—Elizabeth R. Stevens, widow of the Hon. Frank Shaw Stevens, captain of industry, banker, manufacturer, State Senator of Massachusetts, who died in the late nineties. It is surprising to the villager that any one should be so startled on hearing that name in Swansea, the town itself being largely composed of the well-known Stevens donations. There are the two schools, the town hall, the library, the church, and more, most of which were dedicated by the widow in memory of her husband.

Thus Swansea, once you have found it, opens the door unwittingly of an old historic romance to account for many things, including the fateful obscurity of a man who had been the father of the whole West-American staging epoch. Given the public careers of Birch and his friend, one might solve the rest of the story without going farther, without entering the gate of this old house, though it fairly cries aloud to come on, come in—it contains a romance from the old, gold days! It has long treasured the saga of Birch!

And Mrs. Stevens, as it proves, has likewise treasured it. A more than kindly woman of years, she continues actively in the administration of her late husband's estate, and remembers the stories he told her of his stage-coach days in California. She is the second wife of Stevens. His first had been, as one might almost guess, the widow of James E. Birch.

In a room maintained more or less as Birch had left it hangs his portrait, together with that of the young woman who had been his wife, and that also of their son, Frank, with whose death, at the age of fifty, had passed the family name. Yet it is fairly as though the name of Stevens were synonymous. It is as though Birch and all that had concerned him had become Stevens and Stevens's life. The California Stage Company, a painting of whose coach hangs there on a wall, necessarily recalls both men and their early environment. Then the widow of one becoming the wife of the other; the son of one bearing the name of the other; the coaches in the stable having been driven by both, and the house itself having sprung from the gold-dust that their respective stages had borne down from the mines—all this; but it seems also that even the aspirations of Birch, at the time of his death, had been carried along by Stevens.

It fell to him, naturally, upon marriage, to stand

behind the Birch pioneer line across the plains in the matter of its financing; but just as this line would not have sufficed for Birch, neither did it suffice for Stevens. Lured back to New England, as his old friend had been, by the selfsame feminine agency, he too had found himself longing for the whip to vie with that of John Butterfield. The California Stage Company at that time, however, had been anxious to let well enough alone. Its trustees were tired. Travel had fallen off. Through Stevens, now campaigning among the politicians of Washington (again just as Birch had done), they were to have the first mail contract on a line to Portland, Oregon, and intended after that to withdraw. Meanwhile they were dependent largely upon Stevens for temporary financial support. A priceless old file of letters, which the present Mrs. Stevens graciously produced, discloses these facts, and shows Stevens in the exact situation of his old friend, striving toward the selfsame end.

"We think," wrote the California Company trustees, "that you have a sort of an overland mail fever, and if we do not go into the mail business as a company you will go in individually or with others. . . . As we love you, don't for God's sake!" and so on, letter after letter imploring him to desist, and finally managing to dissuade him.

Thus Stevens, out of loyalty, it would seem, to his friends of the Pacific Coast firm, had turned at last away from staging to the life of a "captain of industry, banker, manufacturer, and State Senator of Massachusetts," with only Birch's old toys in the stable, and silver services with coaches engraved upon them, and the picture on the wall by which to recall the things that were, back in the Fighting Fifties.

With these same treasures to-day the old house remains overloaded. Perhaps the most pathetic remnant is to be found upon a certain small marble-topped table, covered with a rich brocade. It is a silver cup, "From John to Frank," and with the added notation:

"Saved from the steamer *Central America,* lost September 12, 1857."

It would seem, incidentally, that the end of the pioneer stage-coach phase might be placed appropriately at that date. Then it was that the first stages were crossing the plains. The wheels Birch had started in behalf of the Pacific Commonwealth were turning then in behalf of the new empire. Others were to carry on.

PART TWO

THE WHIP OF BUTTERFIELD

Chapter I

THE PILOT FISH AND SHARK

A NATION-WIDE financial panic, brought to a sudden head by the foundering of the *Central America* with her cargo of gold, had given fresh impetus to the westward march. More and more those who put out for the new land were taking with them their families, while those who had gone before were establishing homes and turning in considerable numbers from the mud cradle and sluice to the plow. A rather self-sufficient, fairly settled, and promising population west of the Continental Divide was rapidly nearing the half-million mark.

It was a population which, in one respect, was beginning to feel the need of intercourse with the older civilization somewhat less keenly than before; it was beginning, however bitterly, to enjoy the feeling of isolation and independence which had obtained for so long through the apparent apathy of the Federal Government. Yet for the same reason did it view itself with some alarm; and, by the same token, the real need of direct and rapid overland communication was so much the greater.

It was especially so in the light of strained relations between the free and slave States—a condition blamed for all the ineffectual haranguing on the overland mail question since the gold rush of forty-nine. But if at that early date some means of ready intercourse over the plains had seemed necessary, by now there had arisen a very visible exigency. The advent of transcontinental staging was not premature.

Yet the purpose of its earliest manifestation was, and must remain in part, a mystery. The San Antonio & San Diego Mail, popularly known as "The Jackass Mail," may as well have been routed over the poles of the moon for all the good, in itself, it was ever to do toward solving the problem. As a means of communication between the Eastern and Western civilizations it was practically useless. As an aid to emigration it led "from no place through nothing to nowhere," and found, therefore, very few emigrants to aid. Reports, for example, of ten thousand California-bound wagons trekking over the Central or Salt Lake route were accompanied by other reports of no wagons at all west of El Paso on the line of the unaccountable Jackass. Why, then, had it been conceived?

It appears that it had been created to accommodate, in part, government troops stationed along the way —especially such additional troops as might be needed to protect it!

Moreover, there were mines being opened in the Gadsden Purchase, where, as no one could doubt, settlements needed all the encouragement that the Government could give them. Furthermore, El Paso, La Mesilla, Tucson, and San Diego were apt to take new leases upon life at the sound of coach wheels rattling in from far-off places with the mail, and also with the need to buy grain and general supplies from the local markets. Here were the beginnings of new agricultural and commercial developments over a vast and unpeopled land. Settlements would spring up; the railroad would follow, *et cetera.*

In short, Postmaster-General Aaron V. Brown was looking years and decades ahead, and did not intend to be swayed from his far-sighted policies by any mere immediate need—not even with the establishment of a *second* coach mail to California! [1]

This second (in point of contract), owing its inception to the administration of Pierce and its execution to that of Buchanan, had been created by an amendment to the Post-Office Bill of March 3, 1857, and was destined to become the great stage line of Butterfield & Company. Congress had routed it only "from such point on the Mississippi River as the contractors may select, to San Francisco," which seemed fair enough to all sections. But when bids were called for, on the last day of June, it was not long before all were rejected. Not a single eligible bidder had proposed to select a route agreeable to the Postmaster-

[1] The second with respect to contract only. Unforeseen circumstances, as will be noted, were to force earlier developments of a significant nature in the North to meet an emergency.

General!—and the latter was now obliged, almost literally, to draw a diagram so that the mistake would not occur again.

By these strange proceedings everything was arranged very nicely. Contractors having "selected" the route according to the precise wishes of the Honorable Postmaster, the Honorable Postmaster had then "selected" contractors according to the precise wishes of the President. All Southern, like the administration, became the route. John Butterfield's firm—Butterfield being an intimate friend of the President—became the contractors. And the Postmaster-General's home town of Memphis became *the* Eastern terminus, St. Louis being thrown in on a "branch," as a tub to a whale—something to muffle the cries of outrage from the Northern press and populated regions of the Far West.

So much for the projected beginnings of the Great (Southern) Overland Mail, to become the longest stage line in history. From the thirty-seventh parallel it sagged to the Mexican border, and even dropped into Mexican territory *after* entering California. Attempts were made to correct the blunder before it was too late, but the administration remained obdurate.

There was the San Antonio & San Diego line already in operation. By doubling over that section of it from El Paso to Fort Yuma with the Butterfield stages, six hundred miles could be amputated from the middle of the Jackass at a saving to the Government of nearly $60,000 a year! The San Antonio line, moreover, was already demonstrating the practicability of its course. The Salt Lake route was yet unproved and experiments were apt to be costly.

Thus, it appears, the innocent Jackass Mail was acting as a political pilot-fish for a huge political shark. It was the entering wedge for a strictly Southern enterprise looking forward to a Southern railroad and all that would follow, leaving the shorter, main emigrant trail to its crude wagons, mules, and oxen. Given until September 15, 1858, for preparations, the contract of Butterfield & Company had become operative on the same day of 1857—a time when Birch's San Antonio & San Diego stages had already been in action several months.

Birch had had practically no time for preparation. He had executed his contract on June 22, and on the ninth of July, just seventeen days later, the first mail from San Antonio for California had led out, stocking the road as it traveled. It was a road that, west of the Rio Grande, was still in the process of construction, and had never been scored by the wheels of a stage-coach before.

The first mail, however, did not run on wheels until, as it neared El Paso (August 7), it was overtaken by the second—a train of two ambulances, or light covered wagons. This second party had left San

Antonio on July 24 and encountered but one delay. Relay mule teams intended for it along the Devil's River in Texas had been driven off by the Indians. Two dozen animals had been lost; one of their drivers had been killed, another wounded, and some eighteen government troops had been routed in addition. Yet the vehicles had come through unmolested and in very good time under the circumstances.

Ferrying the swollen waters of the Rio Grande near Fort Fillmore was a problem that the first and second mails together met and solved in true pioneer fashion. The current at this season was nearly a torrent; and means of ferrying it were dependent on two diminutive skiffs. The animals, of course, were obliged to swim; mail and provisions were boated. With two wheels of a vehicle in one skiff and two in another, the two small crafts were converted into a catamaran, and it was an odd and rather awkward vessel that splashed out into the current for the steep banks of the opposite shore.

Nor were these crude staging methods speedily improved upon. Had the system continued under Birch, conditions might have been bettered very rapidly, but his death intervened; and it could not have occurred at a more critical and inopportune time.

The line had barely started. Large bills were outstanding. The money panic had brought on creditors in a body, and all the means to meet them, as originally

"FROM JOHN TO FRANK"

"SAVED FROM THE STEAMER 'CENTRAL
AMERICA,' LOST SEPTEMBER 12, 1857."

WHEN THE WORLD ROCKED ON THOROUGH-BRACES

EARLY CALIFORNIA PERAMBULATOR FOR THOSE BORN WITH
WHIPS IN THEIR HANDS.

planned, were inaccessible—tied up with the Birch estate in the probate courts. It was perhaps due only to I. C. Woods, the line superintendent, who had accompanied the first stages out of San Antonio, that the wheels continued to turn.

He had been at one time the very soul and substance of the Adams & Company Express on the Pacific Coast; and as such, in fifty-three, had been obliged to meet a little money panic of his own. Although on that occasion he had tumbled headlong with his firm into bankruptcy, there were few financiers more experienced. In this case he was able to pay a few creditors from his own pocket, but others he managed to stave off for a time, though there were as many wild white men as there were wild red men to jeopardize the stock along his line.

Matters became worse when a certain assignee of the Birch estate, Otis Kelton, stepfather of the widow, came down from Providence to take charge. He was an experienced stageman, but it seems that George H. Giddings, superintendent of the Eastern division, objected as a stockholder to the interference. Upon threatening to "haul off the road," lock, stock, and barrel, he won the support of the Postmaster-General, who threatened, in turn, to cancel the contract. But Woods came again to the rescue and, with other friends of the late Birch, diplomatically smoothed out the ruffles. An agent for the Birch interests having been appointed, Giddings combined with R. E. Doyle, superintendent of the Western division, and the line merged under the name of Giddings & Doyle for a long and rather eventful career.

Chapter II

DURING the San Antonio & San Diego Mail's early struggles for life its passengers suffered the consequences—more ups and downs, at least, than they could readily account for. If only its management could have adopted the regular all-night-and-day system, with stops only for meals and the changing of teams, as a consistent policy throughout; or if it could have employed the method travel-by-day-and-camp-by-night, or even the alternate mode, the traveler might easily have accustomed himself to the life. He was willing to banish old habits if new ones could be had in their stead; but this early stage of California afforded no such luxury. As often as a team of four might be supplanted by the Mexican five or the Yankee six, or as coaches might be exchanged for stage wagons and these for coaches again, so were all other modes of procedure altered at different places at different times, and as often as not without warning.

The vehicle sometimes traveled by night and drew up for rest in the morning; or it did the opposite; or it split the difference; or it went bowling along through several days at a stretch, picking up fresh teams at regular intervals, until suddenly, like a punctured balloon, it would appear to give out—it would go dawdling through a similar period, resting a few hours here and a few hours there, relay animals being driven along with the stage. Or it might be a small train of stages. And often, due to one delay or another, the mail went on ahead in saddle-bags somewhat in the manner of the later celebrated Pony Express, while the traveler, marooned at some God-forsaken station like freight on a side track, waited days for the completion of arrangements which might carry him on.

In short, it was impossible to predict what method or combination of methods would be next employed. It depended not only on the seasons of the year as they might obtain in the various regions, and their supplies of water, forage, and food, but there were emergencies to meet, or the possibilities of them to allow for. There was always the unexpected to expect.

At Fort Lancaster, perhaps, the Comanches had made off with the stock; at Hackleberry the spring had been polluted; at Van Horn the well had caved in; and the Apaches had devastated Dragoon. Neither conductor nor driver could do more than guess what the next mile was apt to disclose. The traveler, whose meals happened as the squaws of squaw-men occurred along the line, whose sleep identified itself with daylight as often as with dark, and never with beds, soon learned to ask no more questions but to take what came, to forget what came not, and to vegetate. It was strange, but in the face of all his vicissitudes he sensed only the most appalling monotony.

Mountains had flattened into mesas; mesas had fallen away into vast plains of bleached grass and yucca; these had become streaked and blotchy, yielding at last to an arid waste of boulders, gravel, greasewood, and patches of Spanish bayonet that flaunted their clusters of white at the broiling sun. But at what place in particular any of these changes had occurred he was seldom aware. Along with the everlasting bounce and sway of the stage-coach he had accepted them as a part of a relentless continuity, a going-on forever and ever. All that was seemed always to have been. And it would continue unceasingly. And he would never reach California.

Out of San Antonio the course had been almost due west to San Felipe on the banks of the Rio Grande. Thence the stage had swung northward to the head of the Devil's River and on over the hostile Comanche country to skirt the Pecos and climb westward again, into the Rockies of Texas and onward to the Rio Grande once more—to Birchville, El Paso, and La Mesilla, and away with a convoy of six guards across the Apache strongholds of New Mexico and Arizona to the adobe pueblo of Tucson. It was a squat, miserable little town of two or three hundred Mexicans and some twenty Americans—a point little more than

two thirds of the distance over the San Antonio &
San Diego Mail route to California.

With one thousand and six miles already traversed,
there were four hundred and seventy more to go. And
all desert. With some eighteen days stretched out at
unbelievable lengths along the road, there remained
ten more—at least ten, maybe twenty!—listening to
the soft greasy chuckle of hubs, to the paddling along
of mule hoofs, the slapping of sweat-lathered harness,
the rattle of chains, the crunching and scuffing, the
rumble and clatter of wheels. Ten or twenty more
days of hard bread, beans, jerked beef, and question-
able coffee; and nights, attempting to sleep on the
ground in smoky huts of mud, or in shelters of brushwood, or with no shelters at all; or otherwise having
to snatch naps from intervals between jolts of the
stage along the road.

With one elbow on the window strap, an arm in
the arm-sling, a leg propped up on a mail sack, a
shoulder supporting the head of a snoring companion,
these all-night runs were apt to be trying. Striving
vainly for sleep, the traveler might start counting
the white pannicles of yucca as they went marching by in the starlight, hoping to be carried off by
the monotony into dreams; but just at the crucial
moment—*bang!* Over the boulders of a washout the
wheels would go thundering, and back would swing
the desolate world, jolting as though to knock the stars
from their heavenly sockets. "Get used to it," was

the advice urged by various stagemen; but these were not always familiar with the nature of this particular line, where time piled up ahead and behind like the surrounding desert mountains.

Long ago, it seemed to the traveler, his companions had told all their stories, threshed out the important affairs of the world, and confided their private histories in shameless detail. He too had been guilty of unnecessary confidences. Now he regretted it. And just as this monotony might have seemed less wearing had there not been so many brands of it, so too he might have felt less lonely now were there no companions at all. The way passengers, the new ones— the ones who boasted a liking for this sort of thing— he found intolerable. He tried to smoke up a screen between himself and their smiling faces; he held himself to a rigid, almost bitter silence; he resorted to drink, which would cheer him none at all; he glared savagely out upon the suffering expanse of desert— something extremely unpleasant to have to gaze upon, yet somehow more in accord with himself. At least it sizzled by day and nearly froze by night and was infested by a thousand devils.

Out of Tucson, on a general northwesterly course toward the Gila River and the villages of the Pimas and Maricopas, the large mesas began spreading farther and farther away till they stood out like sawteeth on the horizon. Lesser ones, close at hand, were breaking up into isolated benches where an occasional

giant *sahuaro* stood meditating in its solitude. All else was greasewood—the dull green, scraggly, and ubiquitous greasewood—and prickly-pears and boulders.

Maricopa, however, brought some relief. There were friendly Indians and some cultivation; but there were also many things about the place with little appeal to any but the most morbid sensibilities. Only several months before this party had come through, the allied Pimas and Maricopas had been attacked by a force of seventy-five Yumas. The latter had expected the support of the Mojaves and Tonto Apaches, but had been deserted. Only three of the attacking warriors had lived to tell the tale of their defeat. And now, since it was contrary to the custom of Pimas and Maricopas to touch their dead enemies, the remains of seventy-two Yumas, filled with arrows and torn by the coyotes, were strewn over the plains within sight of the station house.

If, however, one could disregard this sorry spectacle, here was a haven of comparative rest. It was rest, of course, on the ground, and in a hut of sticks, where a fire burned in the center after the fashion of the Indians and nettled one's eyes with its smoke; but, thanks to the rather industrious Pimas, there was roast chicken for dinner, and there were fresh eggs for breakfast, and similar luxuries to be taken away in exchange for the various trinkets with which these stages were regularly provided. Now, at last, the world seemed to brighten considerably.

After crossing the horseshoe bend of the Gila known as the Forty-mile Desert, there was the sound of running water once more, and the occasional sight of willows, alders, and cottonwood-trees. The stage went scratching through thickets of mesquite, it rocked and banged over the dry river beds, yet sometimes the traveler was able to come up smiling. He could even listen to the old tales of the Oatman massacre and of the murderer of Murderer's Grave, as stations bearing the names of these horrors were passed. The fact was he was nearing California. The approach suggested it. The desert was becoming more desert, but there was the river. At times he could smell the green foliage. There were sparrows, linnets, and even quail.

As though, indeed, this had anything whatever to do with it.

After a hot, heavy pull over gravel and sand along the Gila, after crossing the silent Colorado River, he had only to proceed thence from Fort Yuma some few miles to behold a waste for his ultimate nightmares.

California! State of the journey's end!

A gila monster, hissing from its purple mouth, pushed back beneath a stone. Hissing, too, was the sand in the spokes of the wheels. The hoofs of the sweating mules plunged into it, ankle deep. It spread out on all sides with its wind-worked ribs; it lay heaped in glistening drifts against the escarpments, half filling the arroyos, half burying the few wretched shrubs which had fastened themselves like leeches upon the naked anatomy of land. Lying fierce and defiant in its torture of heat, it was a desolation whose vastness was terrifying; whose bounding rim of slashed and broken hills seemed to hem in some mysterious menace, something that lurked above the silence—heavy and oppressive. There was a desperate urge to hurry, to get away; but the barrier of horizon moved on before the stage, the sand clung.[1]

The soaked and frothy animals, spangled with its glistening particles, pulled heavily into their collars. The driver "touched up" his wheelers with the stock of his whip, while his swamper went stumbling along by the leaders, prodding them with a stick, though he could scarcely haul his own feet through the drifts.

The movements of the conductor [2] were strange. His mood seemed to fluctuate between an utter lethargy and the most acute expectancy. Either he sat with his head buried in his arms, the back of his red, wet undershirt exposed to the burning sky, or he arose suddenly, as though some one had tapped him on the shoulder; he began staring about from his bloodshot eyes. Then mopping himself with a scarlet bandanna, he would grumble something to the driver and wilt forward again.

Even he was aware of something about to happen; but he left his passengers sweltering in their doubts.

[1] Fascinating descriptions of this country are given by John C. Van Dyke in "The Desert," also by George Wharton James in "The Wonders of the Colorado Desert."

[2] See Glossary, Appendix E, as to this later obsolete stage-coach official.

What could happen? Who cared if it did? Spared in
the east by the Comanches, in the west by the Apaches,
and throughout by all the worst of the elements, anything extraordinary now would be welcome indeed.
These ever-dangling menaces were maddening.

But they were dangling nearer. The stage wagon
had reached a point some fifteen miles beyond the dry
well of Alamo Mocho, when the hot air grew definitely
sulphurous; the low sun became dull and tarnished.
A black cloud beneath it arose like smoke from the
jagged edge of a crater. It covered the sun and became
splotched with fire. Long shreds of it tore themselves
from the mountains. A great yellowish shadow spread
over the world; and a black one came waving like a
blanket across the dunes.

Wind-storms were not of frequent occurrence on
the Colorado desert; but they were listed no less among
the potential furies, all of which struck rarely, but
one breed or another of which was likely to attack
in the course of so long a journey. Warning, on this
occasion, had sufficed for some preparations; and the
first hot draft found the animals unhitched, hobbled,
and tied loosely together by their necks, so that, free
of the wagon, they were yet unable to stray and
could turn their tails to the first blast of sand.

When it came it was with a sound like the heavy
back-sweep of a sea. It struck upon the vehicle like a
burst of it, like the green-frothing body of it, breaker
upon breaker. It smashed with a dull impact upon the

leather of the high forward seats and glanced from the boots like driving hail. The wagon trembled and rocked, the stanch covering of its after-part bulging with the intermittent concussions that pressed in from both sides. The animals, with heads nearly down to their forefeet, the blown hair of their hides sticky with the drying sweat, remained as rigid as though made of wood. The gaunt world had turned to a golden yellow; the heavens deep red and gray, one blending into the other, into a sweeping mass, a whistling chaos.

Hours passed. Distant screams came down from forms that appeared and vanished through the blizzard-like waves. They were the forms of the bending mesquite, yet they appeared to be moving, to be stalking into the sand-blast. It was a land for all things unearthly. Yet it was California; the State of the journey's end!

Then night. There were stars, and the wind was gone. And a certain water-hole called Indian Wells had gone with it. So had the covering of the wagon, so had all vestige of road, all landmarks. Mountains would not be visible until daylight; then the hot sun would take its toll of that which the wind had parched. Indeed, if the stage were ever to reach the station at Carrizo Creek, there could be no rest through the night. The contents of the canteens had become precious stuff; there was no water at all for the team. The beasts slogged on over the dry and starry wastes, through hills of sand which had never existed before, over patches of gravel that were new, barankas that were filled, old banks smothered over, strange ones uncovered along with the skulls and bones of other beasts upon whom the sun had once risen too soon.

Carrizo Creek was not far away; but perhaps the stage was not bearing toward it. The conductor was visibly worried. He seemed to be staking all on a driver's "hunch"—

" 'Pears like I recollect that star."

Thus, to venture a composite of several old travelogues published in the journals of the day, came stage-coach passengers of fifty-seven over the deserts to California. Adventures differed vastly, of course, but trials were cut to a pattern peculiar to the "Jackass Mail."

This passenger service was not advertised to commence until October 1857—three months after the inauguration of the mail. The line was then equipped with some 400 mules, the best possible animals for the purpose, and with twenty-five Concord coaches and stage wagons to travel singly or in trains, as the case might warrant, twice a month from each terminus.

From San Francisco the traveler could proceed by steamer to San Diego, thence by stage to San Antonio, thence by various means to New Orleans and the Atlantic Coast. There were also the connections from

El Paso (or from Fort Fillmore farther up the Rio Grande) to Independence, Missouri, by way of Santa Fé. But due to the fact that New Orleans was at least

Courtesy of the Bancroft Library

FROM "THE SAN FRAN-CISCO HERALD" OF OC-TOBER 1857

FROM "THE HERALD" OF NOVEMBER 1857

thirty-eight, and more likely forty-eight, days' journey from San Francisco, whereas steamers thence to New York by way of Panama could now traverse their route within twenty-five or thirty days, obviously the steamers still had their advantages.

The first authentic record of a passenger coach pulling out for a through trip (with no traveling in saddles involved) relates to the first week in November 1857, the chronicler, "B. H. M.," writing for the "San Francisco Herald," being one of the party. Having started from the western terminus, he went no farther than Tucson, whence the stage pulled on. As no attempt had been made to put passengers through on mail time, "B. H. M." had been obliged to devote twenty-three days to a journey of 470 miles!

Another itinerary is provided by a Charles F. Hunning, who was a passenger out of San Diego early in the following month. His party avoided a long detour over the California Coast Range by traveling some eighteen miles on horseback; yet he spent only one day less time than his predecessor on the way to Tucson. He tells of meeting, on his third day out, the west-bound coach, one of whose five passengers was a bride on her honeymoon. Her fellow-travelers "complained very much, and had had a very hard time of it," but this lass was "fat and hardy, and had got along better than any of the men."

It spoke well for the trip. Had the men been subjected to unusual hardships, it is probable that they would not have complained at all. The trials to which they, as frontiersmen, were accustomed were naturally the trials about which they grumbled. Otherwise they were put on their mettle, as in a case frequently quoted from the writings of Silas St. John, an employee of the line.

Over a vast section of the country there had been a famine. Stations, settlements, and military posts were on the verge of starvation. On top of this the playful Comanches had swept over a two-hundred-mile stretch of road and stampeded all relay animals. When the stage pulled through, passengers were obliged to subsist for five days on the grain from the animals' grain bags. Better-humored travelers than these, it appears, were rare. They were hardy men! They were used to this sort of thing! "Hie, Jim! Hook on your nose-bag. Do you prefer corn or barley?"

The ordinary fare provided by the stage company, which was as palatable as could have been soberly hoped for, was seldom so cheerily received; but the traveler was apt to gain weight on the trip unless his ennui drove him to bad whisky. Bad whisky was plentiful along the route; and according to Hunning, it was apt to be very bad indeed.

On this hazardous section of road, lying between Tucson and La Mesilla, he says "we had a very good coach, plenty of mules, and seven men well armed with Colts and Sharp's rifles." The captain of these "side-riders" was one Mr. Holliday, who was further

From an original and technically accurate painting by Chapin of "The Los Angeles Times."

FIFTEEN MILES AN HOUR IN LATER DAYS

armed with two bottles of whisky which he had bought before leaving Tucson. It was "Ratified Whisky." A dealer in this excellent desert grog had guaranteed it as such; but not until this worthy old plainsman had consumed the content of one bottle and begun to contemplate the next could he have vouched for the worth of its guarantee. Without a doubt, the liquor had been put through a kind of "ratifying" process. Four baby rats had been drowned in it, embalmed in it, sealed in it, and there they were.

Whether or not Holliday was used to that sort of thing is not of record; but they were hardy men indeed—these guards through the Apache lands. While the ravages of Indians along their route were frequent, invariably the stage went through unscathed.

In the fall of fifty-seven, during a hostile Indian demonstration in Arizona wherein nearly all settlements from Fort Buchanan to Calabasis were plundered of their stock, a party of forty Apaches attempted to stop the east-bound mail, but was routed in a hurry by the first flourish of arms, a mere gesture from this convoy of six.

"The mail travels so rapidly," explained "The San Francisco Herald," in all seriousness, "that the Indians have no means of making any combination to stop it."

It is true that "The Herald" carried a large advertisement for "The Jackass Mail" (which it mentioned in terms more dignified) ; but, in the face of all odds, the service was not considered slow even by those who wondered whom it served besides the politicians of Washington, D. C. What little mail was carried came through regularly according to contract within thirty days, twice every month and without failure. Indeed, it was building up a reputation for its efforts to better a self-imposed schedule of twenty-seven days.

In March 1858, when four, five, and six mule stage-coaches were well established and running from one end of the line to the other, one mail came through in twenty-three and a half days. Two in the following month were within twenty-five, and June brought a record of twenty-one. It was an average rate over the distance of 1,476 miles of approximately sixty-seven miles per day, nearly two and eight-tenths miles per hour. There was some room for improvement; but the line, as a unit, was given little opportunity for any further demonstrations.

Down from St. Louis and from San Francisco in September came the rumble of the Butterfield wheels —the great overland giant which was to steal the thunder of its forerunner, gobble much of the identity of the pioneer. At El Paso in the east and Fort Yuma in the west, it swept directly into the tracks of the old San Antonio Mail. Predictions were that "The Jackass" would be absorbed. But it was not. Indeed, during the following two months its subsidy was increased from $149,800 to $196,448. It was improved from a semi-monthly to a weekly line, but much of its individuality passed with the improvement. Its central section—that between El Paso and Fort Yuma—was discontinued. It had abandoned some 600 miles of its length to Butterfield & Company and become two lines instead of one. Yet, always as Mail Route No. 8067, it was to continue with various vicissitudes until shortly after the outbreak of the Civil War, ending its long career August 2, 1861, as "The Los Angeles, San Diego & San Antonio Mail": under the firm of Giddings & Doyle, Woods superintending, Frank Stevens of the Birch estate still worrying over its finances.

"It was the pioneer of all these [overland] undertakings," said the "San Francisco Herald," rejoicing in the success of the evolving institution. "The company has been running their stages with strict regularity, and has faithfully performed the terms of the contract, and this was the principal inciting cause to the establishment of the other routes."

But the editor might well have gone back a little farther. He might even have recalled the days of forty-nine when Jim Birch had cracked his whip above the ears of his four mustangs and gone rattling off for the mines.

Chapter III

ACTION ALONG THE RAINBOW TRAIL

A STAGEMAN of more brilliant qualifications and personal resources than James Birch would have been difficult to name; but his death, with its threatening effect upon the San Antonio & San Diego line, makes it evident that President Buchanan had not erred in diverting the major contract from his hands to those of a firm. As it proved, moreover, John Butterfield, as the active head of this organization, was exceptionally well suited to his position.

"Like one or more of our railroad presidents," writes A. L. Stimson in 1858,[1] "he had been a stage driver in his younger days, and a very popular one he was, too." Yet, more than this, he had risen to control all the principal stage lines in the center of New York State. The year of forty-nine had found him expanding broadly into other fields—he was in the Panama freighting business and at the same time was building up a lively opposition to Wells & Company's Express in the Atlantic States. He was known also as a promoter and builder of telegraph systems; as a

[1] "History of the Express Companies and the Origin of the American Railroads" (New York, 1858).

founder of formidable lines of lake and river steamers, and, finally, as one of the foremost expressmen in the country.

His Butterfield, Wassen & Company and his Wells, Butterfield & Company had associated themselves with similar New York express firms in the names of Fargo, Livingston, and others, and were now a part of the grand combine known as the American Express. Of this association Butterfield was the line superintendent, and from it had been recruited various of the joint contractors for the Great Overland Mail Company. With Butterfield as president of the latter, there were apt to be glittering results; but in spite of his sound potentialities and those of his associates—Dinsmore, Fargo, Holland, and the rest—misgivings were broadcast.

From September 15, 1857, these contractors had been allowed exactly one year in which to complete all preparations. Within that period there were 165 stations to be constructed. They were to be fashioned, not of mesquite and willow branches, but of adobe or stone or logs. There were an equal number of corrals to be erected from similar materials. There were many springs to locate, wells to drill, cisterns to dig, tanks and tank-wagons to build, fording sites to grade, bridges, supply bases, and blacksmith and repair shops to establish. Over some 3,000 miles of road, to include a branch, there were to be distributed 1,200 horses, 600 mules, fodder by the thousands of tons, some hundred stage wagons and coaches, together with 750 selected and organized men—superintendents, agents, conductors, drivers, station keepers, hostlers, etc. And what of the wild desert wastes from which almost all of this was to spring? It did not seem possible that these New York expressmen could realize the stupendous nature of their undertaking.

"Were it not for the newspapers puffing of their ability along the whole line," came one rather weighty observance from El Paso, fully three months after the contract had been closed, "no man would ever know that they were in existence as contractors. . . . Their want of action goes plainly to show that they never intended complying with the contract," and so on at considerable length. This correspondent, though anonymous, professed to be a "practical stageman." Having gone into all the intricate details of stocking the line, the idea appalled him. "This thing," he concluded, "is an absurdity." [1]

But it was not simply the stocking of the line that worried John Butterfield. He had been wasting much of his precious time in a futile attempt to bring about an amendment of his contract. He saw no practical reason for adopting the route foisted upon him by the Postmaster-General. Any course bending south of the thirty-fifth parallel, he insisted, would be unnecessarily long. But the Honorable Postmaster having vio-

[1] Correspondence dated El Paso, December 20, 1857, of "The San Diego Herald." See "California Chronicle," February 5, 1858.

lated the apparent intentions of Congress, if not the written law, in behalf of the Southern route, was not to be swayed by any mere contractor now. The route was fixed. There would be no amendment of the contract—that is, unless it were, perhaps, to cut off the Missouri terminus!

For it seemed now that the branch line to St. Louis had been recently surveyed by the Government and declared not altogether negotiable. In short, it appeared that the Postmaster-General's home town of Memphis was the one and only real practicable site for an Eastern terminus!

In the end, however, the threatened northerly branch was spared. But this same branch was, in return, to show no mercy to those who had spared it. It may be mentioned that the spur line to St. Louis was soon to afford such speed to the mail out of St. Louis, that the coach arriving at the junction of Fort Smith, Arkansas, would be obliged very often to wait from twenty-four to thirty-six hours for the mail out of Memphis! And it was to result in such speed in the opposite direction that letters despatched overland directly to Memphis could be beaten by those directed to the same town by way of St. Louis and the river boats! Indeed, no section of the line—not even the Indian-ravished Tucson–El Paso division—was to cause John Butterfield more annoyance than this Memphis branch.

But it was not, by the way, a "branch." The Post-

Office Department, far from admitting it as a use-
less appendage, insisted that its dignity be upheld.
Memphis, it appeared, was on the "main line." *St.
Louis* was on the *branch!* [1]

In the light of such piffle, obviously some of Butterfield's troubles were cut out for him; but what
he was able to make of a route that was either a
political outrage or a stupid blunder might well grant
him the very highest honors among all eminent overland stage proprietors before the railroad. One of the
most noteworthy of his methods tending toward success had to do with his genius as an organizer.

Cutting his long line into two equal parts, joined
by the town of El Paso, the eastern half was given
over almost wholly to an eastern and middle-western
personnel, while the remainder was operated principally by Californians. Not only did this create
standards suggested by the flourishing Pacific Coast
institution, but to an *esprit de corps* which the stagefaring personality of Butterfield might have compelled under any circumstances there was added an
element of keen rivalry which the journals at both
ends of the line were continually whetting.

The route, disregarding the short railroad extensions at the two eastern termini, was further cut into
nine "divisions," the first extending from San Francisco to Los Angeles, the second thence to Fort Yuma,

[1] An amusing account of this affair is given in the St. Louis correspondence
of "The Sacramento Union" of July 27, 1859.

the third thence to Tucson, and so on—El Paso, Fort Chadbourne, Colbert's Ferry, and Fort Smith, whence the two branches extended to their respective rail termini of Tipton (for St. Louis) and Little Rock (for Memphis).

Over each of these divisions was an agent, and over the agents superintendents, all of whom had been chosen from among the most experienced stagemen of the country. There was James Glover of Memphis, a former bidder against Butterfield for the mail contract; there was Warren F. Hall of the old firms of Hall & Crandall and the California Stage Company; A. N. Fisher, the late proprietor of nearly all staging through California's southerly mining district; William Buckley from New York, a veteran of later renown; Charles McLaughlin, owner of all local stage-coaches out of San Francisco, agent for the "Jackass Mail," former general superintendent of the California Company, and one of the outstanding pioneers—all these and others like them were enlisted in the Butterfield service.

Contractors in person, having made this splendid selection of line officials, had traversed the route from end to end; and the work of construction had followed in their dust. Things began tumbling together in the amazing manner of a circus. Soon horses and mules in troupes of several hundred, coaches and stage wagons in grand processions of eight to twelve were coursing the tracks of supply trains, eastward and westward, bound for stations that were still in the process of construction. Gloomy predictions began to go by the board; and, just as stages from the East and stages from the West were soon to come rolling into El Paso, ofttimes within sight of each other's approach, system prevailed all throughout the latter months of preparation. It was a clock-works building a clock; and the very day scheduled by contract for the commencement of service was to see the wheels going round.

Some laudation is due to the daring of many workers who were left in small parties with sundry tasks at the various remote points of the deserts. Mishaps were astonishingly few; but the story of the massacre near Dragoon Springs, Arizona, suggests what hazards there were to contend with besides the hostilities of Indians.

Dragoon Station, located about a mile from the Springs proper and nearly sixty miles from the closest protected settlement, Tucson, belonged to the dangerous El Paso–Tucson division—that portion of road where the tracks of the "Jackass Mail" were still accompanied by the imprints of a half-dozen mounted guards. It belonged no less, perhaps, to the Cochise nation, since the prowling inhabitants of this region had not yet learned to recognize the claims of any company of white men, nor those of any flag. And dangers were increased by the fact that here was a passing point for the Apaches bound to and from Sonora, and that stations, though placed at intervals to average about seventeen miles over the entire route, averaged fully thirty over this particular division.

Even such veterans as Colonel James B. Leach, who had been superintending the construction of a military road—the mail route—between Fort Yuma and the Rio Grande since the spring of fifty-seven, were not given to any show of indifference while traveling through these parts, as witness his approach to Dragoon, some sixteen months later, accompanied by three wagons and a sizable detachment of men.

The date was September 12, 1858—three days before the overland mails were to be despatched from San Francisco, St. Louis, and Memphis on their initial trips across the plains. All along the road, as Colonel Leach's party moved from the eastward toward Dragoon, mail stations had been passed, their flags flying, their builders busy laying on rafters and roofing, storing sacks of grain or tending stock; but Dragoon, still roofless, stood like a deserted ruin.

The stone walls of its corral, built especially high to serve as barricades against Indians, seemed now as likely to conceal a formidable band of them as the mail company's animals. The colonel ordered a detour to the southward for cover, then, with a small force deployed, cautiously advanced on foot. But signs of ambuscade began to diminish. Magpies, crows, and buzzards were strutting along on the naked rafters.

Several of them flapped awkwardly up against the hot morning sky and down to alight upon a heap of bones; the party moved on . . . human bones, a skull, crushed as though from the blow of a sledge, the remainder torn by coyotes. But there had been no Indians here; there were mules, still alive, half famished behind the walls.

And there were men, as it developed, still alive within the dwelling.

The sun beat down between its ribs of roof. Vultures cast shadows that moved sluggishly along the floor—over splattered hatchets, a rifle, a pistol, a sledge of stone. A saddle pillowed the cleft head of a corpse. Time had worked horrors; but death was the least ghastly of all that remained. Two men were breathing—one standing, staring out from mad eyes, unable to speak. His dry tongue was swollen between his teeth; his body was torn like his garments. A strip of rag bound up an arm that had been all but severed.

There were no physicians in Leach's party at the time, nor any yet in Tucson; but while some treatment was being rendered, riders were despatched toward Fort Buchanan, three days' journey on horseback over the only route which any small detachment would dare. It was clear, meanwhile, that there was hope only for the one survivor, Silas St. John, a former carrier for the San Antonio & San Diego Mail, now head of the late construction crew under Superintendent William Buckley. Mercifully, the other lay as he had slept, his head on his saddle, unconscious from a wound which was soon to carry him away. He was buried there in the desert along with one other and the desecrated remains of the third.

St. John, responding to what rude treatment could be offered, said that Buckley had passed through late in August, leaving him with a party of three other Americans, now dead, and three Mexicans to complete Dragoon Station in time for the first Butterfield stages. It must have been about one or two o'clock on the morning of September 9 when the trouble arose. There had been one American sleeping outside the walls. Another, having been relieved from his night watch by a Mexican, had joined St. John and the fourth within the station. All, in short, were intrusting their lives to the Mexicans. It may be that the latter had coveted the stock, or simply that there were motives of revenge. In any event, St. John was the only one to recognize daylight again.

A stir among the animals in the corral, a whistle—he heard it vaguely, and was aroused an instant later by dull, heavy blows, feeble cries. Some chance alone parried the swing of an ax blade which must have ended his life; and a dizzy succession of similar chances saw him, empty-handed, wounded, one-armed at last, bear up through a conflict with two Mexicans wielding hatchets, then three. But by this time he had seized his rifle. One Mexican, on sight of it, fled; the others followed; although St. John, wounded as he was, had been unable to raise the weapon to an aim. He dropped it for a pistol in his saddle holster. But one shot from this and the affray was over. The Mexicans, running, faded off into the dark. The night passed . . . then three more nights.

The companions of St. John had been found beyond help. The man who had slept in the open had been killed outright; a death-rattle had passed the throat of another before the dawn of the second day, and the third had lain insensible, his groans mingling eternally with the barks of coyotes and the braying of half-famished mules, while night after night, with ever-increasing torment, wore through.

A spring of water trickled coolly a mile away, but the survivor had been unfit to stir beyond the meager shade of the walls. One morning a horseman had appeared on the road; but, fully half a mile away, he had decided to come no closer, had passed on a detour. Weak from his loss of blood, feverish from his many wounds, and tortured by thirst, St. John might have ended his miserable life that day but for the opportune arrival of Colonel Leach.

Silas St. John, having come at last into the hands of a surgeon from the fort, survived for a useful life on the plains. His story, related briefly by the journals of the time and at length by his own report as quoted in Farish's "History of Arizona," is not the only one of depredation and murder along the Butterfield line. Lone Willows Station, California, was the scene of a similar massacre a few months later, the wife of the station-keeper being numbered among the victims. Stations were open to plunder, and generally far more worth the plundering than the stages themselves. Indians were soon to realize the fact and to take considerable toll. It was all to be expected; and, in spite of it, the stages, starting according to schedule, continued with an average that was well within schedule; and at no time, until near the last, with the eruption of war, were there any suspensions of operations. No finer record of reliable service can be found in the history of the great overland lines.

Chapter IV

CHIEF BUTTERFIELD AND THE INDIANS

BUTTERFIELD & COMPANY had agreed to carry the mail between San Francisco and the eastern termini of St. Louis and Memphis twice a week, making the through trip within twenty-five days. Common prediction had added about ten days more to this schedule and regarded this rate only as a hopeful possibility. An early pamphlet published in Washington and indorsed evidently by scattered journals, having reviewed the prospects in some detail, reached the conclusion that stages could not be driven across the "Seven Deserts" as proposed "in twenty-five days, nor in forty days, nor at all."

"Human ingenuity," it held, "cannot devise a plan for such an unheard-of achievement. . . . It never has been done. It never will be done." [1]

At the time the first coaches set out (September 15, 1858), Colonel Leach had not yet completed the Fort Yuma and Rio Grande road; nor had Butterfield either completed or established all his stations. More than this, the west-bound stage from St. Louis

[1] See "The Sacramento Union" of September 3, 1857, quoting San Francisco "Town Topics," "The Missouri Democrat" and a Washington pamphlet.

was held up twenty-four hours at the Fort Smith Junction waiting for the Memphis mail. Yet, in spite of it all, and of other delays due to the newness of the vast organization, both the east and the west bound stages, carrying mail and passengers from one end of the line to the other, arrived not only within schedule time, but in less than twenty-four days.

The mail from California having been met by "the cars" of the Missouri Pacific Railroad some hundred and sixty miles west of St. Louis, was received in the latter town with such acclaim as might be imagined. Human ingenuity had achieved the "unheard-of"— twenty-three days and four hours between San Francisco and St. Louis! The town's "Silver Band" was all but silenced by the throat-bursting cheers of a multitude and by the blasting of locomotive whistles, the ringing of bells and the firing of guns. Passengers and mail and John Butterfield himself were seized from the platforms of the Tipton train and borne off in a triumphant march for the post-office. There were speeches of roaring welcome poured out upon the successful contractor, to include a telegram of congratulation from President Buchanan in Washington. But much as the overland mail could mean to Missouri, there was some reason for ecstasy at the more isolated end of the line.

There, due to the delay caused by the Memphis "main line," time across the plains was recorded at twenty-three days and twenty hours—sixteen hours

more than that of the east-bound stage; but it was
fast enough to stand San Francisco on her head.

When the coach itself, behind six sweating, snorting grays, came rattling through her streets, there
were horsemen in advance to clear a path through the
surging mob. Flags were draped from crowded windows and flying from congested roof-tops; while the
driver, proud as Louis Napoleon at the fêtes of Cher-
bourg, nodded a response to a shrieking, whistling
riot with all the dignity of a field marshal. Cannon
and brass band boomed together, "stovepipes" crushed
beneath tramping boots in a howling stream of color
that flooded the plaza. Then a mass-meeting jammed
the Music Hall in honor of "a new epoch" and "the
end of the steamship monopoly."

As the weeks and months passed, and the stages
continued with unfailing regularity, the name "overland" became the word of the day. One bought
"overland hats," "overland boots," "overland coats,"
"overland ponies," "overland chickens," even "overland eggs," to the tune or blast of a real overland
horn whose echoes sounded cheerily through the valleys and over the plains from St. Louis to San Francisco.

"Admiral" John Butterfield, as he was known all
along the line, was in his element, his glory. What
stage driver could ever have been more so? Throughout the several thousand miles of his phenomenal
route he became the recipient of attentions paid to a

traveling prince. Word of his genial presence breathed in any tavern more than filled it. He was the "Great Chief Butterfield" to the Cherokees. He was the Great Father of the "swift-wagon."

The swift-wagon, so called by all the Indians, was received by the tribes of the interior as a marvel of all creation. On one occasion six hundred Comanches, at their proverbial wildest, pounced down upon it in a body. For five hours the driver was obliged to await their pleasure and the passengers to tolerate their insistent company. . . . "*Ugh!*" They looked under the seats. . . . "*Ugh! Oh!*" They unstrapped the rear boot. . . . "*Ugh!*" They examined the wheels; they turned over the mail sacks, inspected the pole, couplings, and trappings. Patiently the driver allowed them their time, though his chronometer may have burned in his pocket. Then, at last: "*Ugh! You go on! Go swift!*" They liked swift-wagons. But not railroad. No. Just swift-wagons.

Their term for coach or stage wagon may have been derived from the obvious; and yet it was very similar to the name of a certain vehicle used very extensively on the Butterfield line—namely, the "Celerity Wagon." The "Celerity" was a type of "mud-wagon" (though evidently no stage was so called at this time). It was adapted especially for use on heavy roads, or for rugged, mountainous country where, given a coach, there might be some danger of capsizing. It was comparatively light, having a trim

body with firm duck superstructure provided with
roller flaps at the sides. Thorough-braces, of course,
were used in place of springs, as in the cases of all
other stages of the West worthy of mention. For
there were, incidentally, various makes and types of
stage wagons to include several splendid Concord vehicles by the manufacturers of the celebrated coach.[1]
But, as was already being realized, there was "only
one coach."

Butterfield was now using at both extremities of
his line, and over an aggregate distance of perhaps a
thousand miles, Troy coaches (saved, perhaps, from
his early staging days) as well as Concords; but the
former type was fast waning in popularity, the Concord being the typical and ineffable. Let a true crafts-
man examine the workmanship involved, and he will
marvel a bit more than did these wild Comanches of
fifty-eight to whom all stages were simply swift-
wagons. Their appreciation, however, was all too genuine.

They knew, for example, that the swift-wagon,
unlike the detested locomotive, depended on stations
—Indian supply stations where stock could be had
for much less than the asking. Among the six hundred braves engaged in that friendly powwow with
passengers along the road, there may have been many
who had recently visited James Glover's division just
east of the Rio Grande and walked off with some

[1] See illustrations facing pages 25 and 161.

(LEFT) OLD EMIGRANT AND STAGE ROAD LEADING FROM THE GILA VALLEY TO OATMAN FLAT, THE SITE OF THE OATMAN MASSACRE OF 1852.

(RIGHT) RUINS OF THE BUTTERFIELD STATION OF OATMAN FLAT.

Photographed through the kindness of William Foeurr.

GRAVES AND RUINS OF OLD DRAGOON
SCENE OF THE MASSACRE OF FIFTY-EIGHT.

thirty-five animals. They had been friendly enough
even on that occasion. They had explained to the
helpless station masters that if, at any time, the mail
company needed the stock any more than they did,
then the mail company could come and take it, just
as they had. But the mail company did not make the
attempt. Naturally, then, they came back.

Thirty-five mules were few compared with the
number they really needed. So they proceeded to
devastate some four hundred miles of the Big Chief
Butterfield's route; and before the section could be
restocked, several stages on passing through were
obliged to depend upon their passengers as well as
their worn-out teams for progress through a considerable part of the plundered region.

On such occasions as this—and they were not in-
frequent—the fare for a through passage, which
varied upward with time from one to two hundred
dollars, may have seemed rather high; but there was
food for the heart of adventure thus to be deprived
of the swift-wagon's swiftness in the very region
where speed seemed most desirable.

The stage, however, carrying heavily armed passengers, was something of an arsenal on wheels. For
every horse or mule that the savage could hope to
capture from its team, he was apt to pay with at
least two "good Indians" shot from his dusty ranks.
The swift-wagon, moreover, had sometimes more
speed even than an Indian cavalcade, whose animals

generally were too poorly fed and cared for to match the endurance of the mail team. The latter, given sufficient head start under favoring conditions, might be expected to outdistance the enemy. In fact, it was not until the middle sixties, when the Indian began fighting for his existence on earth, that the stage-coach became a frequent victim of his attack.

But the stations! The lonely huts of mud on the deserts—these were the objectives for plunder. And the men, or families, living in them—theirs were the bullets to chew. They waited, while the Indians planned, estimating what forces would be needed, what time would be most favorable to them. Then down they would swoop, presenting odds overwhelming; and, resistance or none, they were not always satisfied with just stock.

One rather pathetic account, among many instances of such plundering, relates to a certain Camp Johnson in Texas. Here, in a lonely adobe hut, lived a station master, three attendants, a wife, two children, and two little pigs. This family became aware of callers one morning at sunrise (September 2, 1859) when arrows and bullets from some thirty Indians announced them, several mounted warriors following up to the barricaded door. Being invited to help themselves to the nine mules in the corral, they did so very promptly; then killed a bullock and commenced to eat it on the spot.

A stage was due. It arrived in time to interrupt another firing upon the house, but too late to hope for a fresh team in its travels onward. . . . Swift-wagon! The load had been increased by the woman and her children; the old team, with perhaps eighteen miles to go, appeared scarcely able to put away the first of them. The four men walked along in the rear; and not far behind, waddling and squeaking, came the pigs.

It was a part of the life of station dwellers; and along with the hundreds of horses and mules lost to the Indians by Butterfield & Company, there were some lives to go in the bargain. But there came a time near the end of the Southern régime, when the Apaches in the vicinity of the notorious Tucson–El Paso division, decided not to confine their hostilities to the stations alone. They openly declared war on all travel through their land.

The trouble had originated (February 1861) when an infantry detachment of sixty men under a certain Lieutenant Bascomb from Fort Buchanan had visited a party of Apaches near the station at Apache Pass, a point approximately forty miles east of Dragoon. The intention had been to recover a kidnapped Mexican boy; but the attempt proving futile, the troops moved off to encamp at the station, bringing with them six braves as reprisal. They had captured Chief Cochise himself; but he had escaped, and no doubt with some feeling of bitterness, and some thought of immediate revenge.

On the following afternoon (February 6) the stage from the east arrived some hours earlier than usual—a happening which may have saved the lives of all of its occupants. Apache Pass had long been recognized by emigrants as the most dangerous stretch of trail along the route. It extended westward from the station, coursing darkly through the shadows of precipitous mountains for a distance of about two miles. Slaughter here was as old as travel; but due to a dearth of water elsewhere, there was no possible detour. It had to be risked, and had been risked four times every week by the stages of Butterfield & Company.

This particular stage usually passed through at night. Now, in the late afternoon, it became plain to the driver that, whether or not he was stealing a march on the Indians, at least they had not expected him before dark. The road was blocked with great heaps of loose hay. Where the hay was not heaped, it was strewn; and leading off here and there were long spurs of it which, if set on fire, would soon have converted the entire area into flames. The victims, attempting to escape, would be clearly revealed by the blaze and be fired upon by an enemy they could not see. It was an old trick. And now, even in the absence of its success, there was reason enough for excitement among the passengers. They were clearing the road for the wagon, breaking on through, without knowing at what minute they might be flanked by a hundred arrows from the cliffs above. Soon, however, with the fire trap destroyed and behind them, they reached the west end of the pass. Here there had been an encampment of emigrants. Now there were only the remains. Nine of the unfortunates, chained to their wagon wheels, had been burned alive.

The stage clattered on. Another, from the opposite direction, met it shortly; but though it received the warning, including news of the massacre, all of its nine passengers were determined to risk the pass and reach the station that night. Superintendent William Buckley himself was aboard. They were all ready, they said, for the Indians.

It was perhaps well that they were. Into the echoing dark between the mountains, they had no sooner come upon the remnants of the blockade than the bullets and arrows began to fly. The driver lurched and reeled on the box, yet clung to his lines, cracking and laying on the whip, while a battery of rifles in the hands of his passengers blazed away behind him from both sides. A loud clattering speed was maintained for a moment. Then, suddenly, everything was paralyzed. Two mules shot down, and a piled-up team!

To be halted thus in the midst of such a gauntlet, yet to retain still a hope of escape, was to make some demands upon Providence; but there was promise in the roar of a defensive fire under whose cover Buckley and several others were cutting out the disabled mules.

"All aboard!" The stage was again on its way. A wounded driver, urging on the exhausted remnants of his team, brought his passengers at last, unscathed, to Apache Pass Station. Bringing also the first news of the massacre to Lieutenant Bascomb, volunteer horsemen were despatched toward Fort Buchanan for reinforcements. The stage proceeded no farther. The Butterfield route, for the first time in its history, was blocked.

On the following morning the Indians appeared near the station in large numbers, bearing a white flag; yet none of them would advance to speak their minds. Nor would Lieutenant Bascomb venture among them or allow any of his men to do so; but the station master and one of his assistants, together with F. J. Wallace, a stage driver, strode out, hailing several of the chiefs whom they recognized, and with whom they had been on friendly terms.

It proved a foolhardy move. The three men were seized. Of two who broke loose and fought clear, one was shot dead. The other, scaling a wall of the corral, toppled down the other side severely wounded. Wallace, the driver, was carried off as a prisoner—a subject, rather, for their cruelty. For when the troops from Fort Buchanan finally arrived, his body, together with the remains of three emigrants from the ravished train, was found staked out on the plains and torn by coyotes.

This offense having been promptly avenged by the

hanging of the six Indian captives, bitterness grew. More stations were raided, another stage was attacked, another driver was severely wounded; and, later, Giddings of the San Antonio Mail, was shot and killed.

One rather spectacular encounter occurred early in April, this time about forty miles west of Tucson, where two score Apaches lay in ambush waiting for the stage. There were no passengers aboard. William Willis, the conductor, was sound asleep in one of the rear seats when the discharge of rifles aroused him. He awoke under a raking fire that extended for many yards down the road, and saw the body of the driver fall to the ground. Making his way forward, however, he managed to recover the lines and drive on. Fortunately, in this case, it was the team that the Indians wanted rather than vengeance. At least, none of the animals were wounded. Willis, too, by the grace of chance, was whirled through the gauntlet unscathed, arriving shortly at the refuge of Picacho del Tucson.

The few slight departures from schedule to be noted throughout the history of this Southern mail may be ascribed mostly to this one brief period in the spring of sixty-one—the latter days of the line's existence. Formerly, month after month, the time of arrival at San Francisco and St. Louis varied mostly as the rate of speed was being steadily improved from twenty-four days to twenty-three, and thence to twenty-two. On many occasions, however, the mail came through in twenty-one days, and in several instances twenty. Overland stages of later days, given shorter routes, were to reduce this time to seventeen (Indians permitting), but, on the whole, they were not to equal this reliability. There was to be, in fact, no overland staging more efficient in its management or more worthy of praise than that under John Butterfield.

Courtesy of the Bancroft Library. From an old lithograph.

OLD SAN FRANCISCO

ORIGINAL ILLUSTRATION FROM JOHN M. LETTS'S "CALIFORNIA ILLUSTRATED."

Chapter V

DR. TUCKER'S WILD RIDE

TO embark on a journey which was to involve approximately twenty-six hundred miles of unceasing night-and-day travel by stage from San Francisco to where the rails began was to undertake, at least, a unique experience, and sometimes a real adventure.

"To many people, doubtless, who think more of their ease than they do of robust physical health, a stage ride of two thousand miles may seem a very formidable undertaking. But for those who have a liking for adventure, and a desire to see something of the world, a long ride of two or three weeks, practically in the open air . . . possesses a wonderful charm, especially in remembrance."

H. D. Barrows, writing for the Historical Society of Southern California,[1] goes on to tell of his trip over the Butterfield route. It appears to have been one of almost unadulterated routine—day and night, jog and bump over the deserts. But it was, none the less, an experience which had added some color to the tapestry of his life. It was an experience which the world

[1] The "Annual Publication" of 1896.

had never offered before and was not apt to offer
again in the years to follow.

"I know what hell is like. I've had twenty-four
days of it," was the comment of another passenger,
who had, at any rate, to acknowledge a rare experience. But certainly a "robust physical health" was
needed in order to sense any "wonderful charm." Indeed, out of half a dozen contemporaneous accounts,
mostly from the writings of such hardy newspaper
correspondents as the journals of the time demanded,
there were none to show quite Mr. Barrow's appreciation. It would seem, in fact, that something more
than physical health had been rather necessary.

"One poor fellow went crazy from loss of sleep,
and to prevent mischief to himself and others we were
obliged to strap him fast in the boot and leave him at
the next station"—this from the writings of Dr. J. C.
Tucker, reminiscing for "The San Francisco Argonaut" in later days.[1] Dr. Tucker's story is perhaps the
most graphic of all, his adventures having been well
worth the price of his ticket. Out of Syracuse, Missouri (to which point the railroad from St. Louis had
been extended during the year fifty-nine), he set
forth aboard "an elegant Concord coach" and behind
"six spirited horses." Over the level pampas roads of
Missouri and down through Arkansas he traveled to
the commencement of a romance which is quoted here
at length.

[1] *Op. cit.*, September 29, 1890.

Shortly after crossing the Red River [he writes] we took aboard a party of four—two men and two women—all French. We three men who occupied the back seat, at once placed it at the disposal of these unexpected lady passengers and their escort. While politely acknowledging—in their own tongue—the courtesy, the party at once assumed an utter exclusiveness of manner and ignorance of English. The *patois* of the elder woman and man proclaimed their Canadian origin. The younger man of about thirty-five years, was evidently a Parisian—a haughty, supercilious fellow, who saw nothing but the young and handsome French girl. . . .

But the bright, black eyes of the girl saw everything. Evidently she was fresh from some rural province in France, and hugely enjoyed the novelty of border life in this country.

"Mon Dieux—c'est extraordinaire!" was her constant exclamation.

Somewhere about here, we took on a typical border man—a tall, handsome young fellow in boots and buckskins, bound for his ranch in Texas. With Western familiarity, he was at once addressed as "Texas," as I was saluted as "California." . . .

A few miles further, and a fat German Jew boarded us. It was raining, and this party—now all inside—filled the coach. "Dutchy," as Texas at once irreverently called our two-hundred-pound Teutonic acquisition, insisted upon sitting at the door in the middle seat, and Texas discomfited himself in the middle to give him the fresh air he wanted. It was sultry and close already, but when the rain began to pour down in torrents, and it became necessary to close the windows, it was stifling. The Americans passed around their flasks, joked and told stories. The Frenchmen distantly rejected, in French, all approach at companionship, while Dutchy disagreeably growled at the want of room and air.

Informed by the driver that the French party were professional gamblers, it was not surprising that our handsome Texan was soon broadly returning the admiring glances of the pretty, vivacious French girl. Texas was a blonde—straight, aristocratic features, well browned and bearded, with graceful curling hair falling upon his broad shoulders. His manly, well-developed figure, set off to advantage by the picturesque buckskin costume, long boots and belted weapons, was one calculated, at any time, to attract a woman's attention. Besides all that, while he was evidently educated and well-bred, there was an air of recklessness, an impulsive good nature in every act and word. By the time we took supper at a station near Texarkansas, the Frenchmen were furious. . . . Evidently the men regretted their asserted—"No speck English."

We all wanted to smoke, but the presence of the women restrained us. Just then Dutchy pulled an enormous pipe from his pocket, and, deliberately loading, proceeded to light and smoke it, despite the remonstrances of all. The "Mon Dieux" of the women and the curses of the men only caused Dutchy to open his window to a torrent of rain and wind. Suddenly, Texas snatched the pipe from his mouth and flung it through the window.

Dutchy was disposed to fight, but was deterred by a general acceptance of responsibility by all of the men. After indulging in considerable abuse, which Texas good-naturedly returned, Dutchy slewed him-

From a modern photograph by Keystone.

CONCORD "HACK PASSENGER WAGON"

TYPE OF STAGE REPRODUCED WITH SLIGHT CHANGES FROM OLD ABBOT-DOWNING DRAWINGS.

self around with his back against the door, took a big pull at his flask, and grumbled himself to sleep.

His snoring was equal to trombone practice and so annoying that Texas finally said: "We'll have to get shut of this porker."

Quietly reaching behind Dutchy, he turned the door-catch nearly around. The next jolt . . . the door gave way, and out went Dutchy heels over head into the road.

Texas at once sprang out, helped him up, and in a tone of bantering solicitude, inquired if he was hurt. Dutchy fairly foamed with rage and charged us all with an attempt to kill him. So violent was he that we would not allow him to re-enter the stage, insisting upon his riding outside, which he did to the next station where he started off—the driver said—to get out warrants for the arrest of Texas and California for assault. We stopped here but a few moments; the driver did not care to wait for anybody, he said, and so drove off, leaving Dutchy behind.

The flirtation between the French girl and Texas, by no means unobserved by her attendants, was warming to a dangerous temperature. The little attentions of a wild flower, a helping hand, or an admiring glance, which the dashing Texas managed to give her, elicited oath-garnished rebukes in furious French.

The stage had—the driver called out—rolled across the boundary line into the great state of Texas. It was nearing sunset, and the plain seemed alive with rabbits, antelope, and wild turkeys. In a low tree, quite near the road, sat an immense hawk. As we passed him, he slowly rose in flight, [and] one of the men said: "There's a fine shot!" Texas was sitting at the door window upon that side. He pulled his pistol and with a quick, chance shot, knocked the great bird's head off. Unquestionably an excellent shot, he himself candidly admitted that chance had much to do with the decapitation. Nevertheless, it was noticed that the pretty French girl smiled approvingly and received less frowning censure.

As the dead bird's mate rose just beyond, Texas motioned to the girl to shoot it, at the same time tendering the girl his pistol. Instantly the younger man thrust the revolver aside, exclaiming, in excellent English:

"D—n you, don't address this lady!"

For a moment the men glared at each other, and then Texas, breaking into a laugh, quietly replaced the pistol in his belt.

"Well, Frenchy, you *do* speak English well enough to apologize at the next station," he said.

The Frenchman made no reply, but at once entered into a violent altercation with his companion. Above the woman's sobs, my limited knowledge of French enabled me to understand the fierce denunciations of the infuriated lover of Marie.

A half-hour of grim oppressiveness followed, and then the horn sounded our approach to the supper station. Both men were evidently brave and determined to come together when the women should be out of the way. As the stage stopped, Texas sprang out first and at once passed back of the station house. I was about to follow when the older Frenchman laid his hand upon my arm. "I wish to speak with you, sir, immediately I escort these ladies to the house," he said.

I bowed in reply, and he was again with me in a minute.

"Your friend, Texas, he must give my friend the satisfaction—here—now!"

"That depends upon his wishes," I replied; "after you have explained to him the blood-thirsty desires of your friend, I think Texas will know how to act for himself."

"I will see him," exclaimed the Frenchman, and he followed Texas behind the house.

In a few moments they returned together, and Texas called to me.

"Cal, this fellow brings me a challenge to fight with pistols before we eat our supper. I'm ready. Will you act for me?"

Expressing my regrets at the serious turn of affairs and finding compromise rejected by both parties, I reluctantly assented to his request.

"Now," said Texas, taking me aside, "these fellows are gamblers and not entitled to code recognition. There is a large empty corral back of the house; it has two gates opposite each other—north and south. Tell Frenchy to bring his fighting man to the south gate, and you put me into the north entrance. Then see that Frenchy don't interfere, and I'll fix the other frog-eater."

Returning to the elder Frenchman, I explained the conditions my principal demanded—a free fight to death.

"No, monsieur, it is barbarous—impossible," he replied; "I have the beautiful pistols made to fight the duel. We will fight only with these, like gentlemen, not with revolvers."

"No," I said. "Texas will fight your friend only in the way I've stated. If you don't accept, he will slap your friend's face before the ladies, and force him to use the revolver he carries. Texas knows your profession, and does not recognize you as gentlemen. Besides, we are the challenged party, and have the choice of weapons."

For a moment rage made the Frenchman speechless; then he hissed through his teeth: "D——n the man, he shall be shot in the corral like the beast he is. I will instantly bring my friend to the south gate."

As he turned to go, I said: "One moment—let us understand our position, also, in this affair. We are simply to see that our principals, when they once enter the corral by opposite gates, are to fight it out, unmolested. Until, through agreement or death, they cease fighting neither of us shall enter the corral. Any violation of this agreement will bring us into conflict, also. Do you clearly understand? . . ."

"Oui, je comprends," he replied as he walked toward the house.

Whatever their profession, these Frenchmen were brave men, and it was with great apprehension of disaster that I returned to Texas who remained by the north gate of the corral.

He had not much more than given me his address and that of a friend, to whom I was to write should he be killed, before we saw the two Frenchmen approaching the opposite gate.

These entrances were quite two hundred feet apart, the ground level and unobstructed. Throwing my handkerchief into the air as a signal, the two combatants entered almost simultaneously and opposite each other. They had their revolvers cocked, the Frenchman carrying his raised for a drop, while Texas held his by his side for a rising shot. Sheltered by the heavy gate-posts from flying balls, we seconds watched the principals, who cautiously walked toward each other across the broad corral. While the Frenchman, with upraised pistol, and eyes gleaming malignant hatred, was edging sideways across the tract, Texas was carelessly and more rapidly approaching him with square front.

Suddenly the Frenchman dropped his revolver and quickly fired two shots. At the second discharge, Texas half-wheeled to the left and staggered. His exposed left arm was shattered near the wrist.

As if realizing his carelessness before, Texas now sprang forward several paces and fired. Almost the same instant the Frenchman's pistol again spoke, but neither was touched.

The blood was pouring from Texas' wounded arm as he again sprang several yards nearer his antagonist, who paused, and they quickly fired together. The Frenchman's shot knocked off Texas' hat; but as yet the Frenchman was unhurt.

Then Texas dropped upon one knee, and setting his revolver across his wounded arm, fired with deliberate aim. His antagonist was, at the moment, also in the act of firing, but Texas' bullet reached his heart before he could press the trigger. Throwing his arms wildly in the air, the Frenchman fell dead.

The firing had attracted all of the inmates of the station—not more than half-a-dozen. These—with the two French women—quickly surrounded the fallen man. The driver had eaten his supper, fresh horses were in the harness, and Texas and myself could only squeeze some food and jump into the coach, as the six wild mustangs started off on a fierce gallop. I also carried off the roller-towel and some shingles to splint the broken arm.

The French party remained behind; we saw nothing more of them. Of their history from the driver, an old Santa Fé trader, we heard much. He had known the men as hard cases for many years upon the border. The older woman dealt faro for them, while the younger was doubtless a new acquisition. The men had a wild reputation for bravery and skill with weapons, and had killed many men. They were typical characters of that day—the well-dressed border tigers that met debauchery or death with equal nonchalance.

Dr. Tucker might have met adventure of the more typical kind had he proceeded by the customary route, the notorious Fourth Division, but—

Owing to the Indian troubles and a burned station, we were obliged to cross the Rio Grande just east of El Paso, and go down into Mexico for a day. There was a slight delay in getting horses, but, at a ranch, the usual untamed mustangs [1] were initiated into the harness, and after piling up in a heap a few times, started off. . . . Once started the horses seldom relaxed their gallop until a steep mountain or a station was reached. . . . Once a poor animal dropped dead, and we were obliged to assist the driver in reharnessing but four horses, turning the fifth one loose. We were now in thorough-brace mud-wagons. The mail-bags

[1] It was undoubtedly due to the Indian troubles that Dr. Tucker met so many "untamed mustangs." When stage horses were broken in it was the custom to hook them up along with two or four well-trained animals—this for obvious reasons. "Mustangs," moreover, would have been phenomenal if they existed on the Butterfield or any other first-class line. Strangely, the term "mustang" has appealed to writers more than the animals themselves ever appealed to stagemen.

left scarcely room for our feet; while the seats were narrow for three occupants each. Seated upon the outside end, I tied a hay rope across to keep from falling against the wheel.

Up and down the mountains, through the valleys, streams and gorges, forest and deserts, on we rolled, day and night, seldom stopping more than ten minutes at any station. Our approach to one was heralded by a horn; a fresh team was ready-harnessed; our bacon and slapjack, with a bottle of coffee, ready for us to take into the stage, and the new and impatient driver's "All aboard!" left little margin of time. Twice only we had an opportunity to bathe—by stripping and jumping into a river we forded. . . .

The wearied gunner can sleep beneath his bellowing gun, the sailor amid the roar of ocean storm, but three on a seat in an open mud-wagon, tearing ten miles an hour through a wild country, is a situation calculated to set at defiance any such rest. Youth, health, and trained endurance of loss of sleep in professional clinics, somewhat fortified me, but the extended suffering was intense and poignant beyond description. Greeley's wild ride down the Sierras, with the famous stage driver Hank Monk, was railroading to the bounding we experienced. Three in a row, and actuated by the same instantaneous impulse, we would solemnly rise from our seats, bump our heads against the low roof, and returning, vigorously ram against the rising seats we had incontinently left. You never encroached upon your neighbor, but upon waking you seldom failed to find him lying across you or snoring an apology into your ear. For we did sleep, somehow. The horribly weird feeling that accompanies the effort to resist slumber would give way for a few moments, and the blissful calm of a storm-tossed vessel gliding into quiet waters would fall upon our weary senses. Often did I wake refreshed by a seeming sleep of hours of dreaming, to be told by my watch that minutes only had elapsed. One poor fellow went crazy from loss of sleep. . . . Texas suffered acutely with his wound . . . [but] after the crazy man left . . . was less crowded and more at ease. He got off at Deming. A brave and manly fellow, I was glad years after to meet him in California, when he renewed his expressions of friendship and gratitude for my friendly surgical aid. He had become a staid and wealthy cotton-owner in Texas.

Dr. Tucker's dreary ride on over the deserts of California was one of the usual monotony. In the outskirts of San Francisco, at last, the stage was met by Mr. E. S. Alvord, vice-president (or chief superintendent) of the Overland Mail Company; but the doctor concludes:

I much fear that at that time we failed to appreciate his courtesy. Just then we were happy to arrive and could appreciate almost anything—except a stage and a stage company's vice-president.

PART THREE

THE WHIP OF MAJORS AND RUSSELL

Chapter I

BUCHANAN PLAYS THE PONIES

THE overland mail program of 1858 involved such a splurge of stage lines over the southern deserts that any little crust of consideration favoring the central plains must have come hard.

The Southern system, with the year just starting, had already the Santa Fé & Independent Mail, the El Paso & Santa Fé Mail, and the San Antonio & San Diego Mail. In September, of course, there would be the prodigious Butterfield creation; yet, as though all this were not enough, there was on the Post-master-General's lavish bill of fare a line which, though scarcely mentionable for its utter uselessness and consummate failure, was to start in October with monthly trips between Kansas City and Stockton, California, by way of Albuquerque, New Mexico. All this was to cost the Government, disregarding appropriations for roads and wells, an annual expenditure of about one million one hundred thousand dollars.

Added to this extravagant outlay, however, were further appropriations: $320,000 annually for overland mails in the North—the result of unforeseen circumstances which the Buchanan factions did well to view with alarm.

If the South were to have her Pacific Railroad—*in* the South, for the South, of and by the nation—it behooved her now to countenance the roughshod methods of her political exponents in Washington; to tolerate such obvious legerdemain as had enabled them to dictate the route for Butterfield and thus to bring home the spoils. It behooved the Cotton States, in a word, to grab while their hands were in the basket, and to waste no time even in a statesmanlike gesture. Clearly, there was no time to lose.

Something was bound to occur in the North which might advertise, beyond hope of further disguise, a strange odor in the cabinet of His Excellency.

Given, for example, a mere line of relay horses strung in the hit-or-miss fashion along the Central route; given also a season of year when the snows of the Sierra Nevada and Salt Lake regions would be most "impassable" in the eyes of the Buchanan forces; given this, and a challenge to Butterfield & Company! A challenge for a fair and square horse race, as an impromptu winter sport, across the continent, the long Southern route against the short but chilly Central!

In view of the improvements being made on the latter, makeshift and frail though they were, only a small sum of money would be needed to stock the line for such a contest, and to bring perhaps certain ridicule upon the whole Southern system, the hope for a Southern railroad. It was unthinkable.

And yet it happened—a horse-race melodrama of real life; of virtue, therefore, unrewarded; but with a real villain in it, stealing "the papers," as it will be seen, from "the child"!

Since the summer of 1850 and over a period of nearly eight years the Government had been obliged to maintain for the sake of the Mormons a crude monthly mail service between Independence, Missouri, and Salt Lake City. And since the spring of the following year over a similar period, a service of ruder type had existed onward to California.[1] Both were so primitive in nature that a time allowance of nearly two months between the Pacific and Missouri termini had proved none too liberal. Carriers bound for Salt Lake over one of these joint lines had been known to turn back and forward the mail by sea around to the other. They had been known to hibernate for several months in the course of a single journey. Naturally the service had won few friends . . . beyond the walls of the National Capitol.

But here, oddly, were those who pinned upon it a

[1] Mail over the latter section had been carried on mule-back or, at times through the mountains, on man-back, coursing more often than not an old Mormon trail leading southwestward from Salt Lake to the southern part of California. Over the other—the eastern section, which followed the main emigrant routes—the line had been equipped generally with a few covered wagons and mule teams. But not more than $50,000 a year, to include heavy contractors' indemnities, had been the average cost of this whole service to the Government.

great deal of faith and reliance. That is to say, they could rely upon it to be wholly unreliable. For the grim trials and tribulations of carriers they could well afford to recommend the payment of attractive indemnities and thus feed the files of the Post-Office Department with records to prove the awful nature of the Central route! It might appear, indeed, that these pioneer carriers were the lodestars of anything but the developments that later arose in their trials. Nor had the Pioneer Line provided any immediate incentive for extending the wheel tracks onward. It had opened a negotiable gateway into northern California and was already commencing to flourish, but it had not yet improved itself sufficiently to be wholly winter-proof. Officially, moreover, it simply wasn't being recognized—wasn't being discussed among the best people of Washington, D. C.

The Good Samaritan for the Central—the effectual and immediate God-send—was, as it happened, the "Mormon Rebellion." It was not such a benefactor as other ill winds were to be—the Civil War, for example; but this first windfall had sufficed to set the War Department before Congress with demands for means of rapid and frequent communication eastward and westward from the headquarters of the American troops near the Mormon stronghold of Salt Lake. It was a pressing military need. Congress was obliged to act, and the Postmaster-General to contract for another stage line across the wilderness.

So it was in April of 1858—the month before peace was made with the Latter-day Saints—that an agreement was signed and the first stageman was created for the "Central Overland."

He was John M. Hockaday of Missouri, a young law student barely twenty-one years old, who had done better, perhaps, to have remained with his studies. But as the head of a firm, he had agreed to perform a twenty-two-day service between the Missouri River and Salt Lake City, at a compensation of $190,000 a year.

In June, though by now the Mormons had accepted the President's pardon, the military need of communication remained; and the western section of the joint mail routes was the next to be improved. George Chorpenning, a pioneer carrier of the earliest and longest standing in this region, took over a new contract whose annual $130,000 subsidy called for a sixteen-day weekly stage service between Salt Lake and Placerville, following the old emigrant trail along the dreary Humboldt, and doubling over the tracks of the Pioneer stage line upon crossing the high Sierra Nevadas.

It was in the following month—weeks before Butterfield had completed his preparations for action in the South—that both the Hockaday and Chorpenning lines were actually running. There was a weekly service between St. Joseph, Missouri, and Placerville, California, on the first Central Overland stage line, the mail coming through within the thirty-eight days allowed by the two combined schedules.

Needless to say, it was no speed to boast of in the presence of Butterfield men. They had had a full year to prepare the Southern line, and large capital by which to stock it; while the Central, on the strength of pinch-penny financing, had had scarcely enough time to set up tents for stations at intervals to average sixty or seventy miles—sixty or seventy as opposed to the Butterfield eighteen! Over one three-hundred-mile stretch along the Humboldt, Chorpenning had no relays at all.

Conditions would be ameliorated; but if these contractors dared to invest capital for improvements beyond their barest needs, they would be treading upon very dangerous ground. It was within the power of the administration to reduce the compensation along with the service at any time; and at no time would the political powers be more apt to do so, as history was soon to make clear, than in the face of any threatening opposition by the Central to the Southern route.

Better, indeed, had they infringed on their contracts and brought down the wrath of the press, than to have done what they actually did, as though in defiance of the reluctant hands that fed them. They gave far better service than their agreements called for. It appeared as though they couldn't help it. Stock might stray from drunken tenders, old wagons

ALONG THE GILA

FORT YUMA

ORIGINAL ILLUSTRATIONS FROM "ADVENTURES IN THE APACHE
COUNTRY," BY J. ROSS BROWNE.

might break down, mail parties might rest in camp every night, and count it as fortunate if a forty-eight-hour trek provided fresh teams; still the mail *persisted* in beating the schedule by several days or more.

Meanwhile Chorpenning was buying new stages, of the ambulance type, with accommodations for sleepers. Improvidently, too, he was shortening his route by one hundred miles, and planning to shorten it much further.[1] He was driving, while the world cheered him onward, to his ruin.

For with no more staging facilities than were warranted by the two Central contracts; with no more staging experience than could be boasted by either contractor; and with scarcely a pretense of competing with Southern interests, the dreadful probability was that a casual twenty-five-day service here was forthcoming.

But so was winter. The Buchanan forces may have smiled with the thought of winter. This winter especially. It was bearing down with a cold in the North "unprecedented" in the estimate of "the oldest inhabitants." Some fury had turned on the blizzards and left them running.

---

[1] West-bound, his stages had been hauling around the *north* of Salt Lake into Idaho, passing through the hostile Goose Creek Mountains before reaching the head of the Humboldt. By eliminating the mountains, which he promptly did, the whole distance was cut from 850 to about 750 miles. Further than this, he proposed to pass south of Salt Lake, and south also of the Humboldt—the route to be coursed eventually by the Pony Express.

But the mail ran faster. It ran all the season. It ran, as even the Postmaster-General was obliged to concede, with such "remarkable regularity as to merit special commendation" (if not the guillotine!). "It has received from the people of California the warmest applause and called forth public demonstrations of a most enthusiastic character." [1]

One occasion found Hockaday's stages running so foolishly fast, and another, Chorpenning's running so much faster, that to combine these record trips of winter was to count the joint schedules beaten by thirteen days, with positive proof, therefore, that the Central—the forlorn and cringing Central—could, in winter, exact the demands imposed upon its Southern rival. There was, as the great bulk of all contemporaneous records show, an unqualified victory for the short line; and only upon one occasion had any energetic attempt been made to suggest the real possibilities.

That was the time of the horse-race across the continent—a melodrama that spoke an eloquent volume in one short, tragic act, wherein the *villain* stole *the papers* from an under-nourished, undeveloped, virtuous, and innocent Hockaday-Chorpenning *child*.

The occasion arose in contemplation of Buchanan's annual message—its despatch over the plains to California.

It was known that George Chorpenning and Hock-

---

[1] U. S. Postmaster-General's Report, May 24, 1858.

aday & Company had pooled about $8,000 between them for the purpose of making a record delivery and a cold winter's exhibition of speed. No doubt they were licking their chops as they stocked their lines with fleet saddle horses, providing relays at intervals of about eighteen miles. The indefatigable J. B. Crandall, having sold his interest in the Pioneer (to a Louis Brady & Company) to become a superintendent for Chorpenning, supervised much of the work. Experienced riders to include Howard Egan, Lot Huntington, and his brother of the later-famed "Pony Express," were enlisted and given the orders: "Don't mind a few horses—put the message through."

Fifteen days between St. Joseph and Placerville was the hope. Considering the season, it was an extravagant hope. Butterfield proceeded, therefore, to post riders and fast saddle animals along his own line from St. Louis to San Francisco; while the new Tehuantepec steamers prepared and proposed to beat both!

It was planned that all contestants were to start simultaneously. Advance copies of the President's message had been promised. Before being released to the Eastern press, they were to be on the roads to California. Special agents were appointed by the parties concerned—one by President Buchanan to handle all copies of the document, and to accommodate the protagonists according to their mutual understanding . . . so that there would be fair play.

On the morning of December 6, 1858, the Tehuan-

tepec liner was steaming up in her dock at New York.
The Hockaday courier from St. Joseph had come all
the way down to the Butterfield terminus of St. Louis
with orders not to start thence with the document
until the Southern messenger was on his way.

The Tehuantepec steamer pulled out that morning.

The Butterfield carrier did likewise. And left the
Central route man standing with an empty stare, and
emptier hands—there was to be no President's message intrusted with him!

There was a hitch, some mistake, of course. Anything else seemed too mean a thing to be credible. St.
Louis correspondents, later explaining the juggling,
were not believed in California even by the papers
that published their writings—not until one cor-
roboration was heaped upon another, and there was
only one thing to believe:

President Buchanan had "refused a copy of his
message to go by the Central Overland Route via Salt
Lake, although urged to do so." [1]

One account charged bribery, laying the guilt in
part on Buchanan's appointed agent; [2] but whatever
the facts of the case may have been (biographers of
Buchanan don't discuss them), the Hockaday courier
did not start on his way until, in the ordinary course

---

[1] "Sacramento Union," January 3, 1859. See also "Union" of December 7,
21, 1858, and of January 1, 10, 17, 1859; also "Missouri Republican,"
December 9, 1858; also "Alta California," January 4, and "San Francisco
Herald," January 6, 1859.

[2] "San Francisco Evening Bulletin," January 18, 1859.

of events, he was given a copy of the message by a newspaper editor. And it was not until the fourteenth of the month, not until the Butterfield rider had been more than a week on the road, that the Central route pony was enabled to spring away from the river bank at St. Joseph.

On Christmas night, which followed five weeks of incessant blizzard, its rider came lunging through the drifts into Salt Lake City, where the Chorpenning pony stood ready to receive and carry on.

Almost within the same hour, however, the President's great message, by the Butterfield route, reached San Francisco. It was in the fastest time that had ever been achieved over any route, including the sea, to California, beating the Tehuantepec steamer by several days. The Butterfield line held the record.

But it was a record smartly broken on New Year's Day when the Chorpenning pony came whisking his tail into Placerville—seventeen days and twelve hours from St. Joseph, beating the Butterfield time by two days and its own contract schedule by twenty days, in spite of the villain and the papers.

The cry rang out for a just recognition of this feat, though it was far less emphatic than it might have been if given ordinary justice at the starting point, so that the race in its finish could have told. But it could be argued, none the less, that if the Central held the winter record in its present condition, what chance had Butterfield? If his opponents could better or even equal his time at this season, what would happen in summer?

Perhaps certain politicians knew. Perhaps the strange manner in which the President had *delivered* his message to the Californians was more to the point than anything in the message itself. It was Horace Greeley of the "New York Tribune" who believed it very unwise for a government thus to run in opposition to itself. The Government may have taken this to heart; for it acted effectively toward an early adjustment of this rather vexing affair. Chorpenning and Hockaday should have known better than to play the ponies with His Excellency.

Chapter II

HORACE GREELEY may scarcely be mentioned in connection with stage-coaches without suggesting the fabulous driver, Hank Monk. Yet, before the summer of 1859, both of these distinguished personages were living in abject ignorance of the other's existence. Neither, as yet, could boast of having contributed anything to the other's fame.

But while Greeley was firing off his journalistic whip from the desk of the "New York Tribune," much to the annoyance of the Buchanan forces and to the delight of the Central Overland, young Monk was banging away more or less in the same direction with a modest sixteen-foot length of hickory and buckskin of his own. He had just spent one very severe winter helping to hold down that strategic road which Crandall had opened in fifty-seven over the high Sierras. He had been breaking through snows which were officially declared, by all but an act of Congress, as being impassable. He had been pelting along through blizzards and through rain and sleet, exercising a capacity for endurance which was to give

him a record, eventually, of forty-eight cold and
stormy hours on the box.

Following the tracks of the Pioneer and of a new
and very welcome traffic brought on by recent dis-
coveries of silver beyond the California border, he
had been driving for the Central Overland of George
Chorpenning, using runners where he could not use
wheels, passengers where horses failed him, whisky in
cases of emergency, yet somehow delivering the mail
sack, just as he was prepared to deliver Greeley, "on
time," and becoming very popular in addition. But
now the day was drawing near when the two great
men would rub noses, and give birth, incidentally, to
one of the most pointless stories that ever stumbled
on the threshold of immortality. This day, however,
was happily a few months in the offing.

It was the spring of fifty-nine. The eminent
" 'Tribune' Philosopher," not yet fifty years old and
still in good health, still undamaged in pride or person by any upstart Knight of the Reins, had decided
to practise what he preached to all young men and
"go West." There happened to be new action of interest on the central plains—new tides of emigration,
gold booms, silver booms; humbugs, maybe—it was
his mission to investigate and report. Nor could he
have chosen quite a more critical time.

The remarkable service performed by the Central
Overland during the past winter appeared, for one
thing, to have done its own cause more immediate

BUTTERFIELD STATION OF PICACHO, NEW MEXICO, THE BUILD-
ING ANTEDATING THE GOLD-RUSH, BUT STILL INHABITED.

Photographed by the authors.

BUTTERFIELD STATION OF OAK GROVE, CALIFORNIA—A RANCH
HOUSE TO-DAY.

damage than good. The last session of Congress had closed with a disagreeable slam. The House and Senate had banged their doors each in the other's face; and a vital measure had been caught somehow in the jamb.

There had been the question of overland mail appropriations. Shouldn't the Central be improved? Shouldn't the Southern be reduced? Why continue the Southern at all, now that the short line had demonstrated its worth? Why continue the Central—the Mormon war was over? Many questions, of which these were not the least important, had been left unanswered. The Post-Office Appropriation Bill, for the first time within memory, had failed. Contractors were to whistle for their pay.

Added to this store of embarrassment for the Government, and distress for certain mail contractors, came a supply of dynamite in the shape of a new Postmaster-General. Aaron Brown had died. Joseph Holt of Kentucky was now his successor; but in spite of his nativity, he was regarded as a far better friend of the sea-route mails than even of the Butterfield system.

When he swung into place it was with a belaying-pin; there was overland blood in his eyes, and but little polarity in the action of his swivel-chair—he could turn it southward almost as threateningly as northward. *Any* postal route which did not pay expenses did not rightly belong within the province of his office. The department's business was not to de-

velop new territories. Territories were to develop the
business of his department. And although the weekly
mail by the Central Overland had been all but
swamped by government documents for which no
postal returns could be realized, it made no difference.
The Central route did not pay. No overland paid.
There was to be an immediate overhauling. He whit-
tled his pencil sharp enough to punch holes through
almost any contract. Postmaster-General Holt was a
practical man.

Having been appointed in March, he gave warning
in April that the last day of June would be Doom's
Day. Many would be called, few chosen. He would
completely and properly annihilate the Kansas City,
Albuquerque & Stockton Mail, not one of whose
stages had yet pulled through nor any mentionable
amount of mail. As for the faithful "Jackass" between San Antonio and San Diego—he would knock
twenty-eight trips per annum out of it! Six hundred
miles had already been amputated from its middle;
but now the remainder was to be reduced from a
weekly to its original semi-monthly status. For "whatever the objects, political or otherwise, may have been
contemplated by the Government in establishing this
route through an almost unbroken wilderness," it was
clear to Holt that its continuance, at $196,000 a year,
was "an injustice to the Department." [1]

Then he hauled about as though to deliver a broad-

[1] U. S. Postmaster-General's Annual Report of 1859.

side even upon the strongholds of Butterfield. It may have been a gesture. He did not fire. But he gave it such a thoroughly unpleasant look that John Butterfield ran straight to the President. . . . He was told not to worry. The terms of the Great Overland contract would be respected; there would be full compensation for full service in due time. Thus protected, the credit of the Butterfield firm remained good. Wells, Fargo & Company, proper, stood ready with the necessary advances to cover any overdue compensation from the Government. Wells-Fargo stood ready as a firm, incidentally, thus to pave its way for an eventual début into the West as a stage-coach corporation, having long since gained a foothold as an express and banking concern. But other overland contractors were not so well secured. Those of the Central faced bankruptcy.

The line of Hockaday & Company, as a weekly, had been so burdened with mails that there had seldom been room for passengers. Now with a weekly organization on the company's hands, it was to be reduced to a semi-monthly. The same reduction applied to the western section of Chorpenning; but Hockaday had already been forced to the wall. Unable to stand in the shadow of the pending blow, the young proprietor had worried himself into a state of mental and physical debility; while his partner, William Liggett, had lost the savings of a lifetime—his family paupered. The line was but a demoralized fragment, and passing now (May 11) into other hands.

Under all of these hovering clouds, Horace Greeley was to make his journey across the continent. He had come dodging and hiding from newspaper men through Chicago and St. Louis, bound for a certain overland terminus at Leavenworth, Kansas. Fortunately, he did not have to resort at once to what remained of the erstwhile Hockaday system. There was a phenomenal new establishment running double stages weekly through northern Kansas and onward to a little town called Denver which the late Rocky Mountain gold rush had recently put on the map. It was the Leavenworth & Pike's Peak Express, the first real stage line of the plains to run wholly independent of government support. Still, it appeared to have been in need of more patronage than the Pike's Peak boom had afforded. As the L. &. P. P. Express, it was already ending a career of only five weeks. The last pair of its west-bound stages was to carry Greeley.

"Good-by, Al!"

"By-by, Bill!"

"You oughta got a haircut. The Arapahoes might scalp you!"

There were cheers; and two splendid L. & P. P. "Concords" rolled away. The New York journalist, however, was not yet aboard. He had been lecturing at some of the outlying settlements, and appeared shortly at some remote point farther along the road. He carried an old glazed traveling bag, marked "154

OUTPOST OF CIVILIZATION ON THE "L. & P.P.E."

Original sketch from "Beyond the Mississippi," by A. D. Richardson, who traveled with Greeley

Nassau Street, New York, 1855." He wore a very rusty and well-worn white coat, and carried a still rustier and still more worn umbrella—blue cotton, with a bulge in the middle. His roll of blankets was shoved under a seat; his precious trunk, filled with manuscripts, was strapped in the after-boot. He shook hands with a fellow-journalist (Albert D. Richardson); and they rolled on together over the prairie bottoms of Kansas.

The road beyond the new town of Junction City was marked only by the wheels of the L. & P. P. E. It was a route explored by its original proprietors, Jones & Russell, and led westward between the Republican and Solomon tributaries of the Kansas River, and on to Denver. Beyond Fort Riley and Junction City there was but one more settlement on the road. It comprised two sticks, a bit of sail cloth, two whisky barrels, some pickled oysters, a salesman, and three boxes of sardines.

All other stopping-places were tents and corrals belonging to the proprietors (now Russell, Majors & Waddell). These stands sufficed, however, for frequent relays. The line was commendably stocked. Greeley called his stage "a mere covered wagon"; but it was, none the less, one of fifty thorough-brace Abbot-Downing vehicles not long since imported for use on the line—the first Concord products that Kansas had ever seen. The animals were also the best stock available. They were mules, of course, horses still be-

ing regarded as unadaptable to the plains; but by
means of eight hundred of them, driven in from Kentucky, wagons had been relayed between Denver and
Leavenworth, 650 miles, within ten days, occasionally
eight—in one case it was less than seven; although
Greeley was obliged to devote the better part of two
weeks to his journey as far as Denver.

He sometimes passed the night in a tent; he sometimes slept in the wagon, sometimes under the wagon.
Methods were not dissimilar to those of the old Jackass Mail, and the days were equally wearing. Stream
fringes of elm and cottonwood trees thinned away to
no timber at all; and the drab prairies rolled out and
away forever. It was a country no less monotonous in
its buffalo grass than in buffalo hides and horns. The
beasts were not to be counted; they appeared, literally, by the millions, vast herds shrouding the earth.
One wagon of the line had been capsized by their
thunderous stampeding, and the stage of Greeley was
not to be spared altogether.

One grotesque herd had frightened the team. A
lead line broke; a runaway followed. Then a crash
and a general pile-up. The journalist reached Denver
with a slightly wrenched and lacerated leg which kept
him there a bit longer than he might otherwise have
cared to remain—limping the dirt floor of the Denver
House.

Here, in a long log building, his prospects for making up a week's loss of sleep were obliterated by mid-

night revelers in the bar-room, whence shouts and
even whispers passed through the cloth partitions as
though there were no partitions at all. Yet this place,
with its canvas roof, lean-to kitchen, and bunks un-
adorned by either mattress or pillow, was the only
respectable hotel in Denver. The town was not yet
roaring toward its future. A few quartz mills had
sprung up to drown the cry of "humbug"; but of the
population which had come with the original gold
boom, there remained but a hopeful fraction. Greeley hired a private conveyance and drove on.

He was bound northward for the Central Overland Mail line, which had been sold by the Hockaday
firm to the present owners of the L. & P. P. E. There
was soon to be a consolidation of both lines, and a
bold investment to boot; but it was Greeley's misfortune to happen along before the stock of the failing L. & P. P. E. had been shifted up to the road of
the bankrupt Mail.

He boarded the stage of the latter at Fort Laramie
on June 30. This being the very day that the club of
the Postmaster-General had been scheduled to fall, he
was able to contemplate the action with genuine feeling—he was obliged, for example, to perch himself
at the quaking summit of seventeen shifting mail
sacks. This, he learned, was no exceptional haul. What
then would be the load when postal deliveries would
be made only half as often! The six-mule teams now
used would then be unable to haul it without infring-

Courtesy of the Bancroft Library.

HORACE GREELEY
ORIGINAL ILLUSTRATION FROM "BEYOND THE MISSISSIPPI," BY
ALBERT D. RICHARDSON.

ing grossly upon contract time. "So," comments
Greeley, "they say, 'please let us carry the mail
weekly, though you only pay us for carrying it semi-
monthly.' But no! this is strictly forbidden. The postmaster at Salt Lake has express, written orders to refuse it, and of course he at St. Joseph also." [1]

Greeley's "Tribune" had been a friend of the Central; but it is remarkable that this attitude should ever
have remained after the editor had sampled the route's
wares. Having carried a wrenched leg and several
souvenir bruises to remind him of the L. & P. P.
Express, he might naturally have assumed that the
fates would now treat him more kindly. At least,
stages were not apt to capsize more than once in the
course of one overland journey.

But his six-mule team, while crossing the swollen
Laramie, proceeded forthwith to upset the theory, the
mail wagon, mail, and all. In midstream the leaders
had doubled back. Perhaps the driver was no six-mule
man; for try as he might to discourage the maneuver
by heading off the leaders with his wheel-team, he
was pitched from the box to join all the flotsam that
went drifting down the stream.

That being over and all things adjusted, it was
scarcely within the province of ill fortune that anything of the sort should happen again. But it did happen before Greeley arrived at the Mormon city. This
time the stage pitched him sprawling with an ava-

[1] Greeley, "An Overland Journey," 256.

lanche of mail bags to sample the depths of the Sweetwater; it burst wide its after-boot and belched forth
one trunk full of manuscripts. Greeley rescued his
traveling bag, while the lead-team came prancing
back in a tangle, as though to climb aboard the dere-
lict stage and teach the swearing driver to be more
careful of his language in cases of emergency like this.
The mail, of course, was recovered in due time, being
composed principally of free and worthless government documents. The trunk, however, had gone
bubbling away and under. Greeley "traveled light"
from then on. It was not by his pen that the name of
any stage driver between Leavenworth and Hangtown was ever inscribed for the eyes of posterity—
not even the name of Hank Monk.

But of his drive, from the heights of the Sierras
down into Placerville, he did have something to say.
His coach traveled "just as fast as four wild California horses, whom two men could scarcely harness,
could draw it." Had this been so, of course, Greeley
might never have lived to tell the tale and the world
would have been spared its promiscuous propagation.

"Our driver was, of course, skillful," he goes on;
"but had he met a wagon suddenly on rounding one
of the sharp points or projections we were constantly
passing, a fearful crash was unavoidable. Had his
horses seen fit to run away . . . I know that he could
not have held them, and we might have been pitched
headlong down a precipice of a thousand feet. . . .

Yet at this break-neck rate, we were driven not less than four hours or forty miles, changing horses every ten or fifteen, and raising a cloud of dust through which it was difficult at times to see anything. . . . And right glad was I [at last] to find myself among friends, surrounded by the comforts of civilization, and with the prospects of occasional rest." [1]

Greeley's views and fancies with respect to this drive were very similar to those of the average overland traveler on first coursing the route of the Pioneer—this no matter what driver held the lines. The dangers encountered and miraculously escaped by the journalist were the perils that Monk had been dodging steadily for at least a year and would continue to avoid through some twenty years to follow. Still, no one can be spared the story of "Horace" and Hank—how "the coach bounced up and down in such a terrific way that it jolted the buttons off Horace's coat, and finally shot his head clean through the roof of the stage!"; how Horace then "yelled at Hank Monk and begged him to go easier"; how he said he "warnt in as much of a hurry as he was a while ago," at which Hank Monk said, "Keep your seat, Horace, and I'll get you there on time—and you bet he did, too, what was left of him."

Having recounted this "very laughable thing" three times in succession, Mark Twain [2] adds that the epi-

[1] *Idem.*, 281–282.
[2] "Roughing It."

sode has also been recorded "by every other corres-
pondence-inditing being that ever set his foot upon
the great overland road between Julesberg and San
Francisco." Among those guilty he names Taylor,
Richardson, Jones, Smith, Johnson, and Browne; but
now further references may be made to Mark Twain,
Bowles, Rice, Haskins, Root, Jarett, and, without
question, a dozen or two more as well. Hank Monk,
in his day, might have filled a scrap-book with drivel
to arouse the envy of many a theatrical star. It was
because one day he drove Greeley rather rapidly into
Placerville.

Still, Greeley had been misused. "What was left of
him" escaped from Monk's stage and the clutches of
the Placerville reception committee, to hide, according to the press, in the nearest bar-room, or to be, according to Greeley, "among friends, surrounded by
the comforts of civilization." The old man, in fact,
was more travel-worn and battered than any one
could fully appreciate. But, having been discovered
at the bar, he was rustled shortly to a banquet in his
honor, where, in response to various toasts, he is said
to have arisen from a couch instead of a chair. There
were now, perhaps, more reasons than one why
Greeley favored improvements along the Salt Lake
road.

Chapter III

CHARLIE

"YOU'VE heard o' Hank Monk I reckon. . . ."
Enough people had, at least, to have called forth
this surmise by some writer for the "New York
Sun," [1] although Monk's stamping grounds were
distant three thousand miles.

One imagines that the old Jehu's renown must have
arisen from something more than the one senseless
incident so often rehashed. One is apt to presume
that his glorification must have found nourishment
through some other root—something so elemental
and broadly recognized, perhaps, that it was never
recorded, and thus allowed to drift by the boards. To
a certain extent, indeed, this appears to be the case.

It was July 30, 1858—exactly one year to the day
before Greeley entered Placerville "on time"—that
the arrival of Monk's stage at the selfsame town was
cheered with even greater ado, and that his name,
with a *Mister* and a *Henry* before it, appeared in suit-
able dignity on the front pages of various journals.
It had been his honor, by chance or by special appoint-
ment, to bring the first coach mail by the Central
Overland to its western terminus.

[1] See the San Jose, California, "Pioneer" of April 6, 1878.

As a driver then in the employ of George Chorpenning his route was on the Pioneer road—the same road that knew the sound of his whip, and the streak of white smoke from his black cigar, thence onward through a period of at least twenty years. Thus, having become familiar with this historic line when it was little more than the pack trail as adapted to wheels by old Crandall, he had seen it develop under the hoofs of his teams into one of the most inspiring sections of the Central Overland, and he had remained with it through the palmiest days of its career and onward until long after the advent of the first Pacific railroad.

Monk had a right, therefore, to a kind of distinction; but this particular kind his name has rarely enjoyed. It appears, curiously, that the real tap-root of his fame must rely, as though condemned to an unmerciful fate, upon the everlasting sustenance of the Greeley chestnut. The years were many, and the years were long, but it never failed to provide.

When, for example, Horace Greeley became a candidate for the Presidency of the United States, out ran another branch of this old reliable root, just as promptly as though it had been stimulated by the every-ready ink of press agents. It was *still* a most "laughable thing." Hank, it seems, had written to the candidate, recalling the memorable day when they had enjoyed a pleasant drive together, and suggesting that, in the event of election, some little token of esteem for past services be considered—some lucrative rocking-chair billet, perhaps. It was only fair. But to this request, it appears, the candidate had answered:

"I would rather see you ten thousand fathoms in hell than give you even a crust of bread. For you are the only man who ever had it in his power to put me in a ridiculous light before the American people, and you villainously exercised that power." [1]

Evidently Monk had contributed somewhat to the candidate's subsequent defeat. It was a just penalty. Greeley had aired his views on a certain score about which he knew practically nothing. Like many inexperienced stage travelers by the Central Overland, he had sampled the driving of a Sierra whip and regarded it, published it, broadcast it as a reckless procedure. Monk was not reckless. It was true, perhaps, sometimes he drank; sometimes, according to one of his volunteer press agents, he drank so much that he forgot what he was doing—gave whisky to his horses, and watered himself, thus becoming accidentally sober enough to handle an inebriated team.

But Monk was rather used to this sort of smiling slander; and, whatever the facts may be, his boast was, after twenty years' driving through the dangerous Sierra Nevadas, that he had never injured a passenger. There is little doubt but that he was just as cool and careful as he was deft and fast. It could scarcely have

[1] *Idem.*, May 24, 1879.

been otherwise. He was a veteran on the Pioneer line; he was one of the earliest and longest-tried of all the Sierra Knights.

"You've heard o' Hank Monk, I reckon. . . . Wa'al, there's fifty as good drivers as he ever was," continues the "New York Sun" on the word of "a mountaineer." And while the rest of the article suggests more fiction than fact, this much, at least, rings true.

Monk was one among many, but a chancing popular idol. His relation to his route, in the words of a Nevada newspaper man, was "what the perfume is to the rose, what Boker's bitters is to a cocktail"; and he was even likened to the salt on a scrambled egg—poor Monk! In his life he stood for more than was ever bargained for; but he was no less one of an expert group of drivers—Al Grinnel, Kaiser, Ned Blair, Curly Dan (B. B. Burch), David Taylor, J. J. Crowder, William Norris, C. B. Hoffman, A. Putnam, John Sickles, and many more of varying skill; but, though they were the rank and file of whips in that mountain zone, they were filling a demand for the greatest speed through a country where it was least expected; they were developing an old art toward its acme. Suffice it to say that Hank Monk was one of these.

There were other idols. J. Ross Browne [1] tells of "Charlie." Everybody, he says, knows Charlie. And

[1] "Adventures in the Apache Country," (New York: 1871), pp. 310–324.

"everybody" in Browne's time did know him well enough. Charlie was a type met everywhere. Browne was "proud and happy" to sit beside him on the coach —especially as the night came on with the deepest shadows, leaving the old Pioneer road and the dismal gorges beside it as indistinguishable as though a black carpet had been spread over all. Browne called it a "stage trap."

"The horses seemed to be eternally plunging over precipices and the stage following them with a crashing noise, horribly suggestive of cracked skulls and broken bones. But," he writes, "I had implicit faith in Old Charlie. The way he handled the reins and peered through the clouds of dust and volumes of darkness, and saw trees and stumps and boulders of rock and horses' ears, while I could scarcely see my own hand before me, was a miracle of stage driving." As the stage made a sudden lurch in the dark and went streaming gracefully along the brink of a fearful precipice, Browne found breath to ask: "Do many people get killed on this route?"

"Nary a kill that I know of. Some of the drivers mashes 'em once in a while, but that's whiskey or bad drivin'. Last summer a few stages went over the grade, but nobody was hurt bad—only a few legs and arms broken. Them was opposition stages. Pioneer stages, as a genr'l thing, travels on the road. Git aeoup!"

"Is it possible? Why, I read horrible stories of people crushed to death going over these mountains."

"Very likely—they kill 'em quite lively on the Henness route.[1] Git alang, my beauties! Drivers only break their legs a little on this route; that is, some of the opposition boys did it last summer; but our company's very strict . . . as a genr'l thing. . . . Git aeoup, Jake! Git alang, Mack! 'Twon't pay; 'taint a good investment for man nor beast. A stage is worth mor'n two thousand dollars, and legs cost heavy besides. You, Jake, git!"

"How in the world can you see your way through this dust?"

"Smell it. Fact is, I've traveled over these mountains so often I can tell where the road is by the sound of the wheels. When they rattle I'm on hard ground; when they don't rattle I gen'r'lly look over the side to see where she's a-going."

"Have you any other signs?"

" 'Backer's another sign; when I'm a little skeer'd I chew mor'n ordinary. Then I know the road's bad. . . ."

"How long have you been driving stage?"

"Nigh on thirty years. . . ."

"Why, you must have made plenty of friends during so long a career. . . ."

"Oh, yes, plenty of 'em; see 'em today, gone tomorrow! Git alang!"

And so passed the long hours of the night, Charlie and his chronicler gossiping pleasantly about the risks and charms and the mysteries of the stage driver's

[1] California Stage Company's opposition to the Pioneer over a line later adopted by the Central Pacific Railway.

profession. A hard life was that of the Jehu, he mused, "a life of exposure and peril, and wear and tear, such as few other men experience in this world. You, my good friend," he writes, "who cross the Sierras of California once or twice in a lifetime, imagine you have done great things—you boast of your qualities as a traveler; you have passed unscathed through the piercing night air; have scarcely shuddered at the narrow bridges, or winced at the fearful precipices. You have braved all the dangers of the trip, and can afford to slap yourself complacently on the leg in proof of the fact that you are still sound. But think of Charlie! He has crossed the mountains a thousand times; crossed when the roads were at their worst; by night and by day; in storm and gloom and darkness; through snow and sleet and rain, and burning suns and dust; back and forth; subject to the risk of different teams and different stages; his life balanced on the temper of a horse or the strength of a screw. . . . All hail to thee, Old Charlie!"

The stage-coach was bound upward from Placerville to Strawberry and on over an improved grade that skirted the shores of Lake Tahoe. It had come upon a hard gravelly earth where the hoofs were beating a lively drum refrain, now in chorus, now out again, at measured intervals, in constant rhythm. The tall pines formed a magnificent avenue through which the moon began to glimmer, making a fretwork of silver light on the backs of the animals. Then the beams poured down into a mysterious abyss through which the river was dashing. They fringed the top of the forests "with a frostlike drapery." Nothing could provide a greater thrill, Browne thought, than the many down-swoops and zooms of this grade by moonlight.

Imagine yourself seated in front of the stage, by the side of that gallant old whipster, Charlie, who knows every foot of the way, and upon whom you can implicitly rely for the safety of your life and limbs. Holding the reins with a firm hand, and casting a penetrating eye ahead, he cracks his whip, and away go the horses with inspiring velocity—six magnificent chestnuts, superbly adorned with flowing manes and tails. The stillness of the night is pleasantly broken by their measured tread, and the rattle of the wheels over the gravel echoes through the wild rifts and opening of the cañon like a voice from the civilized world telling of human enterprise. Down and still down we plunge into the gloomy depths of the abyss; the ghostly forms of the trees looming up on our left; to the right, rising far beyond the range of vision, the towering heights of the Sierras; and ever and anon yawning gulfs in front and bottomless pits of darkness still threatening. . . .

The road turns and winds like a serpent, sometimes apparently running into huge banks of granite boulders, then whirling suddenly and plunging into a shimmering wilderness of rocks and trees, where destruction seems inevitable. Yet onward dance the horses. . . . They never swerve from the track . . .

they pursue their way with unrivalled ease and grace; sweeping around the narrow turns; now coursing along on the extreme edge of the precipice, or closely hugging the upper bank as the road winds to the right or the left; now plunging down and whirling with marvelous sagacity over the narrow bridges that span the ravines, often where there is neither rail nor post to mark the way, ever true to the slightest touch of the reins, and ever obedient to the voice of the driver. Is it a wonder that Old Charlie loves his horses and talks of his team with a kind of paternal affection—that he knows them by heart, and holds converse with them through the long watches of the night?

Later, out of Strawberry, in the higher altitudes of the Sierras, the scenery became weird. The earth was of a whitish cast, trees scraggy. Great boulders reared above the wayside, threatening to topple over and crush all beneath them—"thousands of tons of solid stone ready, apparently, at the slightest vibration . . . to come crashing down upon the stage."

"And the verdict of the coroner's inquest 'ud be," said the driver, "eighteen men, six horses, an' a Pioneer stage smashed by the above stone!"

Passengers' teeth began to chatter "like a box o' dice," but the assurance came that those rocks were perfectly safe. Perfectly safe. It was only when the stage came along that they vibrated or rocked a little bit.

He began to hum and sing: "When this cruel

war is over . . ." He knew only one line of only one song, which Browne had the honor of hearing "over a thousand times."

"When this cruel war is over . . ."

What particular Old Charlie is referred to, Browne does not tell. There were a number of them who went by the name—Charlie Crowell, Charlie Watson, Charlie Saddle, "Coon Hollow Charlie"—all well-known whips of the Pioneer in Browne's time. But at one period or another there was one more: Charlie Pankhurst. If Browne's "Old Charlie" happened to have been Pankhurst (and there is no available source to gainsay the possibility), here was one that everybody did not know.

It is true that most drivers were enigmas. Their life histories were not for the world. When they talked—and many of them would not talk except to their teams—any sincere confidence from them could be taken as the highest compliment. Otherwise they were drolly insincere, spinning yarns to be taken with bushels of salt—salt which they frankly passed around for application. Their own lives were strictly their own; and it was exceptionally true of Charlie Pankhurst.

Among the many historic instances of women disguised as men playing the man's part through various masculine walks of life, Charlie Pankhurst contributes a strange case to the annals of staging. From a day

in the early forties when she, as a small girl, escaped
in boy's clothes from a poorhouse, until shortly after
her death at the age of sixty-seven years, her sex was
never disclosed, perhaps never suspected.

With a career among drivers of sixes to be envied,
Pankhurst was one of the most popular whips of New
England long before the gold fever began to call them
away. From the poorhouse to the stables of Ebenezer
Balch in Worcester, she had taken the first step of a
life in masquerade. And she had laughed to herself,
no doubt, when, as a "boy," Mr. Balch had offered
to make a man of her. Clothes made the man, she
learned very early, and went to work pitching hay,
shoveling manure, washing carriages, scrubbing floors,
and so on, with such energy and good-will that when
at last Mr. Balch moved into the What Cheer House
of Providence, Rhode Island, he took the youth with
him and taught "him" how to drive. It was two, four,
and finally six horses—six in a country where the
full complement was no ordinary sight.

But by that time, neither was she any ordinary
driver. Having wandered away from Providence and
back again, and continued all the time in the practice
of her chosen art, she could command from any employer the best team that he owned and be sure to
get it, lest some other employer win her. The wealthi-
est families, when in need of a stable team, wanted
also Charlie Pankhurst. They could depend on her for
a pleasurable trip; and her handling of a certain six

spanking grays had become one of the spectacles of the town. They were horses that she would allow no hands to touch but her own; and they failed to acknowledge her mastery over them only once.

It was on a dreadfully cold night while returning with a coach-load from a dance at Pawtuxet. The horses had been obliged to stand too long, and their driver to wait outside in the snow until her hands were mere gloves stuffed with inert fingers. The cavorting team, pulling out at last, had probably detected her difficulty. Hay-bound, home-bound, the animals were off, Charlie, with more than a dozen lives in her half-frozen hands, unable to check them. Probably one of the most humiliating acts of her life was now when she enlisted the strength of the man beside her to handle the two lead reins.

Her friends in these early days were among the drivers destined to become the most outstanding stagemen of the Pacific Coast. Birch and Stevens, having known her well, had likewise admired her as an expert whip; for no sooner had they become established in California than they sent for her, and soon employed her among their drivers. When the streets of Sacramento were swarming with miners and blocked by vehicles and mustang teams, when runners were crying out their routes and all men swearing as they would never have sworn save to accompany this grand male chorus, Charlie was there, somewhere among

Courtesy of the Wells Fargo Bank & Trust Company of San Francisco, and of "The Sunset Magazine."

HENRY MONK
CELEBRATED "KNIGHT OF THE SIERRAS"

them, rubbing hubs with the next fellow, trying to sober her animals while the clamoring hordes, with their shovels and guns, piled aboard.

She was broad-shouldered, tall, compactly built, and with a complexion, naturally dark, bronzed by the sun. When she called "All aboard!" even her voice could have aroused no great suspicions—it was a strong, masculine falsetto, not very uncommon among men. What may have been whispered behind her back is not of record; but admiration for her skill and daring was broadcast.

Thomas Edwin Farish, author of "The Gold Hunters," having driven with Charlie Pankhurst, gives several examples of this.

He recalls her coolness at one time on crossing a bridge of the swollen Tuolumne River—a bridge that began to reel and rock over a deep churn of water. Her team was walking at the time; but as the structure began to go down she laid on the whip, and reached the other shore only as the timbers and planks behind her fell crashing into the stream. Then, of course, she betrayed few if any emotions, being, as she was, a driver; but once when stopped by highwaymen, it seems she did become angry. At the point of a gun she had been obliged to throw out the express box.

"I wasn't thinking," she said, "of this. But the next time you try to stop me, I'll be ready for you."

And the next time, indeed, she was. Farish writes: "She shot the leader [of the road-agents], applied the lash to her horses and escaped without harm. The body of the highwayman was found by a searching party in an old tunnel near the scene of the shooting." The details are not of available record, but the story is borne out well enough through an obituary item in the papers: ". . . Pankhurst was a noted whip, and of courage once proved conclusively in a fight with highwaymen."

Through most of her career she drove over various roads of California, and, ranking with Charlie Watson and Monk as expert, she was numbered at one time among the select whips of the Sierras. Only during the last few years of her life, when ill health prevented, did she cease to drive. She died unattended and alone in a little cabin on the Moss Ranch, six or seven miles from Watsonville, during the last week of 1879. Friends, coming to call, discovered the remains, also the strange fact of her sex. There were newspapers then that refused to believe it. Others held that it was "too strange not to be true"; but it was likewise too strange not to be investigated, substantiated, and chronicled broadly from the Pacific to the Atlantic States.

Charlie Pankhurst, like Monk, through rather curious chance, has left a few more intimate traces behind than other worthy drivers of the pioneer school were able to do. But they were all so similar that to

know one was to be well acquainted with them all.
Charlie! "Of course everybody knows Charlie,"
Browne writes, "that same old Charlie all over the
roads."

Chapter IV

THE QUIXOTIC PONY

WHEN the Postmaster-General's axe of retrenchment crashed down (June 30, 1859) upon all overland mails but the Butterfield line, there was the able firm of Russell, Majors & Waddell ready to receive the blow and, in spite of it, to carry on and improve what Hockaday & Company had started a year before between Salt Lake and the Missouri River. There was also George Chorpenning, operating over the route west of Salt Lake; but he could not last; he was already staggering. He had had little more than enough strength left in him to put Horace Greeley across the alkali plains and deliver him to Placerville "on time."

Still, with a stubborn pluck and hopes of a brighter day, Chorpenning went on to improve his line, to blaze new trails especially, and shorten the distance. His stages between California and the Mormon capital were already dropping Salt Lake to the north, and awaiting only the completion of a new road south of the dreary Humboldt to initiate the permanent trail for a coming era. With the same spirit, too, he continued the weekly trips, though his remuneration for mail carriage was only for semi-monthly service ($80,000 instead of $135,000 per year). He ran thus until, with the fall of the year 1859, creditors began to foreclose, and the sheriff to sell off his stock.

Even then he continued to stagger. With no stages left on his western division—from "Hangtown" to Gravelly Ford—he borrowed one, and caused it to appear at the Placerville post-office as usual. He might have struggled on for some time in this unaccountable manner; but the case provoked curiosity and investigation. Somebody spied and tattled. It seemed that the borrowed stage-coach ran only to some proximate point of concealment where the mail was sedulously transferred to pack-mules and driven away!

It was scarcely in accord with the government contract. The local postmaster of Placerville, unable to countenance the procedure, felt obliged to make temporary arrangements with another firm—Brady & Company, the successors of Crandall & Sunderland to the Pioneer. Louis Brady, with hopes of favorable recognition in Washington, now hastily extended the old line to Salt Lake.

Still Chorpenning would not admit defeat. Nor would the Salt Lake postmaster acknowledge Brady (a Gentile) as a bona-fide mail carrier on the route. Theoretically there were two stage systems between Placerville and the Mormon city, each one being recognized only at an opposite terminus. Conflicts and failures followed. They foreshadowed the end. It came with the close of fifty-nine, when the contract was annulled in Washington. California, with connections by stage on the Salt Lake route only as far as the Washoe silver mines of western Nevada, was to see no further action until the following spring; but then it was action indeed.

Private capital had come to the rescue in the name of Russell, Majors & Waddell. Private enterprise had conceived the now famous "Pony Express."

"Away across the endless dead level of prairie a black speck appears in the sky. . . . In a second or two it becomes a horse and rider, rising and fallling, rising and falling—sweeping toward us nearer and nearer, and the flutter of hoofs comes faintly to the ear—another instant and a whoop and a hurrah . . . a wave of the rider's hand, but no reply, and a man and horse burst past our excited faces, and go sweeping away like a belated fragment of storm.

"So sudden is it all, and so like a flash of unreal fancy, that but for a flake of white foam left quivering and perishing on a mail sack, we might have doubted whether we had seen any horse and man at all . . ."

And by the same token, moreover, we might doubt it still. There appears to be more truth than mere pony expression in this galloping sketch from Mark Twain. Like a flash of fancy, with but a flake of white foam to dispute the illusion, was the institution itself

—was the entire career of the Overland Pony Express.

It did not involve more than 150 round trips. It did not cover a full nineteen months. Like a belated fragment of storm it came and was gone.

Yet the fact remains: a more glamourous contribution to our historic West than that of this ephemeral Pony would be difficult to name. Within his brief lifetime—a mere flare in the earliest sixties—he was able to identify himself with the new empire as permanently as though he had come racing up all the way from the gold rush to the last spike driven for the Pacific Railroad; as prominently as though he had carried every scrap of communication that California had ever enjoyed, as ineffably as though he were indeed the very trail blazer of the Salt Lake or Central route, the sole champion of its eventualities, the one and only precursor of the first daily stage, and of the first iron horse to go blowing itself across the continent!

It is curious—scribes, in regular relays, have been riding the tolerant animal for nearly seventy years, and have happily disregarded his excuse for living rather more often than not. He has become an immortal Pegasus, striking sparks from his hoofs, and beating out thunder from the rosy top of a cloud—a thing apart, an unapproachable pet of the gods, great for the very fact of his being. Perhaps it were a sacrilege to bid him come down, forget the romance of his life for a moment, and give some general account of himself—his intrinsic value.

The Pony, however, has no few practical-minded admirers. They have many times spoken in his behalf, sometimes with a rather scholarly air. The animal's most vital contribution to the world, they say, is not the most obvious thing. His services as a carrier of mail and other despatches constituted but a means toward an end.

By way of enlightenment, they recall the administration in force at the time of his début (April 3, 1860). It was still that of Buchanan; there was still the old force of truckling politicians behind it. Despite the retrenchments of fifty-nine, the government program called for nearly five times the annual expenditure for stage service over the Southern routes than was appropriated for the same in the North, or over the Central. The latter, in short, was in need of a powerful champion—something to run independent of Federal aid, and that might not be forced to the wall by sectional interests, that would advertise to the world the thorough feasibility of the short line for all purposes.

Here, then, was the Pony's great motive; and there can be no mistake as to that. Relying wholly upon the capital of the new staging firm of Russell, Majors & Waddell, and upon what scant returns could be realized through public patronage, the little animal set out to broadcast the merits of the Central route, to swing popular opinion with such force against political opposition as to compel an immediate reform —congressional action for a first-class line of stages by way of Salt Lake, a telegraph system, and eventually perhaps a railroad.

All this, according to many writers, the Pony actually brought about; and certainly a more conspicuous exhibition of his route's advantages could scarcely have been hoped for. He could not have done better. But it happened simply that he might have spared himself the exertion. His demonstration, as it may be shown, chanced to be wholly unnecessary. He neither caused nor hastened the developments that followed in his trail. Had he never existed, all must have been the same.

One might fairly disregard the fact that stages had coursed the Central route some time before the Pony; that the Pioneer over the Sierras had been running with increasing regularity and success ever since Crandall's historic venture in the summer of fifty-seven, and that Chorpenning and Hockaday had rolled one severe winter under their wheels with such grace that even the prejudiced Postmaster-General (Brown) had acknowledged the commendable service. It might all be disregarded but for the affray in Congress immediately after these Central stagemen had survived their first winter; for then it was that proponents of the short line were thus able to find unqualified support for their arguments, and that they fought hopefully, with no Pony to ride on, for substantial improvements on the Salt Lake line.

That they failed (along with the annual Post-Office Bill) was to have been expected. Still, their campaign in the following year for a daily coach mail left no doubt as to their growing strength. It was all but a victory this time, and, significantly, it was in spite of the fact that the Pony, though now on the road, had not yet encountered a *winter*. Since it had to be proved that the route was practicable through *all* seasons of the year, something besides the Pony must already have suggested it.

So much for the part played by the stage on the Central without benefit of Pony. There had yet to be a decisive victory in Congress. It was still within the Pony's power, then, to compel success. For one thing, his enemies were weakening. No sooner had he started to run than there came a breach in the Democratic party, making it clearly impossible for the Southern branch of it to carry the election in November. Nevertheless, there would be overland measures to debate once more before the Southern régime would be over, and there would be a winter before that time, a good chance for an effective demonstration.

So *still* there remained an opportunity for the animal to prove his worth. He'd keep the road hot. He'd give them plenty to talk about at the next opening of

Congress. Off and away he flew. What wheels could do, hoofs might not prove; but that was immaterial. He could win friends; he could draw eyes; he could perform some marvelous tricks. There was his mission! *Argumentum ad populum!* An advertising agent was the Pony.

He ran weekly at first—and at a rate of nearly two thousand miles in ten days. Who had ever heard of such a thing since Kubla Khan! His biweekly trips commenced with summer. The frequency of service was that of the Great Southern Overland; but the speed! He could beat those Butterfield coaches in the South by eleven, twelve, sometimes thirteen days! Bring on your winter! Bring on the deep, impassable snows! He'd lambaste the hostile faction with some of its own pretty snowballs!

But already this faction had reason to worry about other things. Not only was the Democratic party split hopelessly in half, but it was known by September, beyond a reasonable doubt, that Lincoln would be the next President. The governors of the Cotton States had convened and decided what to do when the expected election occurred; and it was practically agreed at this time that if one State should secede, all would secede. South Carolina took note. The Pony ran on. Come winter! Come winter! Hurrah!

On November 6 he stood at St. Joseph with his ears back, waiting for the news. Legislators of South Carolina, having cast a hopeless vote for Breckinridge electors, remained in session to hear the results for the nation.

Lincoln elected! Fast hoofs were off with the news. Within six days and seventeen hours they had traversed the Central route. Lincoln elected! Buchanan's days were numbered. The Southern régime was doomed.

Thus winter had come for the Pony, and Lincoln with it, the President-elect. What now of the powers hostile to the Central route? They were not through yet, but by the time the express had delivered Buchanan's last annual message (December), there was little left in the Southern camp to care one way or another about that demonstration. Members of Buchanan's cabinet had already resigned; and, before the month was done, South Carolina had seceded.

In rapid sequence six other States followed suit, their representatives and senators withdrawing, one after another, from the national capital. The first shots were fired early in January (from the shore batteries of Charleston Harbor); and it was during a perfect furor in Washington that the measure for a daily line of stages over the Central was again introduced. There was little to oppose it. The Pony was advertising his honey to a hive of bees.

In fact, before the bill was passed, the Southern route of Butterfield had been cut off through Texas. The only rival of the Salt Lake line was out of the picture and beyond consideration, much of it belonging to a "Confederate States of America." The United States, if she cared to spend money on any overland route whatever, was obliged, compelled to look northward, and to spend it all on her own!

Thus winter had come and a few new circumstances with it. Early spring found an unmistakable civil war in progress. The beating of pony hoofs and the rattle of coach wheels could not resound above the thunder of muskets and cannon. A bill had been rushed through Congress for a daily mail on the Central route. The stages and stock of Butterfield & Company, led by the forces of the North, as it were, and fairly fleeing the fire of the South, were in a fair stampede northward toward the one and only alternative route that could be recognized. In so far as the cause of the Salt Lake line was involved, its enemies as well as its friends were acting in accord.

Thus daily stages commenced rolling where the Pony ran; lines of telegraph wires were being hastened faster than ever from both ends along his approximate trail. Nor was the Pacific Railroad Bill apt to remain long dormant, now that the North was no longer opposed.

The Pony may have paused for a moment in his dusty tracks and stared at this amazing action; but even his little horse-sense of modesty must have told him that, in spite of his good intentions, his capabilities, his heroic battle, and his big advertising campaign, he was not quite responsible for it all. He had carried the news of Lincoln's election, yet he had not elected Lincoln. It had all been pathetically destined to happen without his help; and he had hastened the inevitable only if his hoofs had kicked down Fort Sumter and started the Civil War.

What he actually did for the world, therefore, to forget the romance once more, was only the obvious thing. He carried letters.

He carried letter mail for a short time across the plains, and filled the diminishing gap between telegraph terminals with all the despatch that good men and beasts could make possible. His average cargo from start to finish constituted about 100 letters— not very many considering the fact that 6,300, roughly, or at least, had been the ordinary cargo of letter mail by the Southern overland stages in the Pony's time; as many in a week, ofttimes, in these coaches as were known to the Pony's entire career. He was not a popular carrier.

But he was a very popular beast. For, while few could afford his rates of delivery ($5, $3, and $1 as they varied per half-ounce tissue-paper letters in the course of time), not only did he cut the time of the Southern stages in half as a habit, but he delivered news items for the press; and it would be difficult to appreciate in modern times what a luxury this service seemed to the settlements of the plains and to California.

Thus he filled one common want; but considering at what price it was filled—a million dollars, it appears, as a direct loss to the Pony proprietors—even this was more in the nature of a luxury. Certainly it was not an exigency. The Far West had waited nearly ten years for a transcontinental telegraph line. As a substitute for this (pathetic thought!) the Pony served little more than eighteen months. Surely the country could have waited this much longer without suffering material damage, glad though it was to use the Pony while somebody else paid the bills.

Thus the great Central Overland Pony Express appears to dissolve from a vital agent in the building of an empire to a casual benefactor of a small minority and a short-lived popular luxury. Perhaps fame never graced an existence more futile.

Yet fame was his, and may ever remain so. Nor can it be said that he did not earn it, that he does not deserve his immortality. Not only did he make an ambitious attempt, which might have been a triumph had the war not stolen his thunder, but he achieved a national romance. He exploited the daring and hardihood of the youth in his realm, for which alone there may still be a debt in his honor and the price of his glory to pay.

What of all practical attainments in the light of this? Granting the animal all the conquests tacked on to his flowing tail, his material accomplishments would become immaterial alongside of him. As fearless as the great *Don Quixote* himself, he attacked a windmill—or a grindstone which was the world; and though he neither increased nor decreased its monotonous speed, the world had a right to marvel. It were a marvelous trick at any time to make a grindstone spin out some romance.

PONY EXPRESS ENVELOPES OF SIXTY AND SIXTY-ONE

Chapter V

THE PONY'S PIPER

THUS, what benefits were born of the Pony Express is a question better left unasked if the entertainment of a nation is not enough. It was a drama which, under the direction of William H. Russell, its author, first appeared in the great theater of the Wild West on April 3, 1860, and endured a run, night and day, of more than a year and a half.

The settings were of the plains and deserts, the Rocky Mountains and Sierra Nevadas. There was color in war-paint and feathers. There were scenes of buffalo herds, solid masses, extended as a low tufted mesa bending over the horizon; scenes of granite mountains, icy crags where the trails thinned away under the frayed brush of cloud. There were scenes of flooding rivers and torrents, driving rain, giddy whirls of snow and sleet or tumbling hailstones. And through all of this went pattering the hoofs of the Pony.

Besides a fleet five hundred horses, the whole troop involved more than tenscore young men, or boys in some cases, well able to take a man's part. There were Bob Haslam ("Pony Bob"), Jim Moore, Howard Egan, and, of course, the fourteen-year-old Bill Cody.

There were Frey, Randall, Roff, Hamilton, "Boston," Kelly, Richardson, Keetly, Beatly, Boulton, and many more—eighty picked rough riders in all. It was fairly an all-star cast; and the work demanded it. Blood was shed, and nerves were tried, then as now for entertainment. This was no mere horse-play; but it was, nevertheless, a kind of charity bazaar staged at the expense of Russell, Majors & Waddell.

The third member, William B. Waddell, it appears, was innocent of the flapdoodle involved. His most substantial contribution to the pageant was perhaps his name. Nor should the sound business judgment of Majors be hastily impugned—certainly the big Pony show was no example of it. He fostered it because he felt honorably compelled to do so.

His assets amounted to several millions—capital earned, for the main part, independent of his partners and through the struggles and physical perils of half a lifetime. But place it all beside a principle, and to him the money appeared as the proverbial trash. He seems to have been, moreover, one example of Christian gentleman who, receiving a blow on one cheek, could actually turn the other—something he demonstrated rather clearly in the case of the Pony.

Alexander Majors, born in 1814, was a native of Kentucky, but raised from the age of four on the Missouri frontier. As a youth he had been taught to accept the literal word of the Bible; and his strict codes and creeds, even as a young man, were so stringent that he could scarcely make them compatible with the life he desired on the plains. Straitened circumstances on the farm, however, turned him westward to the wilderness. Thence onward through many years his story holds too trite a moral to be told without certain misgivings; nor does it express to this age the man he was.

As a freighter over all the land from the great rivers to the Rocky Mountains, in any event, he neither drank, smoked, nor used profanity; he attempted to enforce sobriety upon his employees; observed his Sabbath in the devil's own stamping grounds and, with his slogging oxen, big wagons, mules and men, marched straightway to success!

During his prospering days he is said to have received a telegram from a remote wire terminal of the plains. It was from one of his train-masters. A wagon had been bogged. The mules were nearly exhausted. The men were discouraged. The one great need, and the only hope, was to swear! Could he swear just once? The request was granted, with the proviso that he do his swearing where neither man nor mule could hear him.

On another occasion a young man applied for employment.

"Can you drive a team?" Majors asked him.

"Can I drive a team? Why, I can drive a team to hell and back!"

Mr. Majors considered the case. Unfortunately, he

told the man, he was not doing business with His
Satanic Majesty this year, and did not expect to freight
in that direction for at least some time to come.

Majors, by now, had become a great government
contractor; he supplied nearly all of the military posts
west of the Missouri and Mississippi rivers; he controlled practically all of the freighting on the plains.
It is no wonder that he didn't swear. Perhaps there
had never been a real occasion to do so; but a time
was about to come when there would be at least the
occasion. It was early in 1860, when William H. Russell, a partner of several years, first approached him
on the subject of the Pony Express.

Russell, it seemed, had given the invulnerable word
of the firm to the effect that the Missouri River would
be joined to California by a weekly or biweekly relay
system of horses, to cover a distance of nearly two
thousand miles on a schedule of nine or ten days.
Senator Gwin had accepted the word at its well-
known value. There was money behind it so long as
Majors was behind it. Now Majors was hearing for the
first time what was already being broadcast to the
world—he was joint proprietor in this extravagant
enterprise.

Russell's Follies had appeared on the plains before.
There had been a certain traveling show, a stage-
coach romance known as the "Leavenworth & Pike's
Peak Express," put on the road in April of fifty-nine
for the benefit of the Rocky Mountain gold-rushers.

Its success had seemed to depend on the elasticity of a mining bubble. Majors had refused to have anything to do with it. Yet Russell, against all protests, had taken his bull by the horns. With a partner, John S. Jones of Missouri, he had organized a company in February, and, independent of the old firm, undertaken the enterprise on the strength, it appears, of a note "payable in ninety days," given and secured by Jones & Russell.

Then ninety days had passed. To save Russell, the old company had been obliged to come to his rescue —to take over the road show of Jones & Russell and encumber itself with a project whose only hope of salvation had appeared along lines of expansion. Toward this end the firm had then relieved Messrs. Hockaday & Company of their burdensome line, taking over the mail contract on May 11, and, with some elaborate improvements during the summer, operated it over the old Platte route between Atchison, Kansas, and Salt Lake City. "The Central Overland California & Pike's Peak Express" became the elaborate title of the original Follies revamped. And now, in order to save the whole, along had come Russell with his Pony.

The need of more Federal support for the Salt Lake stages, the need to pound home to a Southern administration the advantages of the Central route, and the possibility that a horse express might, through its spectacular demonstration, achieve something of the sort, was all clear enough to Majors, the practical plainsman who had done business with the Government now for nearly thirty years. But, by the same token of experience, it was no less clear that the Pony would eat up about ten dollars to every one dollar made.

PONY EXPRESS.

Office, 153 Montgomery St.

THE PONY WILL resume its trips on SATUR-DAY, the 7th inst., and will hereafter run Semi-Weekly. The Regular Days of Leaving will be

WEDNESDAYS AND SATURDAYS.

The public may rest assured that every arrangement has been made, necessary to insure safety and dispatch.

W. W. FINNEY, General Agent.

J. LAMBERT, Agent San Francisco.   jy6-7

Courtesy of the Bancroft Library
ADVERTISEMENT FROM A NEWSPAPER OF JULY 1860

Had the company been paid the million or more which, it appears, the Government still owed on a certain freighting contract incident to the Mormon Rebellion, then the firm proper, rather than the firm in name, might have been able to stand with cash behind the enterprise. As it was, and indeed ever would be, the purse of Majors (in the name of the firm) could be resorted to. Fortunately, he had it to lose. Unfortunately, he had to lose it. Russell had given his word.

It all seems as a melodrama to-day; but it was convincing realism at the time. One hundred thousand dollars in gold had been spent at the outset to make it real; $75,000 was the cost a few months later when there was added a wild Indian raid. Seven station keepers lost their lives in that act; stations were burned, a formidable section of the route was completely devastated. Later there were other raids and counter-attacks. Russell's big show was a thriller; and loud were the cheers as the various actors took up the rôle of hero.

"Pony Bob" Haslam was among those to assume the part. He appeared in a scene of arid wastes, the desert Carson region, where winds blew white with sand and alkali. Indians had played havoc along the the road; and he had reached the end of his route only to take up the burden of another rider's fear by traveling a second. Returning, he met with the necessity of doubling again, a burnt station with charred human remains compelling him this time. Three hundred and eighty-four miles, with but nine hours' rest intervening, he had ridden through this perilous country in order to exact the schedule of the Pony mail.

Jim Moore appears in a similar rôle. With an important despatch from Washington, he had ridden over his route into Julesberg, where another despatch was handed him, his relief having been killed. Retracing his course, accordingly, he had covered without rest a course of 280 miles.

The many parts supposed to have been played by the boy William Cody are known too well—his 390-mile ride, on one occasion, with stops only for meals and fresh mounts, every station on the route entered on time!—or the incident in which he caused his horse to lunge, knock down two highwaymen, and make off; or his fabulous encounters with Indians, and so on. Some legends sprang up around the Pony show; some fiction gave wings to facts. With respect to some of these Pony riders, some paper-back hokum is still parading as history and some history, perhaps, as paper-back hokum. Another generation of sorting and sifting may be needed to segregate it all. Few alleged acts, at any rate, in the whole performance can be compared with that one ascribed to Wild Bill Hickok in the "Autobiography of Buffalo Bill," "by Colonel W. F. Cody."

Wild Bill, despite his great stature, is discovered as a Pony Express rider. He was, indeed, on the line; and he may have ridden at one time to fill an emergency —the autobiographer does not explain. Here, at any rate, he came, the yellow hair of him atumble about the rim of his hat and all but white with the dust. His sharp eyes were fixed upon the relay station ahead —Rock Creek, where a fresh mount should have been waiting, but was not. Neither stock-tender nor the wife of the stock-tender had responded to his war-whoops until, as he swung from the saddle, there sounded from within the cabin the woman's screams.

Wild Bill, like a tall Nordic giant, may have hesi-tated for an instant to identify certain scuffling noises above the wind in the cottonwood-trees; but cer-tainly he did not pause long. With the scream of the woman still whetting his nerves, and the sight of her husband sprawled lifeless in the dust, he sprang to-ward the cabin on the spur of an impulse—but stopped.

He drew and fired. One grizzly form of a white man crumpled down in the doorway. He fired again and crumpled one more. He sprang over his first two dead men, drew a fusillade from four live ones, emptied his gun in return and killed a second pair! With his knife he despatched another. A rifle from the hands of a corpse on the floor sufficed for the sixth and last! "Five at least," tradition says (three according to one good authority), Wild Bill Hickok killed on that occasion!

The scene shifted with the shifting of the old Pony for the new. The unfortunate woman, an outraged victim of the gang, having been left with the newly arrived passengers of the overland stage, Hickok was again on the road.[1]

It was a melodrama which, if not overdrawn by its advertisers, could have been scarcely convincing to the audience even of that day; but the Pony actors did well enough without being given these wild acrobatic rôles; and the whole Pony chorus, as none may ever doubt, remains worthy of all the applause it received while on the road. Over prairies and flooding rivers, over stifling deserts of alkali, desolations of sand, rugged mountains of snow, nearly two hundred miles every twenty-four hours, nearly two thousand miles in ten days, nearly twice as fast as the stage-coach was the rate of travel.

Stations had been built from the eastern slopes of the Sierra Nevadas all the way to the Mormon capital, and there had been stations to stock and equip thence onward to St. Joseph, intervals between them averaging about fifteen miles. Each rider controlled the equipage of his three-station beat and covered, in any case of emergency, either one of the two routes adjoining. His changes from horse to horse occupied but an instant of time; and there was seldom but a few moments' delay in the shifting of riders. For protection against savages and outlaws, he carried his

[1] This incident, like one other (to be noted hereafter) in these chronicles, finds no direct verification in the original sources. William E. Connelley of the Kansas Historical Society, having given the career of "Wild Bill" long and careful study, has told the authors that the story is essentially true, but that the killings of "Wild Bill" on this occasion numbered more nearly three.

six-shooting Colts half-cocked, but did well enough in such times of plight to depend on the hoofs of his mount.

Storm weather found him in a complete suit of buckskin, hair outside to shed the rain. Every measure had been taken in behalf of lightness. He was a light man himself; his saddle was light, with mail pouches, four in number, overlaid in a manner to distribute the load. Nearly all accouterments had been manufactured especially for the service. Even his bowie-knife was unique in design—there was mercury in a tube along its snare which the force of inertia, lent by the blow, would bring smartly to the weapon's point, thus affording a timely extra weight to the instrument.

The horse express was nothing new to the world; the Pony methods in their essence were probably as old as Horsedom, but never, certainly, since the institution chronicled by Marco Polo had there been anything as elaborate, as perfect as this. There was applause from both sides of the continent. Well done, Haslam! Well done, Moore! Well done, Egan! Bravo! Hurrah for Russell! Author! Speech!

Russell's Follies!

Yet it was "what the people wanted," especially if they could have it free. But the purse of Alexander Majors was not inexhaustible. The Pony's receipts were estimated at $101,000, which left a total loss of at least a million, not counting interest on the investment.

The attitude of Majors is reminiscent, perhaps, of a certain old cast of Western pioneer to whom any casual expression of intention by him or even by a partner was, under certain rather commonplace circumstances, like a written contract signed and sealed. Appropriately enough it was on the strength of such a contract that there existed a Pony Express. The system demonstrated that word and bond were synonymous in the eyes of Majors.

Russell's Follies, indeed; but it was an Alexander Majors production, his "super-production," and one of the most impressive of our real Western dramas. Something more than show, more than utility or gold was behind the Pony.

The little animal continued his run until the wires were joined and the telegraph clicked him aside. In October of 1861 his season was spent. In a short time, too, about a million dollars' worth of stock comprising the whole Central Overland California & Pike's Peak Express had fallen into the outstretched hands of Ben Holladay.

Here was the end—Majors bankrupt. The members of the old firm went their several ways. The curtain fell to the tune of "Yankee Doodle"; and there was an ironic smile on the face of the Piper.

PART FOUR

THE WHIP OF HOLLADAY

Chapter I

THE HERITAGE OF BIG BEN HOLLADAY

Well I know who'll take the credit—all the
    clever chaps that followed—
Came, a dozen men together—never knew my
    desert fears;
Tracked me by the camps I'd quitted, used the
    water-holes I'd hollowed.
They'll go back and do the talking. *They'll*
    be called the Pioneers!
                                        KIPLING—*The Explorer*

BEN HOLLADAY climbs to the box of his stage-
coach. Russell and Majors climb down. Ben Holladay sounds his whip with a report to be heard by
posterity. Across the plains he goes bounding. There
are special coaches for him, and scores of special teams
—animals to be driven ofttimes to their ruin in the
course of a single stage, a single stretch of ten or
fifteen miles. From the Missouri River to California
he covers a distance of nearly two thousand miles in
twelve days and two hours, breaking the record of
everything but the Pony Express. His bill in damages
for the trip amounts to ten—some say twenty—
thousand dollars. But it makes no difference.

It made no difference to him. It was too small a

thing in his life, like the emeralds and diamonds he sometimes wore, like his "Ophir Palace" and thousand acres on the Hudson, like the bronze lions at the door of his mansion in Washington, D. C., like the millions he made and the millions that made him, like the twenty-dollar gold piece he could toss out in a tip for his favorite "corn dodger," bacon, and beans.

He was, as William Russell had been before him, "The Napoleon of the Plains." He was, in the cultured mind of the financier Henry Villard, whom he faced on the day of his Waterloo, "illiterate, coarse, pretentious, boastful, false and cunning." "That a man of such character should have found it so easy to command millions in foreign capital was quite a puzzle and shock" to Mr. Villard.[1] But in the mind of John Donaphin, who knew him better, Ben Holladay "had faults of disposition and education, but he was brave, strong, aggressive, talented and generous"; he was a man of "wonderful nerve and activity"; he was "one of God's gifted children. . . . Haughty and dictatorial, he was one of the most companionable of men. . . . Anxious to get the best of every bargain, he would often turn it, with all the profits, to some friend or deserving man. . . . He had faults, but desertion of friends was not one of them."[2]

[1] See Villard, "Memoirs," Vol. II, 273.
[2] "St. Joseph Catholic Tribune" quoted by Frank A. Root and William E. Connelley. "Overland Stage to California," 448–450.

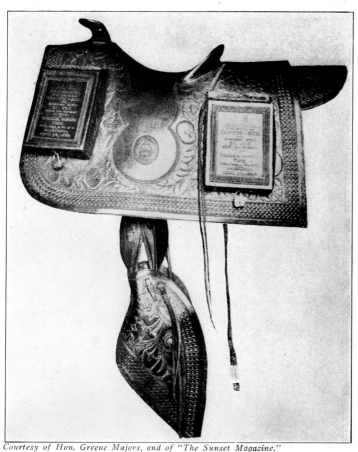

SPECIAL SADDLE WITH ATTACHED MAIL POUCHES USED BY "THE PONY EXPRESS."

Ben Holladay—a Kentucky-born Missouri rustic, keeper of a dram shop, scout, frontier trader, merchant, stage monopolist, steamship magnate, railroad man, and political power in the country at large—was known to have operated at one time a stage route from Atchison to Salt Lake, another from Topeka to Denver, another from Omaha to Fort Kearney, and still others from Salt Lake to the mines of Montana and western Idaho, with various subsidiaries and branches—a total extent of about three thousand miles, with mail contracts bearing at a rate of more than one million dollars a year. A lively passenger business and a convenient freighting business and an express business and a shipping business—all these were contributing generously; and there was the friendship of President Lincoln for his protection. With coaches by the hundreds, horses and mules by the thousands, it was believed that his staging concern alone was the nation's, if not the world's, greatest enterprise ever owned and controlled by one man.

Holladay, in the beginning, fell heir to the daily Central Overland California & Pike's Peak Express, extending from the Missouri River as far as Salt Lake. This line, being the combination of a Salt Lake route that had been driven to the wall, a Denver route that had failed, and the amalgamated upshot of both on the road to ruin, might have offered him a splendid opportunity to demonstrate his capacity as a stageman. Standards had been rather low on the

Central route in the past. Only a modest expenditure of capital and energy might have been needed in order to present a happy contrast between the old management and the new. But it happened now that one did not have to look back in order to draw comparisons. The better part of the original Butterfield organization had been moved up from the South to fill the breach between Salt Lake and the Sierra Nevadas.

This old stagefaring firm had lost something in the recent shuffle, to include a few of its most capable officials; but it was no disjointed affair. It was an organization with set ideals of dependability and new opportunities for despatch. It had brought rather formidable standards to the Central route—they were not the highest; but by them was the Eastern neighbor apt to be judged; and there was needed something more than capital and energy to lift the C. O. C. & P. P. E. from its demoralized state to a position of comparable merit. Whether Ben Holladay was "just the man" for the task may be a question; but it was a very dubious question during the four and a half years of his reign.

It would, perhaps, have been difficult to doubt this new proprietor's genius; but there were reasons, often called "excuses," which prevented him from making any vivid display of this quality along his overland lines. With no glittering exception to be noted in the year of sixty-three, the eastern section of the Great

Overland kept losing the continuity. Generally, it gave poor service. Often, over extended periods, it gave no service at all. Holladay was blamed, of course. He was perhaps the most unpopular stage proprietor that ever lived. But it is very apparent that no one, beset as he was beset by the hostilities of Indians, could have begun, in the slightest, to satisfy the popular expectations.

Holladay, nevertheless, was not a Butterfield or a Birch. Staging, which chanced to become his business, was not and could not have been his profession. Inspired by a love for no calling but the amassing of a fortune, he was apt to tackle almost anything that promised him a fair fight, in the cool business sense, for gold. As an owner of more than a dozen large vessels in the Pacific trade, he was by nature as far from the sea and the ways of the sea as any yokel from his old home town of Weston, Missouri. As an owner of stage-coaches, he was naturally more adaptable. He was a good judge of stock; he knew the ways of the plains; he was practically fearless, and incidentally had once driven, or tried to drive, a stage. But if he was any improvement, in this particular sense, upon the inexperienced proprietors he had succeeded, then the Indian must be blamed for having denied him the chance to demonstrate.

Thus, in many respects, was Holladay handicapped from the start; and while Indians did present by far the greatest of all obstacles in his path, it is perhaps fortunate that his was a phase of only secondary moment in the conquest of the West by stage.

It was on March 2, 1861—about a week after the Butterfield route had been cut up by guerrilla warfare through Texas—that an act of Congress had been approved, calling for certainly the greatest of all American stage-coach undertakings thus far: daily service between St. Joseph and Placerville, contractors agreeing in good faith among themselves to maintain an average speed of seventeen days between the termini, and being bound by contract to a schedule rate of twenty days during eight months of the year and twenty-three through the remaining months. For this service, which included the carrying of all mails to and from California, the annual compensation was to be $1,000,000.

The new agreement was with the old company, the Overland Mail, which, upon shifting to a portion of the Central route, was to make its own arrangements with the firms already established in the other sections. The Mail Company was also privileged to arrange with shipping concerns for the transportation of heavy printed matter, and was to receive liberal allowance to cover the costs involved in moving up from the Southern route. All through the late spring and early summer long trains of Butterfield coaches, wagons, horses, and mules were seen plodding westward over New Mexico and Arizona, and northward

Courtesy of Hon. Greene Majors. From an original photograph.

ALEXANDER MAJORS

OF THE PONY EXPRESS

through California, and eastward along the trail of the Pony Express as far as Salt Lake City. It was the breaking up of the old Southern institution whose Rainbow Trail was fading into the clouds of civil war.

There was some bitterness in the dusty tracks of these stage-coach processions. They were carrying away the old hopes for a Southern railroad; they were walking off with substantial prospects of populating the land, and they were leaving, in certain places, a wake of smoldering ruins where stage stations had once cheered the emigrant, where stage horns had sounded and flags had flown, and where little communities had commenced to lift their heads. But there were certain superintendents of the Mail Company who had not forgotten the inroads upon their stock through Texas. They were burning what they could not carry away—stations and even stores. They were called "Black Republicans." They passed on, doggedly, with "Adios, and good riddance" flung at their sweating backs.

It was all in ugly contrast to the old feeling that John Butterfield had known in the days when he had been hailed as "admiral" and "chief," when even the hottest opponents of his course along the borders of Mexico had acknowledged him as master in the field. But unfortunately or otherwise, during these ugly times he was no longer the head of the Overland Mail Company. He had, some months since, while his line was operating at the height of its popularity, resigned his president's chair.

It seemed he had wished to compete with the Central Overland Pony Express by running a fast line of saddle stock over the Southern route, a route already well equipped for the undertaking. But other members of his firm had opposed him. Differences had arisen. Stagedom, at any rate, had lost him, and could have lost no finer spirit. Now William B. Dinsmore, of Adams & Company renown, one of the original contractors with Butterfield, was the nominal head of the firm. It was still the firm of "Butterfield & Company," but only by virtue of the original contract now amended and improved for the Central service. Reestablished in northern territory, the organization was to be known simply as the Overland Mail, with Ford Cook, an efficiency expert rather than a stageman, acting as manager, and with Wells-Fargo controlling. Personality, in short, had been buried somewhere on the banks of the Rio Grande. In more respects than one, there was to be nothing quite like the old original again.

"The Los Angeles Star" [1] later recalled "the vivid impressions we once had with regard to the certain prosperity, and the growing interest in this section of the country, when the first stage [of the Southern mail] entered Los Angeles, freighted with letters

[1] *Op. cit.*, January 9, 1864.

and passengers, crossing the Saharas of New Mexico
and Arizona, and arriving here in twenty-one days
from the Atlantic States. . . . The regularity with
which the mail was carried, uninterrupted by the vicissitudes of climate or season, and the comparative
comfort enjoyed by those who undertook the long
and tedious journey, tends more to confirm the prac-
ticability of the great highway across the continent
by the southern route than any exploring expedition,
or topographical survey previously made. But almost
before we had time to contemplate the good things
which the Government and Postmaster General had
made possible for us . . . the mail was changed from
the sunny South to the cold and inhospitable North.
. . . But we must not despond. The government is
beginning to see that the Southern route is absolutely
necessary."

In fact, had the war permitted, a coach mail would
certainly have been maintained on both routes. The
Northern, for the sake of a more populated and
promising region, for the sake of emigration and general despatch, did merit greater consideration in spite
of its "cold and inhospitable" nature; but it was not
implied, even by the sectionalized North in the dawn
of its new power, that the Southern route did not warrant some Federal support. Indeed, while the Overland Mail was in the process of moving away, a
contract was being renewed for the continuation and
improvement of the line which Birch had put into
operation in fifty-seven. The old "Jackass Mail" was

to be dignified by the name of "Los Angeles, San Diego & San Antonio Mail." As such it might soon have been made to answer the demands of the country; but the service, having started, was suspended August 2, "due to Civil War." [1]

Thus passed the last remnant of the Southern institution while the Central came into its own. In this advent there was nothing very spectacular. It was a matter of simple readjustment. The Pioneer Line, in perfect trim, flourishing under Louis McLane, answered the problem of the Sierra Nevadas, and stood as the first link of the new transcontinental chain, extending from Placerville to Virginia and Carson, Nevada. The Overland Mail, intact as an organization, had only to occupy the road of the Pony Express from Carson as far as Salt Lake. The C. O. C. & P. P. E., already in action, with a short branch to Denver and connections at Fort Kearney from Omaha, completed the circuit to the eastern terminus of St. Joseph. All three lines, as a unit, were to commence the daily service on July 1. And they commenced accordingly with little ado. There was the feeling that this, the greatest of the world's staging enterprises, was, after all, nothing new. It had been existing for some years in all of its parts and potentialities, requiring only the crack of a congressional whip to make it go. It had been evolving since 1849—years of precious time.

[1] U. S. House Executive Documents, 37th Congress, second session, Vol. V, p. 4 (Serial No. 1131).

Courtesy of the Bancroft Library

ADVERTISEMENT FROM A DIRECTORY OF 1861

But now, with "On to Richmond!" silenced by the advancing Confederate guns, there was the suggestion, at least, of one decisive Yankee victory in the clattering of Yankee wheels, rolling as ever out of Concord, rolling over all the Western empire. The West was conquered. July 2 of sixty-two was to clinch the conquest with Lincoln's name on the Railroad Bill. But there had been certain victories by such as Birch, such as Crandall, such as Butterfield, such as Chorpenning, Hockaday, Russell, and Majors; such too, of course, as "Old Charlie." Their work had been before the crisis. They had proved what a Concord stage-coach could do; they had built up new and very necessary standards, blazed the trails, demonstrated the feasibility of mountain passes, agitated action in Congress and established what firms were now intact, ready for the new staging era. There was the need now simply to carry on and expand with the growth of the land.

This task, however, was not as simple as it might have been; it was not made less difficult by the fact that it belonged to a less crucial phase of Western history. For no sooner had Congress authorized the new million-dollar mail than the War Department made it utterly impossible for the stages to give service worth much more than half its cost. Troops were needed elsewhere. Practically all protection was withdrawn from the plains. Overland stages were to square their own yards with Indians—Indians growing rapidly more tired of the white man's presence in their lands. It was the case, particularly, along that section of road which was soon to fall to Ben Holladay. He was to find himself running a series of Indian wars quite as often as others were to be sure that he was operating a stage line.

A first-class fighter rather than a professional stageman may possibly have been what was needed at this bitter end of the route; for there were stagemen of high standing who did not envy its proprietors. Witness, for example, the trustees of the California Company, writing Frank Stevens in Washington, imploring him "for God's sake" and "as we love you, Frank," don't go into that game!

Frank Stevens didn't; but Holladay did—a roughshod king destined for a little reign of terror.

Men of a more adventuresome cast, braver men, men better qualified to serve Ben Holladay in his long series of Indian campaigns, could scarcely have been found elsewhere. As Pony Expressmen or stagemen, or both, under Russell, Majors & Waddell, many had been "bull-whackers" on the route long before and had become familiar with every mile of it. They were plainsmen. They knew how to protect themselves and the property of their employers from hostilities of all kinds so long as any known resources were available. In the absence of adequate military patrols they were no poor substitutes for soldiers, and had been known to set out deliberately upon war-paths of their own to recover what the Indians had stolen.

When Cody was riding express (supposedly) in the upper Platte and Sweetwater country (modern Wyoming), establishing his record for endurance among pony riders, fighting off the Sioux and carrying on in the incredible manner so typical of the later celebrated "Buffalo Bill," such inroads were being made upon the stock of that division that the company was soon obliged to suspend operations. Colonel Cody's book in collaboration with Colonel Inman, "The Great Salt Lake Trail," [1] tells something of what followed:

While we were thus all lying idle [September, 1860], a party was organized to go out and search for the stolen stock. This party was comprised of stage-drivers, express riders, stock-tenders, and ranch-men—forty of them all together—and they were well armed and well mounted. They were mostly men who had undergone all kinds of hardships and braved every danger, and they were ready and anxious to "tackle" any number of Indians. Will Bill [Hickok], who had been driving stage on the road and had recently come down to our [Sweetwater] division, was elected captain of the company. It was supposed that the stolen stock had been taken to the head of the Powder River and vicinity, and the party, of which I was a member, started out for that section in high hopes of success.

[1] *Op. cit.*, 184–186.

RUINS OF OLD BUTTERFIELD STATION OF VALLECITO ON THE
COLORADO DESERT OF CALIFORNIA.

Twenty miles out from Sweetwater Bridge, at the head of Horse Creek, we found an Indian trail running north toward the Powder River, and we could see by the tracks that most of the horses had been recently shod and were undoubtedly our stolen stage-stock. Pushing rapidly forward, we followed this trail to Powder River; thence down this stream to within about forty miles of the spot where old Fort Reno now stands. Here the trail took a more westerly course along the foot of the mountains, leading eventually to Crazy Woman's Fork—a tributary of the Powder River. At this point we discovered that the party whom we were trailing had been joined by another band of Indians, and, judging from the fresh appearance of the trail, the united body could not have left this spot more than twenty-four hours before.

Being aware that we were now in the heart of the hostile country and might at any moment find more Indians than we had lost, we advanced with more caution than usual and kept a sharp lookout. As we were approaching Clear Creek, another tributary of the Powder River, we discovered Indians on the opposite side of the creek, some three miles distant; at least we saw horses grazing, which was a sure sign that there were Indians there.

The Indians, thinking themselves in comparative safety,—never before having been followed so far into their own country by white men,—had neglected to put out any scouts. They had no idea that there were any white men in that part of the country. We got the lay of their camp, and then held a council to consider and mature a plan for capturing it. We knew full well that the Indians would outnumber us at least three to one, and perhaps more. Upon the advice and suggestion of Wild Bill, it was finally decided that we should wait until it was nearly dark, and then, after creeping as close to them as possible, make a dash through their camp, open a general fire on them, and then stampede the horses.

This plan, at the proper time, was very successfully executed. The dash upon the enemy was a complete surprise to them. They were so overcome with astonishment that they did not know what to make of it. We could not have astounded them any more had we dropped down into their camp from the clouds. They did not recover from the surprise of this sudden charge until after we had ridden pell-mell through their camp and got away with our own horses as well as theirs. We at once circled the horses around toward the south, and after getting them on the south side of Clear Creek, some twenty of our men—just as the darkness was coming on—rode back and gave the Indians a few parting shots. We then took up our line of march for Sweetwater Bridge, where we arrived four days afterwards with all our own horses and about one hundred captured Indian ponies.

The expedition had proved a grand success, and the event was celebrated in the usual manner—by a grand spree. The only store at Sweetwater Bridge did a rushing business for several days. The returned stock-hunters drank and gambled and fought. The Indian ponies, which had been distributed among the captors, passed from hand to hand at almost every deal of cards. . . . The boys became so elated as well as "elevated" over their success against the Indians that most were in favor of going back and cleaning out the whole Indian race.

This incident, like one other heretofore noted in these chronicles, chances to find no direct verification in the raw, original sources such as newspapers of the day, travelers' journals, etc.; but it typifies truly at least the cast of men later in Ben Holladay's employ. And considering the fact that during his time it became the intention of the Indians to "clean out" the whole white race, he could scarcely have asked for a personnel better equipped for the fray. Brave adventure and romance, the Wild West at its wildest, belong to his four and a half years' drive over the plains by stage. He did not operate an exemplary system, he did not run a line according to the finest standards of the West, but it is clear that things might have been worse.

Chapter II

HELL AND HIGH WATER

"INDIAN" barbarities, especially over the several approaches to Salt Lake City from the east, were frequently perpetrated by white men in war-paint, and more frequently, perhaps, by white men and Indians combined, difficult though it sometimes was to distinguish one breed of savage from the other. Atrocities by allied Indians and Mormons upon Gentile emigrant trains may be prominently identified with the middle fifties, most notable of all the outrages being the Mountain Meadow massacre of fifty-seven, when more than one hundred and twenty men, women, and children were slaughtered, and about $30,000 worth of plunder carried away.

But the religious fanaticism of Utah, though it appears to have countenanced such bloody practices in the past, did not generally extend to the depredations of the sixties. Yet the old savage methods of attack and plunder continued to appeal to certain outlaw elements at large throughout the country; with the assistance of Indians or otherwise, these predatory whites continued as a scourge to settlers, emigrant trains, and stage stations.

Photographed by the authors.

STAGE TEAM "AT HOME"

Some time before the advent of Ben Holladay, such was the hostile nature of certain regions along the eastern section of the Overland, that the God-fearing Alexander Majors himself does not seem to have objected when one of the most notorious killers was employed and placed in a position of almost absolute authority over one ravaged division of the C. O. C. & P. P. Express. He was Joseph A. Slade, variously called "Jack," "Alf," and "William," also "The Little Terror of the Plains" and later "The Bad Man from Bitter Creek."

Some men held that he carried twenty-two buckshot and several bullets buried in various parts of his calloused anatomy, others that he boasted twenty-eight slugs from two barrels of a shotgun only, and still others that they numbered but eleven. In any event, there was some added weight to his indomitable prestige, especially since he was known to have worn the ears of "the other fellow" on his watch chain. He seems to have had a strange penchant for ears, having once sent a small package of them, with his compliments attached or implied, to an Indian chief to suggest the fates of certain braves in need of reform. Slade was a reformer. And he was willing to risk hell's fires himself if only he could send others to heaven.

Nearly a year and a half before the deposition of Russell, Majors & Waddell by Big Ben Holladay, Slade commenced his great overland staging career as a division agent, with headquarters at the prominent

station of Julesberg in the northeast corner of Colorado, where Lodge Pole Creek branches off from the
South Platte River. Here, in a long, low cabin, whose
cedar logs had been drawn by oxen over a distance of
a hundred miles, he once offered to share his coffee
with Mark Twain, who "politely declined." [1]

"I was afraid he had not killed anybody that morning, and might be in need of diversion," writes the
humorist. "But still with firm politeness he insisted
on filling my cup. . . . I thanked him and drank it,
but it gave me no comfort, for I could not feel sure
that he would not be sorry, presently, that he had
given it away, and proceed to kill me to distract his
thoughts from the loss. But . . . we left him with
only twenty-six dead people to account for. . . . I
had pleasantly escaped being No. 27."

Of course, Mark Twain at that time was only Sam
Clemens, and hardly worth killing in so far as Slade
could have been aware; but toward certain others who
had chanced to cross his bloody path the Little Terror
had realized his duty. He had fulfilled his commission
beyond the greatest expectations of his employers.
Many men as honest as Clemens himself, not to mention women and children, had no doubt suffered the
consequences; yet many villains had done likewise,
and it was, in all, "for the general good." Drastic measures were very necessary in this land.

The outlaws had formerly been in close coöpera-

[1] See Mark Twain, "Roughing It," Vol. I, Chap. X.

tion with certain station employees. Thefts of stock and stores had made serious inroads on the company's budget. It was in the fall of sixty, while Russell, Majors & Waddell were trying vainly to retrench, being burdened not only by the costly Pony Express but by a heavy competition in the business of staging as well. E. S. Alvord from California, late general superintendent of the Butterfield line, had secured a mail contract over a route between Fort Kearney and Denver, and was running "The Western Stage Company" all the way from Omaha to the Pike's Peak mines. The C. O. C. & P. P. E. had been obliged, therefore, to cut rates in half. It seemed trying enough to be harassed in this manner, without having to suffer other serious losses at the hands even of employees of the firm.

Ben Ficklin, general superintendent under Russell, however, had found some one who appeared to have the faculty of shooting straight from both barrels of the expression. This gentleman—for he did have the manner and appearance—had by that time killed only about a half-dozen men, including Indians; but if he could kill about a half-dozen more, besides Indians, perhaps matters would be adjusted. So it was one day that Slade, as a division agent, walked quietly into Julesberg—a settlement whose station, warehouse, blacksmith shop and store, were conveniently situated near a cemetery known as Boots Hill. It was a graveyard that boasted exactly one pair of boots to every grave; and now, upon the arrival of this new agent, its chance to uphold its old reputation through a period of unbridled expansion was more than passing fair. Slade proceeded to kill six scoundrels purely as a matter of introduction. And he was by no means certain that he would not have to kill more before his conscience would let him rest.

The name of Jules Bené—a notorious Frenchman suspected of being in collusion with stock-rustlers— may have been among those on his list; but it is also likely that the name of Slade was likewise on the list of Jules. There was enmity between them from the start; for it appears that the services of Jules as station-master had been dispensed with in order to make room for the killer; and that the killer had not hesitated to feed the coals of jealousy by hiring an assistant whom the Frenchman had formerly discharged. Evidently Slade was attempting to start a quarrel, believing that his pistol would end it. He became insulting, and is said to have charged the Frenchman with inhuman cruelties toward some rider of the Pony Express. The most likely sources differ somewhat in the details; but Slade, off his guard in the presence of Jules once too often, fell before the sudden discharge of a shotgun, and managed only to shoot twice in return before both he and his assailant were carried away to the hospital, narrowly escaping Boots Hill. That ended the first act.

The next took place about a year later. Jules was

in hiding; but the other protagonist had posted a reward for his capture dead or alive. Slade was no authorized agent of the law; but his authority as murderer-in-chief was undisputed. He had wrought such order out of chaos on his division that, upon recovering from his wounds, he had been commissioned to direct his energy toward another hotbed of thieves —the Rocky Ridge road above Julesberg on the upper Platte. Here not only had he added many new notches to his gun but had actually sentenced three victims to hang, and had properly hanged them, one being a rider of the Pony Express. All the while, however, he had been waiting most anxiously for Jules.

It was in September of sixty-one when the Frenchman, painfully wounded by his captors, was brought to justice—such justice as Slade could conceive. Bound hand and foot, thrown into a corral, he was left to the mercy of the court—such a court as Slade might be expected to constitute. The trial began with a preliminary shooting, a pistol pressed against the defendant's cheek and fired. Then the court adjourned for the night. On the following morning the defendant was alive, but mercifully unable to suffer more from the taunting and gloating of his captor. Slade killed him, cut off his ears, and went about his business.

Ears being no safer than scalps in the bloody realms of this reign, still the little boss of Rocky Ridge had also his lighter moments. " 'Gentlemen,' said Slade, drawing, 'it's a good twenty-yard shot—I'll clip the third button on his coat!' Which he did. The bystanders all admired it. And they all attended the funeral, too."

Some legends were bound to flourish around such a figure as Slade; but this button episode, as related with some credulity by Mark Twain and others, has its convincing qualities. Slade was a "dead shot." Probably he was a "lucky shot" too. And it did happen to be the custom for every one, including the killer, to attend the funeral of the person killed. Certain ideals of decency had to be upheld . . . except, of course, by Slade. He could do about as he pleased. He had done about as he pleased nearly all his life.

As a fugitive from probably his first murder (in Illinois), he committed a second during flight. An altercation with a wagon driver of the west-bound emigrant train had prompted it; but it appears that the driver had been first to draw. He had not, however, fired. In fact Slade, in his quiet manner, had persuaded the other that this little quarrel might be settled more becomingly with fists. One, two, three— they would both drop their pistols to the ground and sail in like good fellows.

One, two, three! The driver fell, drilled through by a bullet from the pistol of a laughing Slade.

Then came the day when, with a score of such murders behind him, he had perhaps a score more bullets with the name of a victim on each of them, and a few extras for women and babies as their cases might chance to arise. An unfavorable comment with regard to the torturing of Jules led Slade straightway to the offender, whom he found in a store tending bar. Slade asked for whisky. The man turned to get it, and was at that instant "deader than any man that ever lived." And no sooner had the widow started off in flight, than Slade had shot her and the child in her arms. Then he proceeded to murder three or four Indians on the place before leaving to call it a day.

He went unhanged until 1865, after having left the stage company and identified himself with road-agents; but he had served Ben Holladay for several years in the interim, and been promoted during that time to the position of division superintendent.

"Best superintendent on the route," [1] William Cody believed—having driven stage under Slade, Cody must have known.

"No one on the line was ever more useful," [2] comes the comment from Frank A. Root, a messenger in the same service, and the very best of authorities.

"We need a dozen Slades on the route," writes a newspaper correspondent from Salt Lake,[3] who had found reason very often to complain of the eastern mail.

Nor do these pronouncements come from pens that

[1] "Autobiography of Buffalo Bill," 52.
[2] "Overland Stage to California," 218.
[3] To the "Sacramento Union," August 15, 1862.

have made any attempt to refute or depreciate the many stories of Slade's exploits, or to justify his acts of inhuman cruelty, cowardice, and murder in any respect whatever. With only a possible exception in the correspondent's case, they are the testimonials from pens that have told Slade's story in more detail than there is room for here. Yet Slade, it would seem, was the "best superintendent on the route," and "no one on the line was more useful," and there were needed a dozen more!

"God help us!" was the traveler's thought. For passengers crossing the plains by stage must have heard very similar comments in Slade's behalf. In a number of cases, at least, upon reaching their destination, they told the newspapers all about it, and pointed to Slade, very naturally, as an *example* of the kind of men in demand on the Holladay line!

Passengers were thus often unjust. There were a number of excellent stagemen as agents and superintendents, and innumerable splendid whips, on the eastern section. But the service there *was* poor. No matter how the delinquencies could be accounted for, this was an undoubted fact; and passengers, even more than those who suffered through the loss or detention of mail, were well qualified to testify on this score.

They could not help but observe, and they seldom failed to comment upon, the striking change of conditions that appeared as they left stages of one man-

agement at Salt Lake to proceed westward in the care
of another. There was noticed at once an improvement in all matters of comfort, speed, system, and
general good manners; and the improvement became
more apparent with the westward progression—as
the influence of the roughshod school of the old frontiers was left farther and farther behind, and that of
the new El Dorado was overtaken. In fact, one was
apt to wonder, Slade being an example of "the best,"
if more blooded stock in stagemen, and less bloody
stock in gunmen, might not have bettered things
somewhat at the eastern end. Perhaps not noticeably.
But certainly the assumption was justified by certain
travelers who did not chance upon some of the over-
shadowing obstacles met by Ben Holladay.

During the hard winter of sixty-two a creditor less
bold than Holladay might have slept through nightmares contemplating a foreclosure on the stage line
between Salt Lake and the Missouri River. C. O. C.
& P. P. E. was then being translated as "Clean Outa
Cash & Past Paying Expenses," with suggestive reasons for it all along the route. But it was otherwise
swamped. Much of it was literally under water, as
were many other things over all the land.

The Gila and Colorado River country being sub-
merged over a distance of one hundred miles or more,
this was one winter that would have paralyzed even
the late Butterfield line. The rivers Carson and Hum-

boldt of Nevada and the deserts in their immediate vicinity, glittering now as a single lake, this was one winter that did paralyze the worthy descendant of the Butterfield line as it ranged between the Mormon city and the Sierras. The Great Basin appeared to be filling. Elsewhere in the nation cabins that had stood since the dawn of the nineteenth century, trees of two centuries' growth, were swept away.

"First mail from the East for six days." "No mail from the West for several days." "This evening aspires to put through the first mail in the last ten days." "Bromley, Division Agent [just east of Salt Lake], a fellow hard to beat out of doors—was three days traveling ten miles."

When the telegraph wires were working, or when a stage-coach managed to pull through, such were the reports from Salt Lake City from January until May of sixty-two. Meanwhile mail matter had also been accumulating to swamp the line; and to add to the chaos of loose letters and bags piled up here and there from one end of the route to the other, the contractors had as yet been unable to contract, as had been their privilege to do, with the shipping interests to carry the bulky articles. Public documents had sometimes served as road-beds for stage-coach wheels! but newspapers and letters were choking all the stations and store-rooms; and it was not until the floods were practically over that arrangements could be made with the steamship men to relieve the congestion. So delinquent was the service on the whole that, despite the protests of the Postmaster-General, payment to the contractors was being withheld pending an investigation—some proof, perhaps, that there had been an extraordinary flood!

Dinsmore's (Western) section of the line, with the financial support of Wells-Fargo, was able to withstand the delay. The Pioneer Line was practically self-supporting. But the C. O. C. & P. P. E. was in very unhappy circumstances. It was an unfortunate goose with a golden egg on which Holladay held a first mortgage. And upon it as it lay, half under water, "clean out of cash," and with all possibilities of paying expenses held up by the Government, Holladay pounced. On March 2 he was the formal purchaser. Bela M. Hughes of Missouri, an able attorney who had succeeded William Russell some months before as president of the line, was retained along with the general personnel. But Holladay assumed full command and became the sole master of the monstrous mess.

Those who had once cheered the Pony Express of the late Russell, Majors & Waddell now hailed the advent of Holladay as a great salvation. Because Ben was a great man. Everybody knew that. On the plains he was "one of the boys." And if, they said, he would only do half of what was expected of him, the daily mail would rise and flourish. It was the general feeling; for Holladay was known nearly as well in Utah and California as he was in Missouri, from whose frontiers he had sprung. Early in the fifties he had bought stores in the East, trekked them to Salt Lake, traded them for stock, driven the stock to California, and sold out at a handsome profit. Incidental to his freighting and stock-driving business, he had also been affiliated with one of the overland mail-carriers (W. L. Blanchard) in fifty-three. In short, he had been hoeing a long road through the West, and was worthy, in the eyes of the West, to drive stages over it—especially since it was believed that he was not the type of man to rest on his laurels.

He reorganized the whole system, adding new stock and vehicles, but continuing for the time with the old name of "C. O. C. & P. P. Express." Great results were anticipated. But they failed to materialize. While the Overland Mail Line was emerging from the floods with all the new life of mid-spring, the eastern neighbor was commencing to offer its excuses. Indians!

And there were Indians; but the world was by now too impatient and too tired to listen. Travelers, moreover, were coming in with reports that made Indian stories seem rather tame. It was well known that heaps of mail had been accumulating all along the route, and that a great deal of energetic work would be needed to put it all through; but now (June) with the warehouse at Julesberg "packed full," and all stations along the upper Platte still hopelessly congested, it was reported that nearly all the mail between the Sweetwater Bridge and Fort Bridger had been destroyed!

"At Sweetwater, thirty-nine bags of United States locked mail, and seven sacks of Wells, Fargo & Company express matter . . . were rifled of their content. At Ice Springs, two bags of mail were cut open, and the station was knee-deep with loose and unopened letters." [1]

Such vandalism could scarcely be attributed to Indians. Informants along the route had convinced one D. W. Pense and other travelers that "depredations said to have been perpetrated by Indians were perpetrated by employees of the company under the direction of different agents." Slade being active as usual at this time, such a charge did not seem wholly extravagant. Ordered to "clean up" any mess, Slade would be apt to "clean" by one means or another. Now, perhaps, instead of making forfeitures for breaches of contract, the contractor would attempt to collect indemnities from the Government for damages by Indians!

It was no wonder now that the long-suffering press had suddenly turned against Ben Holladay and begun to thunder its indignation. Believe in such atrocities? It had to. Witness Slade, best superintendent on the route, most useful man. Holladay, of course, denied

[1] D. W. Pense, a traveler, writing for the Carson, Nevada, "Silver Age," as quoted by the "Sacramento Union," June 26, 1862.

the charge; and subsequent investigations proved nothing against him. Nor, however capable of making money, was Holladay apt to have employed such ruthless methods. Nevertheless, his original popularity was gone at a time when he needed it most. Large bands of Indians, with whites mixed in, were on the rampage all along the Sweetwater, killing and looting, adding havoc to chaos. Troops alone could have brought any order, but the troops were gone.

Chapter III

ALONG THE WAR-PATH OF SIXTY-TWO

THE Sweetwater, having completed more than two thirds of its eastward dash from the summits of the Rockies over the high plains to the upper Platte, makes a slight bend around the southern slopes of Granite Mountains before cutting through the Devil's Gate. Just west of this bend it passes the town of Splitrock, Wyoming; but in the spring of sixty-two, when a small train of stage-coaches pulled westward from this point, there was no town and no Wyoming—there were only the remains of a Split Rock Station, deserted, sacked, and partially burned.

Indian hostilities over this section of the Overland were such that all coaches, daring to venture at all, were obliged to travel in pairs for the sake of protection. A military escort, had such been available, would have advanced here with more than ordinary caution. All the way from Fort Laramie to Fort Bridger, or fairly from Nebraska to Utah, the road was barely passable. One late keeper of Split Rock, a Monsieur Auguste, had met the first of the trouble on the last night of February, during the floods. With a lighted candle in his hand he had answered a summons at his door . . . and snuffed the candle, in the next instant, when his dead body fell upon it. A stock-tender had fallen beside him. The marauders had swarmed in and cut things to pieces. They had set fire to the barn and cleaned out the corral, making off with fourteen mules. Before morning another station, thirty-five miles to the` eastward, had been plundered of thirteen more animals. Since then the whole region had suffered from repeated attacks. Willow Springs, Red Buttes, Dry Sandy, Rocky Ridge, and Split Rock (again) had lost a score more of horses and mules; eight stock-tenders had been reported killed; news had come to Washington that some two hundred miles of overland route had been devastated, rendering further irregularities of mail service unavoidable.

It was the realization of warnings from mail contractors, senators, and military officials during the previous year when the troops had been withdrawn. The Government had heeded the warnings to the end that fifteen hundred California volunteers had been enlisted for service along the line. They were to have marched in order to reach Salt Lake before the heavy snows; but fearing that public sentiment in California might fail to suppress the Secessionist minority, the command had been retained in the State, thus defeating the purpose for which the regiments had been organized, and leaving the stage line to a host of half-starved savages. A battalion of cavalry and a

Courtesy of the Bancroft Library. From an old engraving.

BEN HOLLADAY

ORIGINAL ILLUSTRATION FROM "CALIFORNIA MAIL BAG," OF
AUGUST, 1871.

battery of artillery had later been ordered out from the East, but this wholly inadequate force had yet to arrive and was apt to have its hands full when it did.

The two stage-coaches, now jogging westward out of Split Rock, were well aware of the hazards involved. The party had left the terminus of Atchison, Kansas, on April 2, and given some fifteen days to a journey of about 850 miles! The old Santa Fé Mail, now running weekly wagons out of Kansas City, could sometimes equal this despatch on a route of equal distance with only two relay posts on the entire road. But Holladay, who had been unable to do any real staging in the past, was not doing any at present. His line, as the main part of a million-dollar system, was in a disreputable state; and the occupants of this limping coach train, on reaching the last station, had been fortunate in the discovery of a little scattered hay for their weary teams before driving the animals onward.

A peak of the Windriver ranges was in sight ahead, vague and white, like a mist-cap resting on the hill. The stages were slogging along close together through patches of snow, sand, and frozen mud, the cold morning air making vapor puffs at the nostrils of the tugging mules. Buffalo robes were pulled high about the unshaven chins and the purplish cheeks of passengers; but hands were not far from rifles, and eyes were alert, coasting over the broken plains, the sage-brush, the washed ravines, the broad, patchy sweeps that stretched away on either side to where isolated mountains of rock stood as dark voids bitten out of the sky.

There were nine well-armed men in the party, to include Lemuel Flowers, a newly appointed agent for the Sweetwater division. As next to the last division on the road to Salt Lake, it lay between the most God-forsaken extremes of two others—Slade's on the upper Platte, and James Bromly's beyond the South Pass. Leading through the heart of the Rockies, it was the wildest stretch of road on the line, devoid of any settlements or forts, marked with the graves of emigrants, the ruins of wagons, and the bones of oxen, from its eastern terminus at Rocky Ridge to the other at Pacific Springs.

And of all "stages" of this hostile stretch, that between Split Rock and Three Crossings, twelve miles in extent, seems to have had the least savory reputation. Here William Cody, traditionally, once as a Pony rider and once again as the driver of a stagecoach, had been ambushed by the Indians, barely escaping on both occasions with his scalp. Here, too, had "Lem" Flowers, as an assistant agent, according to the same tradition, been wounded and seen two of his passengers killed. Now, with his party four miles beyond Split Rock where the road sloped upward slightly over a wave of hill, he was about to take part in another encounter.

It was at a point where the sage grew thick even

from the alkaline marshes at the side of the road, and where the wet sand clung and closed at the rims of wheels. Then—a motion in the brush, shadows from behind it, feather-tips, rifle barrels—some one cried, "Indians!" Some one fired into a clump of sage, which immediately responded like the living battery of bowstrings and muskets that it happened to be.

Arthur Stephenson, driver of the leading coach, received the first bullet, yet managed to cling to his lines. He was attempting to reach a point of better vantage at the crest of the hill; but from that quarter, suddenly, a fresh fire suggested the trap; and the wounded driver could do no more than haul over to one side of the road.

Bullets were whacking off splinters as the other stage pulled up alongside, when a galloping troop of lancers, with heads raised like barking coyotes, appeared at no great distance, bearing rapidly down. The teams were verging upon a panic, one animal shot through the mouth, rearing and kicking, others backing and filling, straddling their traces and poles.

They had to be cut out. At any rate, they were being cut out. Half the party had sprung to the ground. Some men were heaving out mail sacks, robes, blankets—all things that might do for cover; while others were heaping them between the wheels, piling up sand, and attempting at the same time to maintain an effective fire. The animals, slapped on the haunches, were off by now in a flying stampede,

Indians hooting their delight, heading them off, running them up the ravine, leaving the other prospects of plunder, such as scalps and firearms, to a feathery horde still large enough to take them.

So the siege was begun. There were the two teamless vehicles side by side on the road; and there were rifle barrels flashing from between the wheels, where all dunnage had been heaped for breastworks. But the conductor, James Brown, was already out of the battle—sprawled in a puddle, stunned or dead, a fast trickle of red down his cheek. The new agent, Lem Flowers, though twice wounded, was yet able to shoot. And a passenger, Phil Rogers, who had intercepted two arrows with one shoulder, was still able to sound an accompaniment along with the rest. James Anderson, another passenger, with a bullet through his leg, remained concealed in one of the coaches to direct the fire and sound the warning in the event of charge. Twice they had come with a yell down the wind; but both times, as rifles were dropped for pistols, they had circled back, somewhat reduced in numbers. Intermittent fire continued thence onward through a long day, while from time to time small groups of Indians were seen to withdraw. Finally the world was quiet.

The stranded party, nursing its wounds, took council. Evidently the enemy was tired, or the prize had ceased to be worth the battle. It was decided that if the disabled men could be moved, a march of eight

JOHN T. GILMER

DIVISION SUPERINTENDENT ON
"THE GREAT OVERLAND"; LATER
OF THE STAGING FIRM OF "GIL-
MER & SALISBURY."

Courtesy of Martha Kimball. From an old photograph.

KIMBALL'S STATION
ON "THE GREAT OVERLAND."

miles to Three Crossings should be attempted. Jim Brown, the conductor, though he had long since recovered his senses, was in no condition to walk. Flowers was in a similar plight. Three others believed they could drag themselves along, but no more. That left, however, besides four able men, a measure of resourcefulness plus the determination and the necessity to be under way; and no time was lost in the undertaking.

The front section of the coach's running gear had been uncoupled. Blankets and robes had been packed upon it in a manner to accommodate Flowers and Brown. Those less disabled found some support behind the truck, leaning against it, or pushing when they could, while a good four-man team did the rest, hauling at the pole. It was a heavy load. It became too heavy, and progress at last too slow. The abandoned coaches had been dropped out of sight, but wisps of curling smoke were rising up in the twilight from that vicinity—Indians were there, at least; perhaps they were advancing.

The truck was discarded in a hurry. Thence onward the two who had been dependent on it depended upon the support of their comrades, dragging and limping on through the dark, through the freezing cold that came with it—a cold that seemed to numb all parts of the body but those that ached or bled. Sometimes they rested, but the chill crept in, prompting some of them on, urging others to remain. Eight

miles, seven, six, a long drag to five, an almost interminable one to four—they were coursing the old
Mormon trail whose milestones might have been tomb-
stones had the graves been spared. They could hear the
plunging of the Sweetwater from the walls of its
roaring canyon. Down from the Windriver ranges
and over the desert plateau it came as though in a
panic to be out of the land. Perhaps at other points of
the route it had passed other scenes of destitution,
other suffering devils, empire-builders being ground
in the wheels of their empire.

And so it had, not much farther up the road—no
farther, in fact, than where the trail crossed the creek
three times. For there, at the nearest ford, stood a
long log station house with barricaded doors; and
under its low sodden roof three children and a woman
were sleeping. Light only from a dark night sky came
through the half-open window, where several bearded
faces and the muzzles of guns glowered out toward
the meandering road.

Ugly things had been happening here. The stable
and corral were empty. Grain and hay had been
spilled. A band of Indians could creep up within sixty
feet of the dwelling before you could get a shot at a
single one. And since they had come, some time since,
guns had been standing by the loopholes. The place
was virtually besieged. There remained hardly enough
food for the children; and no one for days had dared
to put a foot beyond the threshold. If these were

white men coming up the road, they were lucky to be in their head-gear. They were already in view and in range. But they were stumbling and falling; they were bedraggled shadows—nine of them. Easy now to guess what they were: a stage-coach party pulling into the breakfast station! And there was Lem Flowers himself.

T. S. Bordman, one of the unfortunate nine, who recounted his adventures to "The Silver Age" of Carson, Nevada,[1] after having been seven weeks on the road, had had trials enough before reaching Three Crossings, but they had piled up after that like the mountains. Stations all along the Sweetwater had been abandoned. The hospital at Fort Bridger (Utah) had taken charge of the wounded only after two weeks had elapsed from the day of the first encounter; but the surgeon had been able to promise a recovery for them all. At Three Crossings, where they had remained barricaded and besieged for several days, hunger had been staved off only by the fact that some cattle had strayed from the Indians. Because of this chance happening also they had been able to resume their journey. Three oxen and a cow had been yoked to the remains of a wagon to carry the wounded and also the family of station dwellers, who could tolerate the life no longer.

It was becoming the way of this region. Even when the Indians would permit it, life, particularly in the

[1] See "Alta California," May 26, 1862.

case of women, was sometimes defeating in its everlasting suspense, its desolation and loneliness. The distance between stations averaged about twelve and a half miles; but this was to include "swing stations," where only stock-tenders lived; and there were two or three of these to every "home station" where one woman might expect to meet another. Neighbors, few enough and far enough between for the intercourse of men, were thus fewer and farther for the society of women, whose "neighborhoods" embraced a lineal extent of from two to five score miles. Samuel Bowles writes in his journal of travel, "Across the Continent":[1]

How women, especially, can live contentedly in these out-of-the-way places on the borders, working hard and constantly, among rough and selfish men, and preserve their tender femininity, keep themselves neatly and sometimes even gracefully dressed, and not forget their blushes under free compliments, would be passing strange, if we did not see it daily in our journey, and know it by the whole history of the sex. I certainly have seen young women out here, miles away from neighbors, knowing no society but their husbands and children and the hurried travelers,—depending on the mails for their chief knowledge of what the world is doing,—who could pass without apology or *gaucherie* to presiding over a Boston dinner party or receiving in state at Washington. Not all, indeed, are such, but they are frequent enough to be noted with both surprise and pleasure.

[1] *Op. cit.*, 58–59.

Still, there were a few pleasant diversions for these women to which all travelers were not introduced. It was not unusual for a young station mistress to make social calls three stages distant, riding all the way by coach or saddle and returning on the same day or night in time, perhaps, to prepare meals for the overland passengers. "Sometimes, as I happen to know," writes Mr. Root, "they would ride fifty miles each way to and from a dance . . . [and] think nothing of it."

Squaws of squaw-men, so frequently met in the early days along the old Southern lines, had been in a rather appropriate and picturesque setting, surrounded by their deserts, or their walls of mud, pressing meal over their stone *metates,* or baking their *tortillas* in the sun. But here along the struggling "Central," where the primitive life of the old trapper was rapidly passing, where the new white settler was looking hopefully toward his future, and toward the civilization of his land, where he could conjure up in one grand thousand-mile gesture great cities and railroads of to-morrow—here, even in the most desolate spots, were the pathetic intimations of the future that he perceived so clearly: rude walls of mud or logs, but with trim hangings, sometimes, at the windows; wild flowers nodding proudly from a tin cup, or a hooked rug laid on a floor of clay.

The women were coming, more and more, many of them to stay, many to lose heart, some also to return as youthful widows, with a child, perhaps, who had been a protagonist through more harrowing adventures than his children and grandchildren were apt to know in the combined courses of their lives. On the very morning that found Lem Flowers and his party resisting the attack near Split Rock, there were women and children on more than one part of the dangerous road, and in greater plight even than those at Three Crossings.

Beyond the South Pass in Jim Bromly's division, about five miles below the confluence of Big Sandy Creek and Green River, was a home station bearing the name of the latter stream, and a good name in all other respects. Mark Twain had stopped here on his westward journey less than a year before, and had enjoyed a breakfast which, after thirty other overland repasts, was to loom up "like a shot-tower" in his memory thereafter for years. The everlasting bacon and beans and "if you don't like it, help yourself to the mustard!" was not the stock joke at Green River, nor was it the sad state of affairs. Instead, the mistress was apt to serve such rare delicacies as hot biscuits, fresh antelope steak, and good coffee—"the only decent meal between the United States and Great Salt Lake City." But, as a lovely spot in an unlovely land, there was that about the place to inspire good things. In the midst of a tormented wash of desert, it gave life to grass and foliage, and listened to the cold, clear water bubbling by between palisades of green clay.

Mrs. John Mallory was the mistress here, living with a husband and child, keeping house for them and several station hands, serving meals—under normal circumstances—to two coach loads of passengers every day. But nothing was normal any more. Coaches were running wild. They arrived at any time, day or night. They arrived singly or in pairs from either direction or from both directions at once. Five, ten, fifteen passengers or more—you could never guess how many mouths would have to be fed, nor when those mouths might chance along. And all travelers, always, for some strange reason, believed that their arrival was a kind of cosmic advent, eclipsing all known phenomena of the Rocky Mountain roads; and that Green River, of all stations on the line, would surely do honors to the occasion.

It was difficult to keep a self-respecting station even in ordinary times; but there had been floods, and they were not over yet. There had been Indians, and there were apt to be more of them. They were active in the neighborhood at the present time. They had already cleaned out Dry Sandy, two stages distant up the line, and turned the adjoining division topsy-turvy. There was reason to fear for Green River, given the time. But Mrs. Mallory seldom had the time—least of all, perhaps, when the occasion for it thrust itself upon her: when, on the morning of April

17, she stood at the door with her child beside her, heard a volley of shots, and saw her husband, then on his way to the stable, crumple down in a lifeless heap.

It was what she might have expected; it was exactly what had been happening all along the line, yet only what she may have dreamed of, occasionally . . . given the time. She stood for an empty instant staring, like the little tot beside her. He had heard a whistling sound at his ear as a bullet passed through a fold of his mother's apron. He had barely caught a glimpse of the Indians before he was thrust suddenly back. His mother had slammed the door, let down the bar. Other station attendants, nearly capsizing the breakfast things, were cocking their rifles.

What followed, like all that had gone before, was only a current procedure. It happened—it happened all the time; but it was not to have happened here. Until it did. The stable was raided; harness was cut to pieces; grain sacks were ripped; their contents were strewn; the hay was scattered, and the stock was driven away, the vandals, with blackened faces, in a galloping file of rifles and leather rags, being bound, more likely than not, for the next station down the road.

The commonplace nature of the incident, realized more and more through the reports that the stages brought in, was emphasized shortly when a coach from the East stopped at the door. It carried a woman

Courtesy of Ben Powers. From an old lithograph.

OVERLAND MAIL COACH OF THE PIONEER LINE
AT LAKE HOUSE (TAHOE) 1863.

Courtesy of Ben Powers. From an old lithograph.

CALIFORNIA & OREGON STAGE LINE
OPERATED IN THE SEVENTIES BY BARLOW, SANDERSON & COM-
PANY OVER THE OLD ROUTE OF THE CALIFORNIA STAGE COM-
PANY.

and several children. They were the refugees from another ravished station of the Rockies, and with a story to tell very similar to that in which the bereft Mrs. Mallory and her child had played only an everyday part.

Green River Station was to be abandoned. Its occupants were to join the other decamping family and, unless intercepted on the road by the savages, move on out of the country. Clearly, however, the stage was in the wake of new troubles that were only beginning. The war-path was extending itself southwestward along the road to Fort Bridger. Ham's Fork, a stage and telegraph station twenty-two miles ahead, was apt to be the next place taken by surprise. There, moreover, the coach, with its women and children, was apt to roll directly into a trap.

Fortunately, there happened to be a mounted express agent attached to the party—a Mr. Worley, who had been accompanying the stage for some time on its way to Green River. Riding a very fast and long-winded pony, well known in the country as "Billy Buttons," he volunteered to take complete charge of the Indians! It was not too late to overtake them. It would not be impossible to swing around them, lead them a chase to the fork, and sound a warning. He had other ideas in mind, involving the welfare of the coach that would follow along; but there was no time to discuss this matter. Buttons had whisked his tail and started off. It was in a melodramatic rôle worthy of far more recognition than the press was able to grant in that hectic day.

For Worley did overtake the Indians and he did get around them. It was far out on a twenty-mile desert of sage and animal bones. Perhaps, when the Indians saw him, he stopped in his tracks, allowed them to come charging back, then struck out over the plains, around gradually, and back to the road, all hell letting out its Indians at his heels. His luck was with him, at any rate; for when next he flashes back into the scenes of printed record, there is the whole mad troop behind him and Ham's Fork ahead.

But evidently something is wrong. Buttons lags at times—sometimes to the extent that he falls within the effective range. Worley spurs the animal on. But he lags again. Just when the pursuers are on the verge of giving up the chase the pony appears to give out, the savages to take heart and come on, bent upon running him down.

All this, however, Worley understands. At intervals he allows Buttons to feel the bit. He cannot afford to discourage this chase—to have the red devils stop and hear the rattle of wheels behind them! He has not forgotten the stage-coach with its helpless cargo.

So the savages came after the pony decoy, and the stage-coach after the savages; all chasing themselves, so to speak, to Ham's Fork Station; and so, too, had

Worley been able to fulfil both ends of his mission; for by the time the Indians appeared within range of their objective, a detour for them had been made to appear more attractive than the stock in the corral.

What similar dramas grew out of the weeks that followed were probably too numerous for detailed reports. Still, troubles had only started. The same band that had descended upon Green River and chased Worley over the desert had not detoured at Ham's Fork without other visions of plunder well fixed in their minds. Within the same hour of the stage's arrival at the fork, "Granger's," only several miles down the stream (which sometimes exchanged honors with Ham's Fork as a relay station on the route), was attacked before the day was over, and at a cost of some twenty-five horses and mules. Other stations were likewise swept clean during the week that followed, and still more later on, until the line was reported "in the hands of the Indians," and service was suspended again.

Chapter IV

THE WAR-PATH CONTINUED

THE Panama steamship monopolists, with a demure I-told-you-so, had pronounced the overland system "an utter failure." And it was, in fact, so disrupted that during the last week of April, while the Indians were rounding up stock for a future war, all postal matter to and from the Pacific Coast had been diverted to the old sea route pending readjustments on the plains. From Deer Creek on the upper Platte westward as far as Green River, a distance of more than two hundred miles, Holladay's line was deserted. Quantities of mail—some in bags, some in loose heaps, some scattered over the plains—had been left to the mercy of Indians, white vandals, and thieves. Letters undelivered, as reported in May, numbered 53,000; and many of these, of course, would never reach their destinations.

Unprecedented floods acknowledged, Indian hostilities taken into account, Holladay was, none the less, becoming more unpopular than ever. He was learning, if he read the papers, that his line had "no responsible head"; that orders given by some of his officials were being countermanded by others; that his drivers and hostlers were not receiving their wages on time, that they were seizing stage-stock on the principle of *sauve que peut* and striking out for the Cariboo. He was learning that his whole organization was "demoralized"—in a state of "anarchy, confusion," suggesting "the rebel army after defeat"; and that, as rumor in Washington intimated, the direct management of the Central Overland California Mail—the whole institution from Atchison to Placerville—was apt to be given over to "the original Butterfield & Company."

But newspapers could talk and say what they would; senators could froth and business houses cry their dismay—the Sioux and the Snakes and the Crows were making more noise, and troops alone were going to quiet them. Two regiments of California volunteers were forthcoming in time; Brigham Young, in response to a telegram from the Secretary of War, was placing one hundred "thirty-day men" immediately in the field; while from the East, with a force of cavalry and artillery 550 strong, Brigadier-General James Craig was on the march up the Platte, declaring the route under martial law.

Holladay, due at last for an interim of peace, spared no efforts to restore some order and reinstate himself in a cold world's esteem. He restocked his line and overhauled it entirely. To avoid the more predatory natives, he altered his route through the Rockies, abandoning twenty-six stations along the Sweetwater

route and building as many more along the course of
the "Cherokee Trail," by way of Bridger's Pass and
Bitter Creek. This change entailed a cost exceeding
$100,000 and further suspension of service, covering
twenty days of July!

But hopes for the future were rising. Holladay appeared alive to his responsibilities, especially when he
made another one of his flying twelve-day trips across
the plains, coursing the 563-mile Wells-Fargo section, from Salt Lake to Carson, Nevada, in three days
and twenty-three hours, thereby convincing the
world that at least he knew how. Returning, he won
the friendship of Denver by lopping off the triweekly
branch to that town and swinging his main line directly through it. Finally, to advertise a clean sheet,
he changed the awkward name of C. O. C. & P. P. E.
to the "Overland Stage Line" as distinct from the
"Overland Mail" west of Salt Lake. Brighter days
were to follow through the fall and winter. The new
year of 1863, from start to finish, was to find the
Holladay route in step with the Overland Mail, operating as a worthy associate of its more fortunate
neighbor.

But it was during the banner year of sixty-three
that the Overland Mail was given a slight taste of
Holladay's trials in the past. The route between Salt
Lake and the Sierra Nevadas, formerly spared by the
Indians, now became the war-path—a rather short

one and a comparatively mild one, but no less spectacular while it lasted. And that the schedule remained
unbroken throughout this hostile period, there was
due perhaps more than a passing thought, not only
to the drivers who gave their lives, but to the worth
of a thorough and meticulous organization as it obtained under the present management.

Ford Cook held up this link of the chain, Wells,
Fargo & Company giving him full charge of the entire line from Salt Lake to Virginia and Carson cities.
As financial agent and acting general superintendent,
he was in reality the working head, the very line in a
sense, "the Big Boss," as President Dinsmore and all
other stockholders in the New York offices were
pleased to regard him. With headquarters at Salt Lake
City, he was able to concentrate his whole attention
upon a route less than half the length of Holladay's.
Over Holladay, too, he had the added advantage of
an establishment that had come into his hands much
as John Butterfield had left it. Old superintendents
like William Buckley and James Glover from the
Southern route had placed it there; men like Warren Hall (formerly of Hall & Crandall and of the
California Stage Company, etc.) and Jacob Gooding,
both from the Butterfield line, were keeping the ends
tied together, and with many other veterans to help
them; while the well-schooled pioneer drivers from
over the western ranges filled most of the vacancies
that occurred.

Cook knew them all, as they knew him and precisely what to expect from him at any time. Nor could they be certain just when or where he might materialize along the road. For, beyond other extraordinary qualities to suggest the "efficiency expert" of modern times, he had the ubiquity of Stonewall Jackson. Fundamentally, he was not a stageman. He was, it seems, "a pigmy in the stable"; but, clearly, no fear of revealing any lack of horse sense ever kept him out of the stables, or the harness rooms, or the store lockers, or the blacksmith shops, granaries, horse-stalls, corrals, coaches, wagons, sleighs—he was into everything and out again, on his way and back again, taking note of all details, from the cake of harness soap at Sulphur Springs (which had remained too large too long) to the whisky breath of Phil the stable boy (when whisky, contrary to the oldest traditions, was taboo). Perhaps he was not the favorite boss in the experience of all his subordinates; but it is certain that his stringent methods, coupled with a polished, courteous manner, placed him in good standing with patrons as well as employers.

His territory, however, was unpleasant. It was a dreary waste not unlike that along the new Bitter Creek route of the Overland stage across the Continental Divide, with its sage-brush plains, choking alkali dust, and mountains. Walled in by the Rockies and Sierra Nevadas, broken by a succession of crouching ranges, the region, like the floor of a sea gone dry, lay shamed and dead beneath a crumpled overlay of sackcloth and ashes. It drank up the rain, gulped the puny streams that trickled from its snowcaps, absorbed the sweat of its victims, and fairly thirsted for their blood. It was a sweltering or freezing, treeless, birdless basin whose only imaginable use, as Bowles observed, was "to hold the rest of the globe together."

The Overland Mail coach, coursing a route now far to the south of the Humboldt, forded but one stream between the Jordan and the Carson Sink: Reese River whose waters rarely washed the tires of wheels half-way around. Over the Utah section there was the Great Salt Lake Desert to cross—a lifeless sea of gray powder, of dust that towered in combing swirls above the vehicle, half stifling every one, drawing blood from nostrils, pervading and covering everything. It turned men and beasts into stone-colored images; and they had only to remain quiet for a moment, stop sneezing for an instant, to appear as parts of a huge composition carved out of a single rock—the very monument that posterity may some day erect to commemorate these struggling times, to recall the epoch, to portray the past efforts on the part of the stage-coach to hold some of the globe together.

But sometimes at dawn or dusk, when the Great Basin filled with cloud colors, though there were no clouds, and the desert mountains appeared to change, with the change of light and sliding shadows, from

one fantastic form into another, the hours and the
days did cease for a while to pall. At such times even
the grimy Gosiute Indians, those naked, emaciated,
black bags of bones, munching their beetles and grass-
hoppers or the offal of coyotes and jack-rabbits, or
crouching under a bush with an old strip of mail
sack to keep off the snow, seemed not wholly offen-
sive, seemed almost picturesque—dirty little creatures
well suited, at least, to this land. Yet they were more
than that. Exist though they did with only the most
meager and indifferent of tribal attachments, friendly
though they generally were in a cringing way, they
had been known to kill. They were apt to attack when
least expected. They were like "unloaded" guns.

Eight-mile Station (eight miles from Deep Creek),
about eighteen miles west of the Utah-Nevada boundary, had become their first victim of 1863. They
had raided on March 22, murdered the stock-tender,
and fed their savage lust for torture upon the struggling remains of the cook. While the stock was being
driven away, some of them, in quest of more plunder,
loitered about, feeding themselves and their half-
starved animals, and awaiting the arrival of the stage.

One coach was rattling eastward at the time, not
far from the scene of slaughter, Hank Harper driving a snorting team of the finest American horses. The
Overland Mail, having discarded its mules, was stocked
with more than four hundred of these splendid animals. The roads had been improved for their sake; the

average interval between stations was less than twelve miles, and water from wells or tanks was at all points available. There were no longer any thirsting, heart-breaking pulls with exhausted animals puffing in at the end, unable to drag another mile though lives depended; and it was very fortunate now that this was the case.

Hank Harper, however, had not the slightest inkling of danger ahead; nor was his coach even moderately prepared for trouble. Of four passengers, two, riding inside, were boys whose cheeks had not yet grown sufficient feather-down to hold the dust. Their father, John Liverton, was riding with Hank on the box; and the one remaining member of the party, Judge Gordon Mott, a delegate from Nevada to Congress, was comfortably upholstered below, stretched out over seats and mail bags, fast asleep.

The stage, coasting down from a spur of the Shell Creek range, had borne its cargo around a low hill at the foot of the Antelope Mountains where a ragged plain of sage-brush stretched away to the southward. And there, over a powdery clump, appeared the low mud walls of Eight-mile Station—two buildings under one sodden roof, with a cool retreat in between, corral and stable behind, all compactly linked; a miniature citadel, it appeared, standing out in this vastness. There were a few nearly naked loiterers squatting about, mere growths on the face of the land, and always most prevalent where garbage was apt to be dumped. Hank Harper thought nothing of them. He may, at first glimpse, have mistaken their scrawny mounts for his relay; but they were not the kind of animal that he could have mistaken for long. He began to sniff trouble. In the dark passage to the corral between the two buildings, a white figure was visible in the kitchen doorway; and no sooner had he identified it as the distorted and butchered remains of a white man than the Indians were up and tumbling in a body for their horses.

The coach, by now, was no longer in the road. Hank had swerved it to the right out over the plains, laying eleven or twelve feet of whiplash out into air, where it went off with the report of a pistol. If John Liverton heard it, that was probably all. Bullets were already flying after the stage. He toppled forward, doubling over the footboard at the driver's feet. The driver fell after him, half into the boot, drilled through, but still clinging to his lines, still driving—driving, indeed, for all he was worth, and calling to Judge Mott to come out, come up. Another driver would be needed before long.

Inside, the judge was awakened by a yell from the Liverton boys, by a heavy jolt, by a blast of dust from the windows, by shouts from the driver, by everything all at once. Come out! Come up! The judge was coming, his wits still as tousled as his hair, his thoughts and eyes still groping for some means of focus, his hands for the iron rail outside; while the jolting jaws of the opening through which he was trying to squeeze himself aspired to bite him in two. There was no adjusting any such nightmare as this. He could see now—no Hank Harper on the box! No Liverton! A driver, clinging to the lines and calling to him from a tangle of things in the boot! But he reached the box; while the vehicle, bolting over brambles that could scarcely be seen through the enveloping billows of dust, came swinging back into the road.

It was a maneuver that had opened the coach to a broadside—shattering bullets and arrows from out of the gray swirl behind. No need now for further enlightenment on one score; but Hank was explaining another. Deep Creek Station was less than eight miles ahead. The team was good for that distance. But he, Hank, wasn't. And if the judge had never driven stage before, now was the proper time to learn.

Judge Mott began clearing the decks for action. He was attempting to boost the dead body of Liverton overboard in order to make room for his own more necessary boots. But a groan startled him. Liverton was not dead. The judge found another place for his boots! One of them, at least, could rest on the brakestrap—Hank pointed this out, his gray face dripping from fever as he handed up the lines and fixed them carefully between the clumsy fingers of his successor. There were bad places ahead and several turns; but there was also Hank's directing hand, his whip which he continued to use, his calm voice, sometimes addressing the judge, sometimes the horses, letting the animals know that some one could still speak their language, that some one rode behind them besides a delegate from Nevada to Congress.

Several miles passed under the wheels in this manner before evidences of pursuit disappeared, and some distance more before the whip of Hank Harper was still. Within a mile of Deep Creek there was only his voice: *Up, Lady! Yip, now!* Then the voice was still. And the body slipped down.

The story, published a few days later in Salt Lake City, presented the names of two heroes; and yet Hank, after all, had done only what the whole Western world was learning to expect from all drivers, and what all drivers expected of themselves. His cool judgment, his scrupulous sense of responsibility for all things in his care so long as breath remained in his body, was only typical of his race. Hank Harper, with his own fate clearly in view, had taken advantage of all available resources to save his coach and everything aboard it. And he had saved everything but himself. John Liverton had lost a chip of his skull and even some of its vital content, but to no material ill effect for the future. He was now in good hands, but with more narrow escapes behind him than he knew.

Had Deep Creek Station appeared as another ambush, his two sons, being convinced by that time that their father was dead, would have joined Judge Mott in cutting away the teams and attempting a flight on horseback to Cañon Station, twelve miles farther on, leaving Liverton, with the body of Harper, to his certain doom. But Deep Creek had been found intact. An armed party had then proceeded back to the Eight-mile post—to find, however, that the Indians had fled, leaving the place in ruins. Eight horses had been stolen from the station and forty more from a near-by ranch of the Overland Mail Company. The savages were now well equipped for later exploits, which occurred on the rocky road between Deep Creek and Cañon Station, only a few weeks after the Harper tragedy.

It was little less than a repetition of the same drama. The fatal rôle of Hank fell to W. R. Simpson, who was shot and killed, May 19, with the lines in his hands. On the box beside him was Superintendent Howard Egan, former mainstay of the Chorpenning line and celebrated Pony Expressman. To Egan fell the rôle of Judge Mott—he received the reins from the dying driver and, through an ambuscade of rifle fire from the cover of boulders, drove the mail on through.

The road had become so dangerous by now that a "full coach" was generally a coach load of soldiers detailed to protect the mail. Nor had conditions changed three weeks later when, in the absence of a military escort, a driver named Wood Reynolds and one other employee volunteered to assume the risks for the sake of the schedule. Reynolds, along with his companion, about twenty-five miles south of Salt Lake, was also murdered. A herdsman having carried the news to Rockwell Station, a party set out to recover what was left, returning only with the remains of the victims and the salvaged mail. They had found a dismantled coach some distance from the road, riddled with arrows and bullets, two horses lying dead in their traces, another one dying. The bodies of the two men had been discovered near the wreckage, scalped and pinned with arrows and spears to the ground.

Hostilities of this nature, accounting for the death of at least fifteen men along the line, lasted well into July, or over a period of about four months. But during all of this time the mail had been put through with the clockwork regularity of the original Butterfield system, and with the old esprit of the Overland Pony Express. For once in the whole history of the Central Overland California Mail the Postmaster-General, in his annual report at the end of the year sixty-three, was able to commend, without qualification, the regularity and despatch of the service. The several joint lines—"Stage," "Mail," and "Pioneer"—had been running in accord not only with the contract but with the original expectations of the public. It meant that an average speed of about seventeen days between Atchison and Placerville, or about twenty days between New York and San Francisco, had been the order of the day. Still the future was not very certain.

General Edward P. Connor, with headquarters near Salt Lake (Camp Douglas), had arrived in the fall of the previous year with fifteen hundred California and Nevada troops to protect the route; yet even this added force, though it had served to good effect, was far from being adequate. The incursions by the white men upon the Indian hunting-grounds were already threatening the primitive existence. White emissaries of peace were being received with scorn by the old chiefs of the plains; and in view of the stock and firearms recently accumulated by the savages, it was well suspected, especially by the settlers of Colorado, that they were organizing for a war of extermination.

In the spring of 1864 it began.

It was a general uprising of the Sioux, Comanches, Ciowas, Cheyennes, and Arapahoes, belonging to the annals of Indian wars rather than to those of staging. Indeed, for long periods of weeks at a time, on Holladay's Overland Stage Line, there was no staging at all; and during other weeks coaches with escorts traveled again in the manner of wagon trains, stopping at cinder heaps instead of stations, and expecting no relays at all; while the steamers wallowed once more in their oceans of glee with the overland mail piled aboard!

Emigrants were being cut off and settlers raided

continually. Overland trains, upon which whole communities were depending for their supplies, were hemmed in at various points along the road. In July, Governor Evans of Colorado begged that the militia be called into Federal service; but, as the request was not granted, matters became rapidly worse. Settlers along two hundred miles of the Platte, and from all other parts of eastern Colorado, deserted their crops in the fields and gathered to build block-houses as fortifications. Denver, becoming crowded with refugees, was soon to organize several armed companies to defend the settlements. But, with only a scant protection along the Overland Stage Line, a large portion of it was doomed to utter destruction in spite of all the resistance and determination that the military could muster and what courage stagemen could display.

Robert Emery, a skilful driver from Maine, happened to be in Atchison in August when the worst of the rising storm began to concentrate itself directly upon the stage route, and when all the old whipsters in the town were determined to remain there, it being only folly to venture out on the road. But Emery had reason to view the circumstances in another light. He had, or had had, close relatives and friends at Liberty Farm, nearly two hundred miles away on the Little Blue. It was a home station which, according to rumors, had been raided and burned, its occupants probably massacred. This report was more than the young driver's anxiety could digest without immediate action. No escort was available; but, as it happened, there were seven men and two wilful women prepared to start out with the first coach. Emery, therefore, volunteered at headquarters to take them.

Frank A. Root, messenger and mail agent, who knew at least half the Overland Stage drivers during this time, records this drive of Robert Emery's as being among the wildest ever witnessed on the plain. The driving, however, is portrayed as being anything but wild. Young Emery was evidently a typical whip, unflustered in the face of fifty charging Sioux and a full load of panic-stricken passengers; for he had both to contend with before noon of his first day out.

He had reached the crest of a low hill and barely started down over a spur toward the bottom-lands of the Narrows, when a war-painted troop in full regalia broke into view not forty rods ahead. Most of his party, bold enough at the start, were now terrified. The road being cut away on either side by deep ravines, left little room for turning; and with the first maneuver of the team, swinging deliberately around on the proverbial dollar, passengers were up on their feet, tripping and falling about, all control of themselves and all faith in Emery blown up in a puff of dust. Their cries of dismay and condemnation mingled with the hideous yells from behind; for the Indian cavalcade was now clamoring and lunging up the hill. The cool motions and words of the driver, before he could feel justified in letting out his team, placed him in the light of a madman in the distracted eyes of his party.

"Keep your seats! For God's sake sit down, gentlemen, if you value your lives!" he kept saying, though one arrow grazed his cheek and another clipped a rosette from the head of a wheeler.

The coach, by now in a vibrant clatter, rocking and swaying with the beating of sixteen hoofs, appeared still too slow for any hope of salvation. One warrior, mounted on a better-kept pony than most Indians possessed, managed to make several complete circles of the stage and, at each circle, send forth a rapid succession of shafts. Still, at two points of the road, where the danger of capsizing was imminent, Emery brought his team to a walk and his passengers to the point of apoplexy. Fortunately, no arrows took effect at these times or at any other; and there was refuge in sight ahead. It was an ox-train of some two dozen wagons. Its conductor, having seen the stage coming, had corraled his vehicles and was soon to welcome the party inside—a party whose unbridled consternation now turned into unbounded ecstasy. Emery, and even his puffing horses in their lather of heat, became the victims of feminine embraces.

Public palaver for good results, public condemnation for bad ones, whether justified or not, was the lot of all stagemen. Holladay was learning this apothegm through one kind of experience; and Emery

LOUIS McLANE

PRESIDENT OF THE PIONEER STAGE COMPANY—LATER OF WELLS-FARGO'S EXPRESS AND THE GREAT OVERLAND MAIL.

was perhaps not wholly unconscious of it upon finding himself pedestaled as a hero. Later, it appears, he would never speak of the incident. He had only driven his team, and not forgotten that a good one required driving at all times regardless of circumstances. His passengers, once the danger had passed, realized the fact and remembered it; for it was about a year later that they came to him as he lay with fever in his dying bed. Waiting for one of his moments of consciousness, they slipped a gold ring upon his finger, given and inscribed ". . . *in acknowledgment of what we owe his cool conduct and good driving on Thursday, August 9th, 1864.*" [1]

The stage driver was, indeed, a singular personage, introduced into the world and then snatched away, leaving no one like him, no group-character by which to draw fair analogy. He has been likened to a soldier for his observance of duty, his pride of organization, his fearlessness; to a sailor for his skill and resourcefulness, his fatalistic attitude, his love of tradition; to a ship's master for his feeling of absolute responsibility, command, and equanimity; to a musician for his art and eternal love for the same; to a mountaineer for his drolleries, his inscrutability, his genuine fondness for good whisky and a chew of tobacco; to a knight for his proud yet unassuming bearing, his quiet and chivalric manner.

---

[1] Frank A. Root and William E. Connelley's "Overland Stage to California" gives the account in full, with an extract from an old newspaper likewise describing it.

Those who regarded him as arrogant, as indeed some passengers did, had generally traveled but little by stage, or had not yet been introduced to the hazards and hardships of his life. A certain traveler upbraiding one of the most celebrated and popular of the later Sierra reinsmen for his lofty demeanor, had the naïveté to refer to him as his coachman!—no slur intended. Perhaps he had tried to tip this "coachman"! If so, unless it were a cigar, or a box of cigars, or a new hat, or a good bottle of whisky, it is not surprising that this "coachman" appeared a bit patronizing or overbearing. For no greater *faux pas* could be made in Western Stagedom than to assume that the driver, though his income were but a tithe of the average among his passengers, did not place himself on the social level of any one aboard. *While* aboard, in fact, he ranked them, and had sometimes to let them know it for their own well-being.

Samuel Bowles, the journalist, traveling overland with the Vice-President of the United States, was rather surprised, upon arriving in the wee hours of night, to see his eminence refused "breakfast" by the station mistress for his having arrived at such an extraordinary time; but Bowles was *not* surprised when the request was finally granted upon the mere mention of hunger by the Vice-President's driver. Bowles was not surprised because he had traveled considerably by stage.

"There is no king on the route," he comments, "like

a stage driver,—he has a 'dreadful winning way' with him, both for horses and women. The philosophy of it I do not understand, but the fact is universal and stubborn; he is the successful diplomat of the road; no meal can be begun until he is in place; and there are no vacant seats where he drives,—even the cold night air would not send our girls off the box, and inside, during the long ride." [1]

Eulogies to the Knight of the Ribbons, being fairly as numerous as the old journals of stage travel, one is apt to wonder if any driver was ever guilty of any wrongful or really infamous act. Sketch after sketch of the lives of these men as presented by Mr. Root, and as corroborated by many other pens, glitter with splendid deeds of heroism, with but one instance of a driver who, while driving, betrayed his trust.

This fellow, *alias* Frank Williams, shocked the world, splattering the escutcheon of his order with the most repelling of bloody stains. He had driven his stage intentionally, and according to careful plans, into the hands of robbers. Five of his passengers had been killed in the encounter. At least sixty thousand dollars in plunder had been stolen. And of this loot Williams accepted his share, paying the penalty later on, however, upon the scaffold.

There are other instances, in some number no doubt, of drivers giving up the whip for the mask and gun; but certainly there are very few who, like

[1] Bowles. "The Switzerland of America," 32.

Williams, revealed either the black streak, or the yellow, while actually engaged with the reins. There must have been, and there was, a charm and an inspiration involved, that compelled the very highest qualities of manhood from all qualities of men, and made the race worthy of its unquestioned place on the honor roll of this Western history.

Chapter V

AN OVERLAND JOURNEY WITH MR. DEMAS BARNES

WELLS-FARGO'S "Overland Mail Company," operating stages between Salt Lake and Carson, Nevada, had been holding a blanket mail contract over the entire route from the Missouri River to California, subletting the Atchison-Salt Lake section to Ben Holladay, and the Sierra Nevada section to the Pioneer Stage Company of Louis McLane. This contract was to have expired in June, 1864; but it was extended a number of weeks due to slight complications involving the new arrangements.

Dinsmore, representing the Overland Mail Company, had submitted the highest of four bids. Holladay, though he had not entered the lowest, finally won through expressing his willingness to accept the low figure, its proponent having withdrawn. Now, however, rather than sublet to Dinsmore, it proved convenient for Holladay to cause two separate and independent government contracts to be drawn. It proved convenient, moreover, for him to meet Dinsmore's high terms and accept for himself the lamb's share. He was to control the Atchison-Salt Lake section at an annual subsidy of $365,000; while Dinsmore (who was to make his own arrangements with the Pioneer), was to control the route between Salt Lake and Folsom, California, for $385,000. Dinsmore, in short, was to receive twenty thousand dollars more than Holladay, although operating a line of half the length!

Still, it seemed Holladay could afford it. His monopoly over the eastern section, which forced Wells-Fargo to accept his terms and rates of express, was one method of squeezing the difference through his rather small end of the horn. He had also been squeezing passengers—many more than Dinsmore could ever hope for. Holladay's nine-passenger coaches had been packing as many as twelve and fifteen to a load, while an average of nine would have been worth more than two and a half million dollars a year.

"How do they like it?" he asked an old driver.

"They don't seem to like it at all," the driver confided. "Always complaining, always too crowded. . . ."

The eyes of Ben Holladay were all aflash. "That's it! Pack 'em! Pack 'em like sardines!"

So they were packed in the great, red rolling boxes for Big Ben to shake well while using. They were paying $350 in fare from Atchison to Salt Lake City; they were paying a dollar or two more for every so-called meal to include "the mustard," and an extra rate of $1.50 for every pound above twenty-five pounds of baggage. They came in droves, bound not only for Denver, Salt Lake, and the various points of Nevada and California, but for the new mines of the great Northwest. The gold fields of Idaho and Montana were already glittering, bringing more opportunities for stagemen.

Holladay's program for 1864, in fact, was to add about 900 miles to his former system, one route extending northward from the Mormon city to the Bannock and Virginia mines of Montana, another branching northwestward to the diggings of Boise, Idaho, and connecting there with the splendid Thomas & Ruckle lines through the Blue Mountains of Oregon to Walla Walla. In short, he was to operate for the present about 260 Concord stages and nearly 6,000 horses and mules over an aggregate extent of some 2,200 miles of mail route in his own name. As the first proprietor to manage more stock than the old California Company of the middle fifties, he was taking the second enormous step in his staging career.

In a way, it was like the first.

He plunged into another maelstrom. There were floods along the Platte for old memory's sake; but the Indian war-whoops, with the usual newspaper accompaniments blaming Ben Holladay for everything, were such as he had never heard before. No sooner had he arranged with the Postmaster-General for the final settlement of the new contracts than reports of the unprecedented hostilities reached him in New York. It was the same news that had come to Atchison, August 9, when Robert Emery undertook his wild drive.

This was the beginning of an almost endless campaign against the Overland stage, and of five months' concentrated action. Already in its eastward and westward extensions from Fort Kearney, over a distance of more than two hundred miles, the line was in ruins and strewn with the bodies of forty or fifty whites. The westward egress from the fort was wholly blocked. To the eastward settlers were organizing for mutual protection along Alvord's Western Stage Company branch to Omaha, thus enabling a few coaches to pull through on that road; but Holladay's main line to Atchison was nearly obliterated. Elsewhere, as stations were abandoned and stock hustled to various strongholds, all hope of restoring any semblance of order was deferred indefinitely. Once more, with a sigh, the overland mails were returned from the eastern stage termini to the Atlantic Coast to proceed by steamer to California.

October 1 was the date set for the commencement of operation under the new arrangements; and there was to have been, in spite of the reduced subsidy, an improved schedule—a daily sixteen-day service during eight months of the year and twenty during the remaining months. But at this date, on Holladay's Overland Stage Line, there was scarcely any service at all. One coach, under military escort, but without any mail, did manage to reach Salt Lake early in the month—the first coach from the east in four or five weeks, with only the gloomiest of prospects for the future.

New Year's Day of 1865 found Holladay's stages just able to limp over three fourths of the route; but the remaining fourth could show not even an attempt. Between Denver and the important little settlement of Cottonwood Springs the road was lined with the graves of white men; the plains were littered with the decomposed bodies of Indians and animals, torn and scattered by the wolves. The packed sand by O'Fallon's Bluff continued to soak the blood from persistent ambuscades; Julesberg lay, with its dark memories, in ashes; and other heaps of cinders, where stations had stood, exposed charred human bones. Stages did not cross here. Blue uniforms and fixed bayonets, with wagons for the mail, slogged back and forth through the snow. Such angry wounds as this were naturally a long while healing; but so crushing had been the blows struck over all, and so heavy were those still to come, that the line was never quite to recover.

All through sixty-five, however, with the capable stageman William Reynolds as the new general superintendent (in place of George K. Otis), and with agents of sound experience all along the line, some efforts were being made to restore the fine order of 1863. Tents had sprung up where old stations had fallen; half the remaining mules were sent up to do the Bannock business, and fine new horses were distributed over the greater part of the line. In the early spring, coaches were running out of Atchison at precisely eight o'clock every morning, and returning within a half-hour of the schedule time. Four or more cavalrymen, with pistols at holsters and rifles slung in the saddle, galloped along behind, from station to station, passing garrisons of troops at every one or two hundred miles. There was some security; but it was not enough.

Late in May, only about a hundred and forty miles out of Atchison and on a section of road so well patrolled that it was considered the safest of all, there had been an ambush in which several soldiers were killed, while a stage-coach carrying six or eight men, women, and children provided a running target for some twenty-five warriors. Speaker Schuyler Colfax and his party, to include the journalist Bowles, having been given special escort, special coach, special everything that there was to be had, pulled safely through to Salt Lake City shortly afterward; but, having been delayed west of Denver several days when the Indians broke up some fifty miles of line directly ahead, they had skirted disaster rather closely on several occasions. Once they had interrupted an attack on a small band of returning Mormons, their escort hauling up in time to drive away the offenders; while just behind and just ahead of their coach as it labored on, stations were being pillaged, stock-tenders and soldiers were being killed.

It was hardly a country to suggest the kind of stage travel that persisted over it. One might associate it with occasional parties of adventurers, and with border men, settlers, miners, and all the dusty herds of the plains. But there were frail and pale young ladies, with neat bundles and parasols, who tucked themselves in beside the coach windows as though dust would not have the heart to touch them, as though Indians lived only in paper-back novels which they knew nothing about. There were bustling dames in crinolines who hoisted their hoop-skirts loftily behind on squeezing through the narrow coach doors, perhaps beseeching some gentleman, meanwhile, to hold the baby until space could be found for the baskets and bundles and things. And there were gentlemen generally willing to help in such matters— men who had formerly regarded their great city limits as the boundaries of the livable world. There were all types of both sexes and all ages.

And there was also Mr. Demas Barnes.

Mr. Demas Barnes was a mineral inspector bound for the Nevada mines. He represented So-and-so for Such-and-such, and did justice to his true importance. His burnsides were charmingly tufted, like the brisket of a cocker spaniel. He was friendly, too, like a cocker, but with far more grace and *savoir faire;* and he was very human. Lines of humor sheered down from the corners of his sensitive mouth; but it was a quiet humor; and the lines were like neat cords attached to his cheek whiskers to hold them precisely, so.

It was only a few weeks after the eminent Colfax party had set out that this personage sat pivoted on the box of a stage-coach, the plains of gray bunchgrass rolling away on all sides and placing him conspicuously in the center of the firmamental focus, like a bottle bobbing on the sea. Folded in a trim linen duster and holding up an umbrella to shield his complexion from the sun, he was counting wagons as they passed. It was the season of heavy traffic, with emigrants setting forth as usual in the spring; but there were also new mines opening; and freighting, after its long paralysis, was being resumed in full force. Mr. Barnes counted a thousand wagons in one day, and passed one train that was five miles long.

He made note of all this—he was writing a book; [1] and wagons kept him counting all the way to Denver; but there must have been times when he lost all count, or suspended the operation in despair. Sitting with his umbrella in the hot sun, and turning it occasionally to ward off a puff of dust, or a wet sneeze from some rude horse, clouds had gathered very suddenly. The thermometer had sunk "thirty degrees in ten minutes." A "hurricane" had blown up, compelling him to take in his awnings. It had then proceeded

---

[1] "From the Atlantic to the Pacific Overland."

to pelt him with dirt until the clouds opened fire
with lightning and thunder, accompanied by torn
sheets of rain.

Seeking shelter inside, he had so added to the congestion that it had seemed only right that he hold the
baby and balance the grateful mother's bandbox on
top of his head. Windows closed, everything stuffy,
passengers sick, baby bawling, rations giving out,
water brackish—Demas Barnes had lived through it,
had beheld it with sober eyes; for the whisky had been
so utterly abominable that the drink itself had en-
forced prohibition. Yet he had seen the proud owners
of potatoes along the route asking a gold dollar a
potato! He had seen the driver, when his party complained of having no chance to wash, plunge the
whole grimy "outfit," coach and all, into a flooded
stream, smiling jovially as the water rose a foot over
the floor, filling boots, drenching bundles, splattering
dry clothes, turning dust into paste, and drifting
crackers into pads of dough. Six days and six nights
of this sort of thing! And nearly a week's delay in
Denver due to Indian blockades ahead! Mr. Demas
Barnes had a sense of humor, but it was wearing out;
and there was nothing funny at all about the road
ahead.

This was the Rocky Mountain transit, called the
Cherokee Trail, adopted by the stage company several
years before upon the abandonment of the Sweetwater
section. From Denver northward to Medicine Bow

Creek on the Laramie Plains, and westward through Bridger's Pass to Bitter Creek, and down this stream to the Green River, it continued a little farther to join the old road at Ham's Fork Station, 445 miles out of Denver. Mule teams, pioneers always for the overland stage, were still used over this dreary road. Most of the country was desert, or a medley of deserts, a crazy-quilt of desert samples in many exotic moods.

Where roved the Bitter Creek, like a dish-water drain, through a vast dump yard of alkali, or of soap and soda, was one weird sample in silvery gray which might have fallen from the lumpy white face of the moon. Ashy powder, six inches deep on the road, filled the air and tarnished the sun. There was the White Desert, the Red Desert, and the Twenty-mile Desert, all seven thousand feet above the sea, sweltering by day and freezing by night. Winds whirled and loaded themselves with sand. The lonely clay buttes and rocks obtruding from the plains farther east toward Bridger's Pass, and which might also have tumbled out of the sky, were bitten and chiseled by the recurrent blasts into fluted columns and spires, into walls, forts, Gothic cathedrals, ruins in clay and stone.

But there was still another kind of desert for Mr. Barnes to cross before reaching this oddly furnished floor. Less of a desert, but more of an ordeal, it was that vast summit basin of the Rockies called the Laramie Plains. Embraced and drained by the great hook of the North Platte with its tributaries, it afforded some life to other than the ubiquitous sage. Wolves and cinnamon bears roved down from the adjoining mountains; there were antelope, bounding like fawns over all the land, and sometimes elk or black-tail. Here the Colfax coach and escort, constantly entertained by the ridiculous pranks of prairie-dogs and black-striped squirrels, had been obliged at one time to swing from the road where a grizzly lay snoozing in the dust. And the grizzly in these mountain fastnesses was little more welcomed by the hunter than the sight of Indians.

But Mr. Barnes and his eleven companions were trying not to believe in Indians, although they knew why the stage-coach stopped over every night at a station, and why sentinels were posted outside; and they knew that their heavy equipment in rifles, which they had been especially advised to carry, was not for grizzly bears.

Stunted trees and canyons of tumbled rock had been left far behind. The coarse vegetation of the lower plains grew rich and green in their memories while, imperceptibly, the road had lifted them up to the snow line and a rolling plateau. The coach had crept rapidly into the heart of the Rockies, but it had seemed that the Rockies had crept around the coach, using all the cloaked methods known to their unpleasant inhabitants. Somewhere up here on the top of the world, as Mr. Barnes learned from the driver, some five thousand head of stolen stock were grazing.

"Five thousand, plus six new mules and a dozen new scalps and a neat pair of burnsides" was apt to be the next driver's story on the next coach to follow. Mr. Barnes looked back for the escort. He wished it would keep just a trifle closer. Unlike all his fellows, he had no rifle. His umbrella and pistol seemed inadequate.

"We whistled," he said, "to keep up our courage." But early one morning, six miles beyond Cooper Station, where the road leaves the Laramie Creek for the Medicine Bow, "some horsemen came riding down upon us like lightning, crying 'Indians!' . . . The coach wheeled about so quickly as nearly to tip us over—and if we did not make a race, I am no judge. We ran our mules five miles, until we intercepted an emigrant train, and also a company of cavalry."

That was better. And this was to be no ignominious retreat after all. Forty-four military and twenty civilian strong, the coach turned again and followed now in the dust of a charge. The Indians, crouching low on their ponies, retreated, but circled round to the flanks; and one youth of the escort who had pursued them too far, reeled under their fire and fell into their butchering hands.

We recovered the body [writes Barnes]. They had stripped him entirely of his clothing, dug out his eyes, torn off his scalp, opened both his breasts, taken out his heart and entrails—a tribute to his bravery—cut

Courtesy of the Bancroft Library.

"STOP, LOOK AND LISTEN!"

UNION PACIFIC RAILS ACROSS THE CONTINENT

ORIGINAL ILLUSTRATION FROM "BEYOND THE MISSISSIPPI," BY ALBERT D. RICHARDSON.

off his feet, cut his head nearly off, and otherwise dis-
figured him—leaving one bullet in his head and eight
arrows through his body. They afterwards intercepted
us at a crossing of a gulch and at the brow of a hill.
We were in for a fight, and drew up in line. . . . We
approached on a slow trot; got in firing range, the
bullets flew from every gun. Their leader fell, and,
our force being large, they skidaddled as fast as they
could run. . . .

This is only a sample of what is daily occurring.
Two of our pilgrim companions were killed the same
day. The stage company is minus horses, the government without a tithe of military force, and the
people without sufficient to eat. There is not force
enough here to guard the station, let alone hunting
Indians. . . . Tons of mail are abandoned at the different stations. I have seen it, Mr. Holladay, and my
name is at your service.

Mr. Barnes was writing all this at Fort Halleck,
July 1, only about a day after the encounter. All his
baggage had gone under water at Boulder Creek;
and now, using his valise for a desk by the side of a
hut, and surrounded by a dozen or more of his dis-
appointed traveling companions, he was trying to
dry his clothes in the sun. His escape from the Indians
was recounted with only slight variances by the newspapers shortly afterward,[1] and his complaint against
Ben Holladay was but the rising voice of the time. The
Overland Stage Line was falling more rapidly than

[1] See (Salt Lake) "Vedette," July 8, and "Sacramento Union," July 15,
1865.

ever into disrepute. "The Austin Reveille" of Nevada now spoke of it as "a bilk":

. . . The eastern line—at least from Denver to Salt Lake [more accurately, Fort Bridger]—has never been respectably stocked, and from the reports we have always had, it appears that the drivers are fully as base as the poor brutes they drive. . . . The mail seldom comes through, although passengers who are willing to pay a liberal sum to drivers can be forwarded after a manner. . . . It is true that Indians are on the line, but Indians are not the sole cause of delay. The line is in the hands of the wrong man, and the service will never be performed until someone having the ability to manage, and conscience enough to impell him to his duties, takes charge.[1]

Yet if it were true, as estimated in the writings of Root and Connelley, that Indians and outlaws were costing Ben Holladay as much as all other overhead expenses combined, then it might appear that even a "superman" could not have upheld enough spirit in his organization, even during the short interims of peace, to run an efficient, or a fairly efficient, stage line. His new subsidy was small; he depended largely on passengers; yet, with every loss in stock and stations involving a suspension of service, not only did there come a depression in the passenger business for the period, but such an accumulation of mail that passenger carriage had to be cut down for some time

[1] Quoted by the "Sacramento Union," July 17, 1865.

to follow. Such incidental losses to Indians were fairly beyond estimate; but complainers did not consider them. Their own hardships and inconveniences were so involved that they were seldom in any frame of mind to be just.

There was no disguising the fact, at least, that Mr. Demas Barnes, whenever he expressed himself with regard to Ben Holladay, was in a terrible humor. He admitted it upon reaching Salt Lake. There, ten days behind time, he had expected to receive some important correspondence and to reply before going on; but the telegraph wire as well as the stage line was cut off behind him. There was no corresponding with the Eastern States at all.

By now, however, he had become a seasoned traveler. He was able to sleep on the bounce or, perhaps, to wash in one end of a horse trough while horses splashed their noses in the other. His complexion was probably ruined; but the complexion of the world soon grew brighter. Holladay had given him experience enough to enable him to appreciate the line of Dinsmore; and his humor rose accordingly as he proceeded westward in the hands of Ford Cook and the rapid coaches of the Overland Mail.

This section of the line, happily exempt for two years from all inroads of Indians, and close to markets of supplies, was still in good condition. From Salt Lake to Austin the Colfax coach had covered the distance of 385 miles in fifty hours; and the remaining distance to Virginia City, 200 miles, in twenty-two hours, with "teams that would shine in Central Park or Fifth Avenue equipages—with drivers, generally, intelligent and better dressed than their passengers." Whirled over the rough mountains and plains of this uninhabited region, rarely passing a house except the stage stations, never seeing wild birds or beasts, the speed of the coach had ranged between seven and twelve miles an hour, rarely falling below eight; and "so wisely was all arranged, and so well executed, that not an animal suffered; to horses and men the ride seemed to be the work of every day, as indeed it was in everything but the higher rate of speed." [1]

It was what should have been, but never was, over the entire line. Mr. Barnes, however, was not whirled along quite as rapidly as Messrs. Colfax and Bowles had been several weeks before; but, considering the roughness of the road, he was happier as it was. Indeed, there came a time when he felt that things were being hurried altogether too much. At "Egan's" he met a "perfect beauty"! Like the heroine at the pleasant station of Virginia Dale long remembered by Bowles, like the other at Green River never forgotten by Mark Twain, this one, "light and bright as a bird," captivated Mr. Demas Barnes.

"Her house was tidy, mountain flower bouquets upon the table, standard authors upon the shelves, carpets upon the earthen floor." And the breakfast

[1] Bowles, "Across the Continent," 132–139.

that he received from her dainty hands was "splendid."
In fact, he believed her worthy of a better position;
he believed . . .

"All aboard!"

He believed . . .

"ALL   ABOARD!"

He believed he knew who was going to give her
one; and he could not help envying the driver. As
for himself—he had to make the best of another.

There *was* another in the coach. A grass widow!
And this in a day when a newspaper editor could
write, seriously and soberly:

Divorces and highway robberies in various parts of
the state, are unhappily too conspicuous in the annals
of the twelfthmonth, yet not more prominent than in
other years.[1]

There were comparatively few highway robberies
on the Overland; but a grass widow might be encountered anywhere. This one may have been the
pristine pioneer of Nevada; and with her, in the same
coach, *vis-à-vis,* night and day, sat Mr. Demas Barnes,
alone! Alone, that was, except for her four children;
and they—all under eight years of age—only made
matters worse.

"Each," he explained in his journal, "had a specific
want at least once in twenty minutes, which, divided

[1] Editorial in the "Sacramento Union" of January 1, 1861.

by four, gave me a gentle hint exactly every five
minutes. . . . The first night—each one clambering
for the soft place and crying over the accidental
thumps, assisted by the gentle raps and kicks of the
mother, who insisted upon their keeping perfectly
still, and occasionally asked the gentleman if he would
not reach the canteen or open the basket—was charming to a man who had six full days of sleep owing
to him."

The next day found the children all covered with
molasses, the stage with crumbs, while the ashy dust
poured in unmercifully over all. Mr. Barnes, meanwhile, had been saddled with the profoundest of do-
mestic responsibilities, which he assumed like a gentleman much to her growing distrust. Whether it were
worse to fight Indians for Holladay, or take care of
infants and grass widows for Wells-Fargo, began to
be a dubious question. Nevertheless, when night came
again he was busy removing the middle seat, piling
in mail bags, blankets, and shawls, tucking in the children and letting the stage-coach rock them to sleep,
his mind singing lullabies which he dared not breathe
aloud.

"They were so well tired out I heard nothing from
them till morning. But the woman!—dear me!—not
gifted with Eve's gentle confidences, posted herself
upright in the further corner, and insisted she would
not sleep a wink all night; and I think she would have
declared she had kept her word had I not had to climb

out for her lost bonnet once or twice. The Lord forgive her awful suspicions!"

Mrs. Martha Vance Kimball, wife of William Henry Kimball, who maintained a station not far from Salt Lake City throughout the entire stage-coach phase, recalls the period now, at the age of one hundred years, with little pleasure. "One great trouble was," she said, "few passengers knew how to take care of themselves. Drivers were different. At least they could keep themselves clean where cleanliness was possible. But the passengers! I hated to see them come into my house." She shuddered and mentioned the unmentionables.

"Do you remember the Colfax party? Do you remember Mark Twain, or Demas Barnes?"

"How could I remember any of them? They came in droves." And she sighed wearily at the thought. "I had to feed them. And they were so filthy, so helpless."

It was plain, however, that Mr. Barnes was given more to take care of than himself; and that he, as no more than an average traveler on a typical trip at a typifying time in the representative year of sixty-five, had not yet seen the end of his responsibilities. Down, staggering, into the bouldered gullies, over chuck-holes and rocks, and up the hill at a drumming gait, six glossy horses, frosted over with the dust, were whirling the coach along as though the road were a masterpiece in macadam. Mr. Barnes, having escaped from the widow, was sitting beside the driver, where he could discuss the new Johnson administration and the fall of Richmond in peace.

It was near the end of his journey. He could look back over hundreds of miles, and over days that stretched out interminably behind him. Broiled by the sun, blown by the storm, drenched by the rain, starved, soaked in the streams, delayed, chased and beset by the Indians, cut off from communication, jerked away from an incipient romance, thrown to a grass widow, employed as a nurse for four sticky children, and suspected of ulterior motives for his gentlemanly conduct, and now peace, but peace short-lived—blasted into the culmination of all the unhappy events which he had neither expected nor bargained for.

The coach had stopped at some deserted wayside place at the top of a hill. The driver, asking Mr. Barnes to hold the lines, had climbed down and sauntered away, leaving two fumbling hands with six ribbons that had never before fingered more than two. The lively animals were stamping, craning their necks, feeling their bits. One bully leader shrugged up into his collar. The other did likewise. Mr. Barnes tried to check them, but the other four beasts had already started, and the coach was lurching forward on a down grade.

He yelled for the driver; but the team was already at a trot. The hill was becoming steeper. A gorge at a bend below was horrible to look at. He pulled on the lines—it made matters worse; for, while the team responded, the coach did not! The double-trees came in contact with the legs of the wheelers; they jumped and stretched into a gallop.

Mr. Barnes had only a slight, or a dangerous, knowledge of driving. To his shattered wits the dilemma had suggested only one thing: "the wheel horses had no breeching"—no harness by which to check the coasting of the vehicle. To stop the team, in so far as he could judge, was to run over them, wreck. To let them go was to plunge headlong over an embankment. So, "yelling and bobbing about on the high seat like a rush in a windstorm," down he drove, clattering and banging, his cargo of passengers in terror. One thing to do, and only one—he did it! He pulled the leaders into the bank! They fell and rolled, swings and wheelers on top of them, coach over all!

No breeching. . . .

The driver came up as the dust cleared away. Broken pole, broken harness, broken nearly everything breakable but bones—the greatest misfortune of all, he may have thought, as he glumly surveyed Mr. Barnes. No breeching! He swore lustily. "Did you ever happen to think of using the brake?"

Mr. Barnes was glad, on July 16, to see this journey's end, and found reason then to be thankful to his thankless world. Not another coach had passed the Rockies since his had fought its way through; and

the papers, having already published the story of his
own little engagement, now carried the news of fresh
outbreaks on the eastern plains. It was the beginning
of more troubles to last throughout the year.

Early in August a coach from the East arrived at
Fort Halleck with news of another emigrant massacre
—a train burned, nine men and women killed, three
women carried away. In the following month, between Denver and Salt Lake, there was no longer an
effort to maintain the daily service. Triweekly coaches
running eastward out of the Mormon city went only
as far as Green River. Thence onward through the
Rockies there was but a weekly military train to pack
the mail. During the several months remaining, Indians, busy again on the lower Platte, were destroying
telegraph lines, chasing stages, burning trains, killing
soldiers, emigrants, and stagemen. Still the line remained open after a fashion, and still the passengers
came, coaches seldom venturing forth without a full
load of them—all kinds of them, all ready and apt
to meet as many trials and mishaps as those recounted
in the journal of Mr. Demas Barnes.

Chapter VI

THE LAST DAYS OF THE GREAT OVERLAND

CRITICISM of the Overland, adverse and otherwise, was naturally most prevalent in the Pacific States, especially in California and Nevada. As the direct beneficiaries of the system and its chief dependents, the people of this section were sensitive.

What they had expected of the service, moreover, was in part what they had been led to expect through an anomaly. It was not wholly through the past demonstrations of the old Butterfield line, nor through the present good record of its progeny now running under Wells-Fargo's control between Salt Lake and the Sierra Nevadas; but their expectations had been largely influenced by the standards of their local institution, one that had been developing since the early fifties under the most favorable of circumstances.

They were apt, therefore, to be harsh critics. Ben Holladay was apt to suffer through their judgment of his line. Their experiences had not been his. What they knew of staging was the nation's best—a quality which had prompted the remark from our friend Demas Barnes [1] after his ride across the plains: "I must

---

[1] *Op. cit.*, 83.

say, this is the first real staging I have experienced";
and from Bowles: [1] "There is no stage-riding, no
stage-driving, left in the States,—I doubt if there ever
was any,—at all comparable to this in perfection of
discipline, in celerity and comfort, and in manipulation of reins"; and from C. L. Brace: [2] "I have seen no
such coaching since years ago in Old England"; and
from J. Ross Browne: [3] "If we are behind times in
railroads, it is certain that there is no such a country
in the world for feats of horseflesh."

One of these writers (Barnes), was referring to the
California Stage Company's line across the Sierras;
while the others were speaking particularly of the
Pioneer Stage Line under Louis McLane, Brace referring to it as it was in its later days of decline.
But Bowles describes it briefly as it appeared in the
summer of sixty-five, when it was running several
coaches daily each way over "a stage road one hundred
miles long from Carson to Placerville, watered as city
streets are watered, to lay the dust for the traveler!
. . . day by day, all the summer season." There were
then few up-grades that were not negotiated at a
trot. But the west-bound traveler was most impressed
by his journey over that portion extending from Lake
Tahoe to Placerville, seventy-five miles of well-graded
road, up to the mountain summits, and down the
western side. Of this section Bowles writes:

[1] "Our New West," 310, 311.
[2] "The New West," 187.
[3] "Adventures in the Apache Country," 315.

. . . The drive over it, made in less than seven hours, even surpassed any that had gone before in rapidity and brilliancy of execution. With six horses, fresh and fast, we swept up the hill at a trot, and rolled down again at their sharpest gallop, turning abrupt corners without a pull-up, twisting among and by the loaded teams of freight toiling over into Nevada, and running along the edge of high precipices, all as deftly as the skater flies or as the steam car runs; though for many a moment we held our fainting breath at what seemed great risk and dare-devil performance. The road is excellent, hard and macadamized . . . and therefore far different from that whose rough remains and steep passages are occasionally met on the mountainside, over which Mr. Greeley made his famous ride six years ago. . . . Mr. Colfax well said, in one of his speeches, that . . . he was sure much more was necessary to drive a stage down the Sierras as we were driven than to be a member of Congress.[1]

To average more than ten miles an hour over a stretch of seventy-five miles down this congested Alpine road was one thing, but to average nearly nine over the whole of it from the Placerville railroad terminus of Shingle Springs, *up* to Virginia City, 116 miles, was a feat—the record of Louis McLane, who gave thirteen hours and forty-five minutes to the trip. The average rate between the termini, except in winter, was between seven and eight miles an hour. Winter reduced the speed to the common overland rate of

[1] *Op. cit.,* pp. 310–311.

approximately five; but, as the heavy traffic packed the snow for the teams and sleighs, wherever sleighs were necessary, a very dependable schedule was maintained.

But it was not the sort of staging that any one should have hoped to find all the way across the plains. There the incentive was lacking. The overland enterprise from its inception had been looked upon as a temporary measure pending the advent of rails; and the obstacles over so wild and long a route were about as numerous as the advantages favoring the Pioneer.

The Pioneer, with about eight years of development behind it, was the product not only of the best practical staging ability, but also of Nevada silver and California gold. Louis McLane had felt justified in an investment of between three and five hundred thousand dollars for improvements on the road alone. Tolls collected in one year had amounted to about $600,000. Twelve million dollars had been collected by the freighters. Since 1860, winter months excepted, the Pioneer Stage Company had been obliged to run extra coaches as a habit to accommodate the crowds. Mail contract or none would have made little difference. The line had grown out of that kind of prosperity which had created and glorified the California Stage Company in the middle fifties. And, more than this, there was the California Company itself as a rival. It was operating two other trans-Sierra routes, and forcing Louis McLane to toe the mark.

Even in midwinter, both lines were making friends.

"When it comes to staging," writes one January traveler to the "San Francisco Bulletin," "the Pioneer via Placerville, and the California via Dutch Flat to Virginia City beat the world. . . . They may be considered as standing on equal footing; and yet we must give the Pioneer Line the credit of being the leading spirit in staging." [1]

This keen rivalry, of more than three years' duration, had of course worked the usual charm. It had made lofty mountains shrink into mole-hills; it seemed even to have melted the snow. Other opposition had lived and died; but it was well within the province and power of the Pioneer and the California Stage companies to run on indefinitely and prosper. It happened only that the latter, grown tired after ten years in the harness, wanted to sell out, whereas the Pioneer wanted to buy and expand. Accordingly a bargain was made in the fall of sixty-five. Birch's old corporation closed its books. The rivalry was no more. The Pioneer, soon to slide under the name of Wells, Fargo & Company, forthwith began to decline.

Thus it might seem that among those things which Ben Holladay may have needed for his Overland Stage Line was a rival. Troops would have helped him more, no doubt; but a good opposition man—the kind that could reduce mountains and melt snow—might also have reduced such obstructions as Indians consider-

[1] Quoted by the "Sacramento Union," February 6, 1865.

ably. California and Nevada, while accepting the Indian as a serious hindrance to the service, had never quite recovered from their old suspicions. Nor did Holladay dispel their incredulity in the least when at last he did meet his opposition man.

It happened in the fall of sixty-five that a new line sprang up between Leavenworth and Denver to vie with a section of Holladay's Overland Stage. Head of the competing firm was one David A. Butterfield, who, not to be confused with John Butterfield of the Southern Overland, seemed to have dropped into the arena from out of the blue sky where he had had some freighting experience and been endowed with a rare personality worth money in any enterprising venture.

David Butterfield was not unlike William Russell in some respects. He was a typical promoter, and a successful one, having managed to organize a joint-stock company in New York under the name of "Butterfield Overfield Dispatch." The "B. O. D.," as it was called, was to run a fast freight and triweekly stages over a line paralleling Holladay's for half its length. The new route had been explored early in August; and like that of Russell's L. & P. P. Express, it was a short-cut to the Rocky Mountains, coursing the whole length of the Smoky Hill Fork, then cutting straight across the desert to Denver.

This Smoky Hill route, being nearly seventy miles shorter than Holladay's road along the Platte, offered the Dispatch certain advantages; but, like the L. & P. P. E. again, there was no mail contract to cover it. The new line was to depend solely on the returns from passengers, freight, and express, along with the good-will of Colorado settlers. Plans were to expand, in the event of success, with a stage line from Denver on to Salt Lake and another to Santa Fé, with through bills of lading for freight to all points of Colorado, Utah, New Mexico, Arizona, Idaho, Montana, and Nevada.

Holladay did not appear to worry; and while the B. O. D. stages, warmly applauded, were running to some effect before the end of September, open warfare between the two competitors did not start at once. The first show of opposition against the Dispatch sprang up in the shape of Indians; but the story, as reported to the press early in October, left room for some doubts and suspicions. It seemed that a party of thirty war-painted scoundrels had stopped a B. O. D. coach near "Monument Station." They had, in a most unaboriginal manner, motioned the driver to turn back; but the driver had refused, whereupon the marauders had pounced. How it was that all the passengers had escaped was among those things not explained; but the coach had been burned and the stock stolen. And the villains *were not Indians, but whites in disguise.* Agents of the company were investigating "the cause of the attack," which was to be "ferreted out." [1]

[1] "Atchison Champion," October 10, as quoted by "Sacramento Union," November 2, 1865.

Holladay's route, meanwhile, had been in a deplorable state. Through the Rockies, at least, for the past several months the line had been limping with the aid of weekly military mail trains, and was now only commencing a daily service. This sore spot, however, being unharried as yet by competition, could not have mattered so much from the strict business standpoint; and the time had come for Holladay to attend most strictly to business. The Atchison-Denver half of his line, always the better half, now called for his special attention; and there, in October, though Indians were chasing the coaches, burning trains, and taking many lives in addition, things began to shine in an alarming manner before the eyes of the B. O. D. By November, watches might have been set on sight of the cantering Holladay teams over the Atchison-Denver road. It had suddenly become a race-course with a regularity and despatch to match the standards beyond Salt Lake—of Wells-Fargo's Overland Mail.

Over the Wells-Fargo route, from Salt Lake to Virginia City (565 miles), the usual time was 120 hours—five days; and one recent trip had been made at an average rate, to include all stops, of 8.7 miles an hour. Holladay, over his Atchison-Denver section, was doing fairly as well. Five days instead of six were often sufficing for his longer run of 653 miles, while one recent trip over that distance had been made at an average rate, to include all stops, of 7.9 miles an hour.

David Butterfield, meanwhile, was not being showered with compliments. Neither was Holladay, for that matter. The west-bound traveler could expect real service only as far as Denver. To the extent of the B. O. D. opposition, he traveled behind well-fed teams, changed at frequent intervals without loss of time.

But beyond Denver! There, according to one passenger, the stage was drawn by "half-starved mules" that "had to live on sage-brush." It was "hard to find the animals when wanted—especially at night, and then again . . . harder to catch them when found." [1] The inhabited stations were far apart, and if a passenger got one poor meal a day, he was fortunate.

Perhaps Holladay needed more time in order to restore this Rocky Mountain section and raise it to the standards of his Atchison-Denver half; but time worked a different effect. By December it happened that the Overland Dispatch had run itself nearly to death, so that there was virtually no more competition. Holladay could rest on his oars, and rest in peace; for there were no Indians now to molest him. There were only the newspapers to go on tattling tales: his line was "in a wretched condition"; it was "without system or regularity," [2] and so on. But he was used to that.

[1] See "Sacramento Union," November 16, 1865.

[2] *Idem.* December 23, 1865. See also "San Francisco Bulletin," December 15, 1865, and the "Alta California," January 8, 1866.

The trouble, now that the Indians had withdrawn, was winter. The old proponents of the Southern route might have risen from their political graves to cry with the steamship men, "I told you so," but for the fact that the same winter, with at least the same severity, had dropped a thick white blanket over the Wells-Fargo line and affected it not at all. There, over the Nevada deserts, where the thermometer rested often far below zero, where the road was covered with snow ranging from fifteen inches to fifteen feet in depth, the stages not only continued to run regularly, but they were running to a summer schedule.

"This company," writes a correspondent from Ruby Valley at the time, "was never in finer condition for winter service, having an abundance of grain for their horses, as well as hay, plenty of provisions for their men, and sleighs and light coaches distributed so well along the route, that it is impossible for snow or anything else almost to stop them. Unfortunately the company east of Salt Lake have lost the continuity, but this is nothing very unusual for them." [1]

Ben Holladay, of course, had been caught unprepared by an exceptionally cold winter—the coldest since sixty-one it was called—but he was probably far too busy with other matters to let it bother him. Having bitten off more stage line already than it

[1] "Alta California," January 8, 1866.

seemed he could chew, he was about to take another bite. He was about to take the third and last big mouthful before retiring. He was training for battle. Wells, Fargo & Company had unsheathed an ugly blade.

Wells-Fargo, through its Western representative and general manager, Louis McLane of the Pioneer, was taking root in the California stage world, and was well intrenched thence onward as far as Salt Lake through its control of the Overland Mail Company. Now, being dissatisfied with Holladay's terms in the matter of express transportation, this powerful firm was hobnobbing with the unfortunate stockholders of the Overland Dispatch. It was well within the power of Wells-Fargo to put the Dispatch back on its feet, and extend it, as originally planned, from Denver to Salt Lake, thus controlling a line of stock, independent of Holladay, from the Missouri River to the Pacific Ocean. This plan, moreover, was to be carried out unless Holladay would reconsider his policies.

He politely declined.

Messrs. Root and Connelley [1] tell the story as it was given to them by David Street, an eye-witness of the action that followed:

"Mr. Holladay quietly formed his plans; he instructed David Street, his general agent in the West, to send a competent practical stage man and a clerk

[1] *Op. cit.*, 404-406.

over the line of the B. O. D. Company as passengers—
not to make themselves or their business known—
and to make . . . as complete an inventory as possible."

This task accomplished, and the data digested,
Holladay received a note signed by the American,
the United States, and the Wells-Fargo express companies, repeating their demands and adding the threat.
If Holladay refused this time to comply, they would
stock the gap between Denver and Salt Lake and be
rid of him.

Holladay, filling a desk chair in his New York
office, "arose, as if sniffing the battle and eager for
the fray, and said, 'Now, I am going to take the bull
by the horns.' "

He did not respond at once to the note from the
express firms, but sent a messenger to the president of
the Park Bank, now also the president of the Dispatch, asking this important person to lunch with
him at his office. Holladay's office, writes Mr. Root,
"was on William street, just off Wall street, and not
far from Delmonico's Beaver street restaurant. He
told the clerk to go down there and order a fine lunch,
with wines and cigars, to be served at his office.

"The bank president came on time, and Mr. Street
says he can remember well Mr. Holladay's putting the
case to him. In stature he was a small man, and Mr.
Holladay a large one; and the latter, in the domineer-
ing though pleasant manner of his, had crowded him

up into a corner." He knew more about the Dispatch than its owners knew, he was saying. The line was already out more than a million dollars, and was apt to be out a whole lot more very shortly. But the proposition was this—Holladay explained it and named his figure. He told the president of the Dispatch to think it over, but to send a decision that afternoon.

It came before three o'clock. There had been a meeting of stockholders; and the bargain was closed. Holladay was to be the new owner of the Overland Dispatch. If, now, Wells-Fargo cared to stock a line from Salt Lake to Denver— "Tell them to stock and be damned," he told his secretary. And the express men again sheathed their blades.

"This," says Root, "really paved the way for Holladay selling out the whole overland business to Wells, Fargo & Company."

But at this particular juncture—February, 1866— he had eight or nine months to go in his fullest sway. Under the new name of "Holladay Overland Mail and Express Company" he consolidated the Dispatch and the Overland Stage, to include his Montana and Idaho lines, and added the route between Omaha and Fort Kearney formerly owned by the Western Stage Company.

Thus the early spring of sixty-six found him operating over the Smoky Hill route, between Topeka and Denver, 585 miles; over the old Platte route between Atchison and Denver, 650 miles; between Fort

Courtesy of the Bancroft Library

ADVERTISEMENT FROM THE "SALT LAKE
UNION VEDETTE" OF APRIL 27, 1866

Kearney and the railroad terminus near Omaha, 150
miles; between Denver and Salt Lake City, 600 miles;
between Salt Lake City and the Montana mines,
roughly 600 miles to include subsidiaries; between a

junction on the Montana line and Boise, Idaho, 370 miles; and about 40 miles of local lines out of Denver —a total of nearly 3,000 miles of stage route in all. Securing a mail contract over the Smoky Hill route, he held mail contracts to cover his entire system, these bearing at a rate of about a million dollars a year. Meanwhile he was running steamers out of San Francisco to Oregon and Mexico; but his stage-coach system alone was, as it had been even before this sudden expansion, the nation's greatest enterprise to be found in the hands of one man.

To disregard, for a moment, a mass of chronicles relating to Holladay and published during his active career, and to consider only the later-day publications, is to be left with the postulate that the man was, in the best sense of the expression, the greatest stageman that ever lived.

To disregard, arbitrarily again, all the more recent publications, and to consider only the contemporaneous matter such as newspapers and public documents of Holladay's time, is to behold in this most dominant figure of the stage-coach world anything but a genuine stageman. It is to feel, without being assuaged by very many conflicting opinions (mere drops of clear water in the bucket of mud), that Ben Holladay, like the Indians that beset him, simply exploited the institution for all that it could be made worth to him within the bounds of public toleration; that his grasping business ingenuity, rather than any sense of professional pride, dictated his various policies for better or worse; and that not only was he party to an unmistakable decline of the old system as built up by such men as Birch and Butterfield, but that he contributed liberally toward it.

Thus, strangely perhaps, the Holladay that exists in tradition is a very different personage from the Holladay that stood before the scrutiny of his own world. But to accept him wholly as popular opinion beheld him would be to accept also a mass-prejudice which, but for Indian hostilities, might not have expressed itself so bitterly. To accept him, on the other hand, as tradition has painted him for the bulk of modern writings would be to accept also a great deal of pure hokum from those lavish brushes that dipped into paper-backed novels for their color, those that were wielded often by capricious ghost-writers and press agents—dime-novelists, in fact, who were given liberties with many names not their own.

This much, however, may be said: Few, if any, well-known stagemen, either before or during Holladay's reign, ever opened themselves to more criticism, were ever obliged to make more excuses, ever revealed by their actions a character less suited to their responsibilities, or ever stood in a more compromising light.

His attitude toward his important public duty may be only suggested by the condition of his line when the B. O. D. opened competition with half of it.

Then, indeed, he could talk about Indians. He could likewise point back to the peaceful year of sixty-three when he had run an efficient stage line. But at that time there had been a great contract to hope for in the following year; there had been a long siege of public pressure against him and his political prestige; there had been unpleasant rumors afloat in Washington to jeopardize his future; and now, if not then, there was reason to wonder if all these circumstances had not had some bearing on that sudden burst of efficiency and display of good intentions. Had he given some evidence of those same intentions during his last year of power, when again the Indians were quiet, the question might have answered itself in his favor.

But then it was that Ben Holladay demonstrated, more clearly than ever before, that he did not really belong to the institution he controlled. It belonged to him. The Pacific States especially suffered the consequences. During the spring and summer of 1866 California and Nevada spoke their minds, as witness the following (greatly abbreviated) paragraphs from the "Sacramento Union," "Virginia Enterprise," and "Carson Appeal":

. . . Since the establishment of the so-called Overland Daily mail, the average will not show over a tri-weekly mail service. . . . The fault of which we complain does not lie between here [Virginia, Nevada] and Salt Lake. . . . Indeed, there is probably no mail service in the world of the same length performed with greater punctuality than that from Sacramento to Salt Lake . . . The fault lies with the portion of the service under the contract of Ben Holladay. . . .[1]

. . . The trouble about the Overland Mail is owing to Ben Holladay's grasping and speculative spirit. He has so many enterprises on hand that he does justice to none . . . At the present time he is making money by his stages and express to Montana, and, therefore, neglects the transportation of the Overland Mail, knowing full well that he can make it all right with the government by and by at Washington.[2]

. . . We unite with our brethren of the press in requesting . . . the better protection of the mails against the abuses of one Ben Holladay . . . Mails which are carried between here [Carson, Nevada] and Salt Lake go regularly enough; but east of there, in Holladay's dominion, they are scandalously delayed. . . . Thousands of letters are lost. . . . It would be a benefit to the Pacific states if Ben Holladay were declared by congress a nuisance that ought to be abated. . . .[3]

. . . Ben Holladay . . . has never transported a daily mail to and from Salt Lake, while proof is equally positive that a daily mail has all the time been carried between Sacramento and Salt Lake. . . . If an investigation should be ordered by the Post Office Department, a most shameful condition of affairs will

[1] "Virginia Enterprise," May 24, 1866.
[2] "Sacramento Union," May 26, 1866.
[3] *Idem.* of June 7, 1866, quoting the "Carson Appeal."

be found to exist in the Holladay transportation. . . .
The cry of Indian disturbances was made the excuse
for the non-fulfillment of the mail contract for years;
but we opined that all the savages that ever infested
the plains have not been as great an obstruction to the
transportation of the mails as has been Ben Holladay. . . .[1]

. . . We received by Overland Mail yesterday
[July 3] a letter postmarked at Philadelphia, February 17, 1866. If it takes four months and a half for
Holladay to transmit a letter . . . how long, in the
estimation of the Postmaster General, should his mail
contract continue. . . .[2]

Whether the subject of all these remarks was sub-
sequently advised by his confidants in Washington to
withdraw for the good of the service, or whether he
had come to believe it advisable to "get out from
under" for the good of his purse, a rumor "from reliable sources" was published before the end of August to the effect that Holladay had sold out to Wells-
Fargo.

"This," said "The Reese River Reveille" of Nevada, "seems almost too good to be true." [3]

And it was, indeed, a little premature. There appeared no more reports of the transaction until two
months later. But during this interim, no doubt, ne-
gotiations, through a third party, were in process;

[1] "Virginia Enterprise," May 26, 1866.
[2] "Sacramento Union," July 4, 1866.
[3] Quoted by the "Sacramento Union," August 25, 1866.

for, by the last week of October, Holladay appears to have sold and Wells-Fargo to have purchased—("bought out Eugene Kelly and S. L. M. Barlow, the successors of Ben Holladay")[1]—consolidating the whole system under the management of Louis Mc-Lane. Ben Holladay, now or shortly afterward, was definitely out of the stage-coach world—the greatest stageman that ever lived, if he was really a stageman.

But the end was very near.

As presaged by the Railroad Act of sixty-two and the subsequent land grants, vast preparations for the rapid extension of rails from the East and West toward Salt Lake had, even before Ben Holladay's withdrawal, begun to materialize measurably. Now, with promise immeasurable, the ties were clattering down upon the dusty road-bed and the rails were being spiked into place.

The length of the overland stage line was shrinking, stage for stage. Soon it would be division for division until, at some uncertain point, at some indefinite time (much earlier than many minds could believe), the gap would be sealed; and the world's greatest undertaking on hoofs and coach wheels would be an achievement of the past.

If, during these final years—from the last months of sixty-six to the spring of sixty-nine—Louis Mc-Lane, as the president of Wells-Fargo and the man-

[1] "Sacramento Union," October 27, 1866.

ager of the entire system, had been able to raise the standards of his shrinking line to those of his Western section, then the critics of Ben Holladay's sway might have crowed a last refrain. The Indians, however, once more attacked all possibilities of fair judgment. The year of sixty-seven was comparable only to sixty-four from the point of hostilities against the line, winter pouncing on a disrupted organization, mail congesting the route, complaints renewed, as ever.

But the Iron Horse was fast devouring all this trouble, gulping half the eastern section (as far as Cheyenne) before the end of the year; while Wells-Fargo, with some alarm, began to realize that the most extravagant predictions in behalf of the railroad would be realized if not surpassed.

The company, in spite of the Indians, had made many costly improvements. Bowles, going over what was left of the route in 1868, writes: ". . . The horses are gayer and go faster than three years before; and the meals at the 'home stations' are greatly improved; no more single-roomed turf cabins, bare dirt floors, milkless coffee, rancid bacon, stale beans, and green bread, and 'if you don't like it, help yourself to the mustard'; but comfortable little taverns of dressed timber and planed boards, with carpeted parlors and separate dining rooms, fresh meat and milk and butter, trout and eggs, everything 'square' in fact, and a hearty welcome." [1]

[1] Bowles, "The Switzerland of America," 31.

Among these better accommodations, moreover, were fifty new Concord coaches, all of which would soon be a drug on the market, and a thankless loss. Cheers from the side-lines in this losing game arose only at the sound of steam whistles. Second fiddle, and a cracked one at that, was the Wells-Fargo accompaniment to the march of the Iron Horse.

Between the moving terminals—the traveling towns, the collapsible camps of brawling inebriates that moved with the railroad workers—between Hell-on-Wheels and Hell-on-Wheels, as these termini were called, the line of coaches continued to run until squeezed at last into extinction.

Other chronicles could be made to follow the stage through its second twenty years of ventures and adventures in the West—its career in the hands of such great firms as Wells-Fargo, Gilmer & Salisbury, Barlow & Sanderson, Flint, Bixby & Company, and many more, operating through the Northwest and the Southwest and along the Pacific shore. It was lively staging in many cases, and immaculate work in some; but to follow this stage were to join the funeral procession, where the horn of Gabriel is the railroad whistle, and the cross on the grave is marked, "Look out for the cars!"

But once stagemen did not have to worry about the cars. Once, in the summer of 1850, a Concord coach came around Cape Horn. Once again, just a few years later, scores, even hundreds, of them came

DOWN THE SIERRAS IN SIXTY-FIVE
ORIGINAL ILLUSTRATION FROM "BEYOND THE MISSISSIPPI,"
BY ALBERT D. RICHARDSON.

around, and the horses were driven in from over the plains. That was before there was anything better than trekking lines on "The American Desert"; it was when the Gold Coast Forty-niners were growing up with their isolated system, realizing for themselves, and demonstrating for others, that a fast coach mail across the continent was truly no visionary's dream.

That was when the largest staging firm in the world, the Birch monopoly, was likewise the very finest, and when rare color, unknown to the Eastern institution, was being blended in a manner to distinguish a coming era. It was when the pioneer system had only its endowed ability (and quantities of gold dust) to depend on—when mail contracts, politicians, and Postmaster-Generals didn't matter.

That was when the threadbare strands of Union were beginning to part; when trans-Rocky Mountain republics, no less than "Confederate States of America," appeared before many sober eyes as writing on the wall. But that was also when James Birch, with a living example of his own work to point to, strengthened the opinion that iron was not the only material that could be used as a bond of intercourse. Soon then it was that he stretched the first life-line across the Seven Deserts; and soon that John Butterfield came along with another, drawing it out from the West and the East and tying the knot in the middle. It was when the "impassable" had been passed meanwhile by Crandall, "the prince of drivers"; and when Hockaday and Chorpenning began pioneering the short Central trail.

But the historian of so much glamour must be carried away, saving his inevitable lack of bias, by that directness and stolidness of aim that these men had. Unquestionably that period must have been an æon (even) in our American times, when the conception of directness counted. It is a sorrow that this conception has had so few literal historians; for most of us, or even of the past generation, are inclined to look upon it only as a bold and fictional adventure. It was that era in fiction in which we conceived the stage-coach as drama solely, and gave it but little further thought. Some dignified the vehicle as a precursor of the railroad—precursor it was, indeed; but there is a sense of grandeur, more than a handsome gesture, added as we pause to wonder: What would have happened to this empire but for the Concord, the men who made it, the men who drove it and foresaw its unheard-of capacities?

AN AFTERWORD

THE WHIP ITSELF

by

Captain William Banning

AMONG the pupils of the old British school of staging there have been some able writers; and the art of driving the British four-in-hand remains happily of permanent record. Among these writings, however, are incidental attempts to compare the English modes and methods with those of the Yankee —attempts to compare a system which the writers understood with another so foreign to their experience, apparently, that its most elemental principles are not even suggested.

It seems, indeed, that the only documentary evidence of the practices involved in the American system has been confined to these few misleading sources. And from them we are apt to form the impression that the Yankee, as he faced the task of putting his world on wheels, chanced to adopt certain ways and means of his own because . . . Perhaps he didn't know any better.

Obviously, he didn't.

In view of his fairly incomparable problem, he was unapt to turn from a solution which he could regard as adequate to one which was clearly and utterly inadequate. For the British coach, in the eyes even of

one of its most devoted exponents—Fairman Rogers
—was in nowise adaptable, from points either of
capacity or strength, to the American needs; whereas
the coach of Concord, New Hampshire, was adaptable beyond any question of doubt. During the period treated in these pages, in fact, the vehicle was
regarded as one of such excellence that there was little
any one could ever do to improve it, and nothing
any one could ever do, besides Abbot, Downing &
Company, to duplicate it, or to create anything comparable. But, though the colonies of England were
obliged to use the coach very largely in preference to
any that their home institution had produced, still
the British school was apt to smile upon the Yankee
masterpiece as a rather crude thing after all.

"It is sometimes supposed," Fairman Rogers tells
us, "that the American coach [he refers directly to the
Concord] was invented especially for the use on the
early, rough American roads; but it is evidently the
European vehicle of the latter part of the eighteenth
century *arrested in its development* because the conditions of the road in those parts of the United States
where coaches were used resembled the conditions existing at that time in Europe."

The italics are mine. We are to believe, perhaps,
that if the development of the American conveyance
had not been *"arrested"* (due, strangely, to the obstacles that it had to surmount in its evolution), then
the Yankee might have had something rather fine,

something, it may be, like the British mail coach; although Mr. Rogers is frank to admit that this mail coach would have gone to pieces in the first half-mile over certain roads coursed by the Concord with safety and despatch.

I suspect, however, that we may understand the workings of Mr. Rogers's mind in this case a little better than he understood the workings of the minds that built the Concord.

Since the body of this vehicle is supported by leather straps, or thorough-braces, he observes: "This is exactly the mode of suspension of the European carriages before the introduction of springs, which, as it will be noted, are wholly absent in the Concord coach." But they were happily absent, as we have already pointed out in an earlier chapter. If our stages were being drawn by horses to-day, I am convinced, in spite of all the improvements that the steel spring has enjoyed, leather thorough-braces would still be in great demand. Nor would they be the thorough-braces of the eighteenth century, but an ingenious development from these as known to the wheelwrights of Concord.

There was a time, indeed, when American stagemen were justified in looking back upon all steel-spring stages, to include the English variety, not only as something wholly unsuited to their own particular needs, but as something which, from a mechanical and scientific standpoint, was the inferior. The most important function of Concord thorough-braces has already been explained. It has been shown how, by allowing the heavy body to rock fore and aft, they enable the force of inertia to supply the timely boost to relieve the team of strain due to obstacles of the road. The horse was the vital consideration. The less taxed, the more he could pull and the faster he could go. The coach that could run the easiest with the greatest load was the best for the horse. And the Concord was that coach.

Thus, in rough country, or in any country after all, the thorough-brace principle, as applied to the team, worked a benefit. In any country a team could haul more with greater despatch while drawing a Concord than while drawing any other known conveyance. That was *why* the Yankee called it the most perfect traveling vehicle in the world. Still we are told that it was a coach "arrested in its development." Arrested, indeed, when at last it was found that there was no room for further improvement.

Misconceptions as to the modes of driving fostered by the American coach are as prevalent as those pertaining to the coach itself. For, as it happens, the principle of the thorough-braces as described had some bearing upon the methods of harnessing the team, and hence upon the driving of it.

The stage-coach has passed; and an old art, typically American, is about to become a lost one. The nature of it, however, may be held on record; and toward

CAPTAIN WILLIAM BANNING

LAST OF THE ACTIVE DRIVERS OF SIX.

this end it is my hope to supplement what the English already know of their school with that which the Yankee may some day care to learn of his own. I shall not try to explain "how to do it," but only "how it was done" by those drivers who achieved the highest, those who were known as "reinsmen."

A reinsman was a master driver who, by virtue of his exceptional skill, was able to drive each span of his complement wholly independent of the other.

As most teams were harnessed, however, this kind of driving was at once impossible. With breast-straps (pole-straps) and traces drawn taut, or nearly taut after the old English mode, there was a team so hitched that it could not possibly be "reined"—the separate spans could not be driven independently.

Many notable and excellent six-horse American whips did, it is true, drive a tight-laced team, one whose wheelers and swings were so rigidly strapped to their respective poles that their traces were never quite slack. The animals could scarcely move without moving either the pole or the vehicle proper. Nor —which is more to the point—could the pole or the vehicle move without affecting these particular animals.

But the drivers of these strapped-up teams, however well they drove, *were not reinsmen*. And they sacrificed, along with certain elements of grace and certain practice in the most delicate sort of fingering and brake work, a great deal of efficiency to include power, speed, endurance, and ofttimes much hide from their wheelers' necks.

The wheelers (the span nearest the wheels) were, of course, first to show the ill effects of this inferior method. Harnessed so that the pole between them could not swing freely, they were taxed with the unnecessary duties of constantly checking or preventing that inevitable action. Let a man take hold of the pole (the fixed tongue) of a Concord coach, drawing the vehicle across the stable floor; then place some small obstruction under a front wheel and observe how promptly he is thrown from his balance by the consequent motion of the pole. One may sympathize, then, with a strapped up span of wheelers in their more rapid pulling over larger obstructions of the road, and realize why some drivers sought to devise a means of sparing their animals such hardship.

Nor were these obstacles of the road the only agents to torment the poled-up wheelers and drag down their spirits. The movements of other horses in the team —the actions of the swing animals when not pulling straight ahead—all came back on the collars of the span behind, adding vastly to their everlasting punishment. That the swings themselves paid part of the penalty is obvious; for they too, being strapped up, were obliged to resist the motion of their own pole as imposed by the other spans.

But given six horses harnessed for a genuine reinsman—breast-straps swinging liberally—and observe a few of the advantages.

TEAM LOOSELY HITCHED FOR THE REINSMAN

"a" (breast straps) and "b" (traces) showing the relative and coördinate slack allowed for the necessary freedom of a well-reined team

A shock due to a front wheel's thump into a chuck-hole—but the pole, swinging suddenly as a result, spends the brunt of its energy in the air, having put strain upon the collar of no animal. At a turn, observe how the leaders may be swung deliberately without dragging, or tending to drag, the second span off-side; how the second, upon reaching the pivot point, may be swung without affecting the third; how, in short, there is, at all times, a maximum horse-power drawing the coach at a minimum strain upon the beasts.

It was a happy team whose driver was a reinsman. His horses showed it; he could let them show it; he could permit the romping of any animal, knowing that the others would not be taxed by it, though they might be reminded they were free to join the dance.

Most drivers understood the theory once it had been demonstrated to them; but there were only a few sufficiently skilled to put the theory into practice. Those few were the pioneers of a new art; or else they had taken an old one and carried it to the heights of Olympus. It was an American contribution that could look back upon the four-in-hand of older times as too crude a thing for the finest work.

I can hear the protests of the old coachman of England, with his tight and shining pole-chains, his trim bob-tailed team, his fastidious observance of etiquette born of splendid tradition. His eyes, trained for a hundred niceties unknown to the Yankee school, are apt to look upon any harness that dangles as one indication of a slovenly driver. But for us, of a different environment, forced away from the older régime, those tight traces and pole-chains, those bob-tails and iron springs can only be viewed as the bluff-bowed, balloon-sailed old hulks of the sea were regarded by the clipper men. It was a case only of natural evolution, the Yankee being obliged to carry on at a point where the Englishman was able to stop.

Where the mountains in America were loftiest and most rugged, where the roads were most narrow and threatening, there, above all places, was the greatest demand for the whip who had learned to "rein," the driver who had mastered the most difficult of modes of driving. His was strictly a triplex power plant of duplex units operating on twenty-four hoofs; and if, by means of his six lines and his brake and whip, he could exact from all of its parts and potentialities a maximum degree of efficiency at all times, then he was a master of masters. He was a reinsman indeed. He was one in a thousand.

He was, to recall by far the greatest in my own life's experience among the whipsters, a man like John J. Reynolds of California. Reynolds, like most drivers, was a reinsman in his own estimation; but, very unlike most, he was acknowledged as such by every stageman or connoisseur that had ever seen him drive. Fortunately, I had the opportunity to observe him in action and to study his technique through an acquaintance of many years. He demanded the closest scrutiny; he was not given to explain or demonstrate anything. He seldom talked while driving; one was flattered to receive a monosyllable from him, flattered to think that he could show the respect for human beings that he always bestowed upon his horses.

Even his coach was comparatively silent. All couplings were so well leathered fore and aft that one was conscious only of the dull clucking sound from the sand boxes (around the axles). It was a sound with an effect upon his team, as drum taps upon marching soldiers, and seemed to call for the silence of anything that might mar that needed rhythm.

Yet that rhythm was sometimes marred by a sudden *bang*.

You might see a deep rut ahead, and know that, if

John wanted, he could shave that hindrance so closely that his passengers would call it chance; and yet, *bang* into it he might go, with a spinal concussion for the pilgrims to remember and complain of for the next mile or two. They would swear that where chuck-holes were avoidable the same should be avoided, if only for the sake of the blessed beasts in the traces. But John Reynolds could make no such sweeping rules; and, as it happened, whenever he began jolting the daylights out of his passengers, he was using more judgment than textbook.

His horses, loosely harnessed as they were to enjoy the full benefit of the shock-absorbing thorough-braces, were, in the first place, largely immune from the jolting felt so keenly aboard the coach. In fact, he could generally spare his animals more unnecessary hardship by simply allowing them to follow the road than by constantly swinging them hither and yon in order to dodge the rough spots. But this consideration was not all. In this case the welfare of his passengers obtained. During this trip or another, dark night with thick weather might fall. Sooner or later he could expect to be uncertain of his bearings. A team conscious of the bit even over flat desert country would expect the bit at all times, storm, fog, or none; whereas the team allowed, wherever possible, to follow the road, would be ready to supply a very necessary instinct when the judgment of the driver failed in its sense of direction.

But John was as silent about all this as an automaton with wheels inside; and, like most of his kind, he "bumped the eternal bump" with his beloved art stuffed away in his brake boot and gloves. He was not a large man; but he was a powerful one—solid, clean-cut, blond, and as high-strung as the teams he drove. The pay he received was exactly twice that of any other driver in his sphere of action. With opposition at white-heat, the man who could beat his opponent, yet impose the lighter tax upon his horses so that he could outdistance the other still farther on the following day, was worth a bit more per month than his weight in silver. John Reynolds was the unvanquished champion. And, while stage-coach races were to be deplored in the few cases where circumstances demanded it, still the contesting team of the reinsman was well off indeed.

Reynolds, moreover, had exceptional qualifications for racing as well as for everything else involved by his career. His apprenticeship entailed not only teaming but the driving of fast trotting horses over various courses of California and New York State. He understood horses, and was especially equipped for the handling of the finer ones and for the promotion of their finest qualities. With muscles in his wrists like spring-steel cords, his deft fingers could play upon the lines—slipping this one, holding that, and climbing up on the other—with the easy yet almost invisible promptitude of a prestidigitator.

As a child, it seems, he had practised these tricks of the fingers. He had shoved six stakes in the ground, tied lines to each, and led them all back to be arranged properly in his fingers. The game was to draw back one hand, letting any one line slip while holding any two, or any two while holding any one. It was to draw back both hands and do likewise. In one movement of the arms he would try to dislodge any one, two, three, four, or five of the sticks without disturbing the remainder.

It was not child-play. To appreciate the nature of the exercise, one has only to flatten out both hands, fingers together, then suddenly command a certain two fingers of one hand and a different two of the other to spread—to do so simultaneously and immediately without affecting the other members. And while this experiment requires but little of the muscular action embodied by John's boyhood game, it is surprising with what reluctant obedience the appointed agents will respond, and with what stupid persistence the unappointed will volunteer. But with six lines to handle, and about three times as many exercises as there are fingers involving them, it will be found that reins to be slipped will hold, those to be held will slip—the telegraphic system between mind and fingers may seem a very awkward affair.

John Reynolds, however, when it came to six real lines and six real horses, could work this telegraphy to perfection. It was a vital faculty which most

CONJURING BACK THE OLD DAYS

MAJOR FREDERICK R. BURNHAM AND CAPTAIN WILLIAM BANNING ON THE
BOX—FROM A RECENT PHOTOGRAPH.

drivers could boast only to a slight degree. The lack of it demanded tight breast-straps; the presence made possible the loose ones and the most delicate or finished kind of driving.

In this, the brake was used conjointly with the reins. It was, in fact, made to act upon the reins. It served as an integral part of the actual driving processes, and this in a manner entirely unknown to the older schools.

I have seen John's team given credit by passengers for having made a very graceful turn—no credit for John, because, apparently, he had done almost nothing toward the execution of that maneuver. Perhaps it was observed that he had applied a slight pressure to his brake (wanting to slow down "or something"); and that the tip of his whip-stock had tapped a wheeler on the back (as it might do almost any time for some reason or another); but certainly, as any one might have sworn on the witness stand, he had done nothing more. Yet his horses had gone streaming around a curve, one span after another, as precisely as a double-timing, crack column of squads when given "Column right!" and *"March!"*

The impression was, whenever this happened, that his team had been sent around that particular turn so often in the past that now it knew just when, and exactly how, to execute the maneuver. John did not have to bend a finger. He simply left it to habit and horse-sense.

It was far from being the case.

Given a level cross-road of light surface, and John could send his team swirling in either direction; he could do it as well, if not better, over a road never coursed by his animals before; and, in so far as passengers were apt to observe, it would be without a movement of the reins.

Presuming that the turn contemplated is to be right: the six-horse team is trotting along toward the cross-roads, all traces swinging, as they would swing on a light level road most of the time. For under these free and easy conditions the driver need not wait for his arrival at the turn before adjusting all of his lines. Some moments before his horses have done anything to attract especial attention he has fully completed these adjustments.

His lines have been drawn up slightly, lead line on the off (or right) side to a greater extent than those on the near (or left). It being true that, when the movement begins, the swings and wheelers will almost invariably try to cut off the leaders, the wheel and swing lines on the near side have also been drawn somewhat tighter, care having been taken in these manipulations that no animal has felt the bit, and that all traces, as nearly as possible, remain loose.

So the stage rolls on, the driver with his hands resting lightly on his knees, where they are to remain henceforth inactive. But now the leaders have reached the turn. We hear a slight scraping of brake—just a touch which seems to act at once upon the ears of the horses rather than upon the motion of the stage. Every animal has heard in this sound a signal of execution. And, simultaneously, all have felt, for the first time, a tension on the bit as planned and arranged by the driver some moments before. The driver, to repeat, has not moved his hands. *But the brake has retarded the motion of the vehicle just enough to tighten the reins.* It has put the proper strain on the various bits of the entire complement exactly as pre-arranged.

Thus the movement has commenced; and, as the leaders swing, the driver drops the tip of his hickory on the off-wheeler's back to encourage him into the collar and prevent any cramping of the stage should the leader swing too sharply.[1]

The use of the brake in this one simple maneuver is noteworthy; for the same principle was observed more or less in many others by all reinsmen. If before reaching the cross-roads mentioned above, the driver had drawn up his lines, all to an equal extent, and later given the same signal of brake, then the team, in his motionless hands, would have come to a stop, although, of course, a more holding pressure of brake would have been applied. And the same method, modified, or varied, obtained under other circum-

[1] Incidentally, I have seen lazy wheelers watch this situation with the keenest interest, and, should a wheel scrape its rub iron, *jump* into the collar and throw the wheel clear again—something the more remarkable for the fact of the wheeler's laziness.

stances where the lack of tension on traces and various other conditions permitted. But all this was strictly within the province of reinsmen. Clearly, in the case of a strapped-up team, the brake would fail to act to such consummate advantage upon the lines.

The brake, however, was vital to all American drivers. I have never seen one of them who did not stop his team by first applying the brake. Some roads in the early days were so steep that perhaps on rare occasions the driver was justified in causing his wheelers to "set back in the breeching" *at a walk* to aid the brake or skids in retarding the stage. During the first ten years of my driving my wheelers were equipped with this breeching; but because during all of that time, over a wide range of country, I found no occasion ever to put this part of the harness to use, I discarded it (as many drivers did) and drove four or five more decades, and continue to drive, without it.

Even as emergency equipment, as in the event of a brake's carrying away, two wheelers, by means of their breeching, could scarcely be expected to avert further accident. The American stage-coach was too heavy for such contraptions; and horses, for the same reason, were the more to be considered.

As it may have been observed, horses, and everything to make life easier for them, were the chief considerations. The whole soul and body of the West-American institution was based on practicality. The reinsman himself was a progeny of practical endeavor; his team and its harness were an expression of the same thing; his coach the supreme expression.

Some fifteen years before the automobile had begun to invade the last strongholds of the stage-coach I clipped several pages from "The San Francisco Argonaut" (September 9, 1889) and treasured them long afterward as the most sensitive tribute to the reining of six that I had ever had the pleasure to read. The author, Captain Robert Howe Fletcher, whom I was delighted to meet not long ago, had never been professedly a driver; although on numerous occasions, it seems, he had held the reins. As a cavalry officer, however, horses and all that they stood for were naturally a source of inspiration.

"To the music of clinking chains, and buckles, and creaking thorough-braces," he could imagine the oaks that dotted the valley through which he drove as being "regular road-agents of trees, standing sturdily in the middle of the highway as though they would stop us and try to rob us of our hats as we sped beneath their branches." Of the chap with the whip he observed that "it belonged to the eternal fitness of things that the stage-driver should be a silent man, that his name should be 'Jerry'; that he should be big, broad of shoulder, and brawny armed.

"Going down the grade, when we were all searching for something to cling to, Jerry bade [my] little boy hold on to his arm, stalwart fellow that he was; with six impetuous horses in his hands, and a ponderous brake under his foot, a little boy, more or less, hanging on to his arm was nothing to him."

High up on the mountains at last, and swinging suddenly around a sharp curve, "we found ourselves," he writes, "confronted by nothing—that is, nothing but blue sky. Looking down we saw a hawk pass beneath us, and beneath the hawk were dark green, forest-covered mountains, and at the foot of the mountains was a lake—a silver-blue ribbon—so far away that but for the signals flashed from its surface by the sun, it would have been indistinguishable in the silver-blue distance of the surrounding hills. As we hung there, on the verge of creation, we had a good idea of what it felt like to be a bird. And, after the descent began, the sensation became still more realistic.

"With the horses trotting loosely in their harness, and the driver on the brake, we streamed around the curves, at one moment swinging over the abyss until one's hold on one's breath involuntarily tightened, and the next, swinging back easily toward the bank. In some places the shoulders of the mountains jutted out so abruptly that we would lose sight of the leaders around the curves before we would get there ourselves.

"They were dainty, elegant little animals, those

leaders; at one moment, with their reluctant heads reined around toward their flanks, they danced like wild deer along the verge of the precipice, and the next, the inexorable driver was grinding them against the bank—but never a sign did they give of leaving the road, so thoroughbred were they. The swing horses, a trifle larger, followed the movements of the leaders, but more sedately. The wheelers, big steady fellows . . . [And] all six moved in fearless obedience to the guidance of the two hands, clad in a pair of buckskin gloves, whose taciturn owner, with one foot on the brake and another on the footboard, made me think of a skilled musician playing upon a familiar instrument."

Here is one casual bit of writing ringing true in all its detail. I have purposely (and awkwardly) omitted a phrase describing the movements of the wheelers—the big steady fellows that "held the stage back," etc.—this being evidently a slip of the pen, since no man could have handled that team, as it seems "Jerry" did, with wheelers holding back.

Captain Fletcher told me that whereas he had forgotten many scores of good whips, he had never forgotten Jerry—Jerry the "silent man," whose happy team "trotted loosely" in the harness, and who suggested "a skilled musician playing upon a familiar instrument." Such a driver was not apt to be forgotten, being, as he must have been, a reinsman.

These masters were few enough in life; but I have seen only one, only Jerry, appear and live from the pen of any man.

The average writings are anything but stagefaring; the average are enough to cost the heads of most stagemen their last remaining strands of white hair. There is need for more Captain Fletchers to recall the things that were. The significance of the old staging system, its vastness, the excellence of its qualities, the dignity and pride vested in its operations, the character of men it employed, the art it developed, and the brave romance it entailed would seem to warrant the same respect by all who might attempt to portray it that has been elicited by our clipper ships; and yet, before such respect can prevail in this nation, there will be more to unlearn than to learn.

As a motion-picture man once told me: "We don't *want* to present the stage-coach as it was. We must show it as the people *think* it was. Or else they won't believe us."

BIBLIOGRAPHY

Sources in General

The main substance of this writing, not having been compiled from histories, biographies, memoirs, or other reflective matter, was obliged to depend above all upon the periodicals belonging to the period treated, and to a very large extent upon the Federal documents, travelers' journals, and other contemporaneous materials; although the pertinent works of later times were not overlooked.

There are, moreover, two authentic and very worth-while publications of the present century affording further study into certain important phases of this topic: Dr. Le Roy R. Hafen's "Overland Mail" is a recent and thorough work tracing the history of the mail and, incidentally, that of the stage, much as we have sought to trace the history of the stage and, incidentally, that of the mail. And the voluminous monograph, "The Overland Stage to California," by Frank A. Root and William E. Connelley, contains without doubt more information on Ben Holladay's line than could be found in any other one source, having also a full background to cover the whole overland era. (See Secondary Sources below.)

Perhaps the most readable journals of stage-coach travel are those of Borthwick, Bowles, Browne, Mark Twain, Richardson, Barnes, and Davis. (See PRIMARY and SECONDARY SOURCES.)

The more obscure itineraries may be found in the "Sacramento Union" of June 11, 12, 13, 15, 16, 17; July 17, 1857; January 10, 19, 20, and October 4, 1858; also in the U. S. House Executive Documents, Serial No. 1000; the Postmaster-General's Report of 1858; "New York Times" of June 30 and September 22, 1858; "Alta California" (San Francisco) of October 14, 15; November 6, 20, 23; December 7, 1858, and May 26, 1862; "San Francisco Bulletin" of July 21, 1859, and June 10, 1864; "New York Tribune" of December 5, 1865, and approximate dates.

The only monograph of the earlier American staging world (in New England and elsewhere) appears to be Alice Morse Earle's "Stage-Coach and Tavern Days," treating in a charming manner the history and life of the old Eastern systems—a reading that might be supplemented to advantage by Stanley M. Arthur's article "On the Old Boston Post Road," which appeared in "Scribner's Magazine" in November, 1908. There is also Edward Everett's "Stage-Coach Travel Forty Years Ago," reprinted from the New York "Ledger" in the "San Francisco Bulletin," July 22, 1859.

Old English coaching is well represented by Violet A. Wilson's "Coaching Era," and W. Outram Tristram's "Coaching Days and Coaching Ways." Technical works on the same subject are listed with the SECONDARY SOURCES below, opposite the names of Adams, Rogers, Straus, and Underhill. See also Stratton.

Sources named in the following lists include only the most important ones used in the process of compilation, PRIMARY SOURCES being those belonging to the period treated, and SECONDARY (of far less importance here, with the exception of the books mentioned above) being those of later or earlier publication.

PRIMARY SOURCES

Periodicals:

Almanacs and directories of Western cities and States, files 1854–67.

Hayes, Benjamin. Files of scraps from newspapers of 50's and 60's. (Bancroft Library, University of California.)

Hutchings' "California Magazine," miscellaneous files 1856–60.

"Los Angeles News," miscellaneous files 1856, 1858, 1863.

Marysville "California Express," September 10,

1852; "Herald," September 11, 1850; September 11, 1852; "National Democrat," August 27, 1851.

Nevada (California) "Journal," April 19, 1851.

"New York Times," files July–November, 1857; "Tribune," files 1865–66.

"Sacramento Democrat," September 28, 1853; "Democratic State Journal," August 28, 1852; "Placer Times," March 30, 1850; "Placer Times and Transcript," September 24, 1851; "Transcript," July 3, December 25, 1850; "Union," files 1853–69.

Salt Lake "Union Vedette," files 1866.

San Francisco "Alta California," files 1849–60; "Bulletin," files 1855–69; "California Courier," July 1, August 20, November 6, 30, December 25, 1850; "Herald," files 1852–69; "Pacific News," files 1849–50; "Picayune," files 1850–51; "Whig," files 1853–54.

Shasta (California) "Courier," files 1852–55.

Wilmington (California) "Journal," files 1865–67.

Books and Pamphlets:

BARNES, DEMAS. "From the Atlantic to the Pacific Overland" (New York, 1866).

BARTLETT, J. R. "Personal Narrative of Explorations" (New York, 1854).

BATES, D. B. "Four Years on the Pacific Coast" (Boston, 1858).

BORTHWICK, J. D. "Three Years in California" (London, 1857).

BOWLES, SAMUEL. "Across the Continent" (Springfield, Massachusetts, 1866); "Our New West" (Hartford, Connecticut, 1869); "The Switzerland of America" (Springfield, 1869).

BRACE, C. L. "The New West" (New York, 1869).

BROWNE, J. ROSS. "Crusoe's Island" (New York, 1864); "Adventures in the Apache Country" (New York, 1871).

DAVIS, W. W. H. "El Gringo" (New York, 1857).

DELAND, ALONZO. "Life on the Plains" (New York, 1857).

GREELEY, HORACE. "An Overland Journey" (New York, 1860).

HAYES, BENJAMIN. "Emigrant Notes" (a Bancroft manuscript).

HEAP, GWINN HARRIS. "Central Route to the Pacific" (Philadelphia, 1854).

HELPER, H. R. "The Land of Gold" (New York, 1855).

HUNTLEY, SIR HENRY VERE. "California" (London, 1856).

McCUE, JIM S. "Twenty Years in California" (San Francisco, 186–).

MARRYAT, FRANK. "Mountains and Molehills" (London, 1855).

RICHARDSON, ALBERT D. "Beyond the Mississippi" (Hartford, 1867).

SIMPSON, JAMES. "Report of Explorations Across the Great Basin of Utah" (Washington, 1876).

STIMPSON, A. L. "History of the Express Companies" (New York, 1858).

United States documents, to include all reports of the Postmaster-General from 1848 to 1870 (Washington, 1849–71).

WADSWORTH, W. "Wagon Road Guide from St. Joseph to California" (San Francisco, 1858).

Letters:

CRANE, J. M. From Utah to editors of "Placerville Democrat" ("Sacramento Union," July 13, 1857).

DUNBAR, E. E. From Las Cruces, N. M., to C. D. Poston in California ("Alta California," March 13, 1858).

FARWELL, J. M. From various overland stations to editors of "Alta California" (November 6, 20, December 7, 1858).

GWIN, Senator W. M. From Washington, D. C., to President Buchanan ("Sacramento Union," October 12, 1858).

HAWORTH, JAMES, president of California Stage Company, from Marysville, California, to F. S. Stevens, vice-president, Washington, D. C., during January, 1860. (Scrap-book of Mrs. F. S. Stevens, Swansea, Massachusetts.)

MOWRY, Lieutenant SYLVESTER. From New York

to the "New York Times" (July 10, 1857).

RICHARDSON, A. G., superintendent of California Stage Company, from Sacramento to F. S. Stevens, Swansea, Massachusetts; files 1859–61. (Scrapbook of Mrs. Stevens.)

SECONDARY SOURCES

ADAMS, W. B. "English Pleasure Carriages" (London, 1837).

BANCROFT, H. H. "Chroniclers of the Builders," seven vols. (San Francisco, 1891–92.)

BARNARD, HELEN M. "The Chorpenning Claim" (a Bancroft pamphlet, 187–).

BARROWS, H. D. "A Two-thousand Mile Ride by Stage" (annual publication of the Historical Society of Southern California. Los Angeles, 1896).

BARRY, T. A., and B. A. PATTEN. "Men and Memories of San Francisco in the Spring of 1850" (San Francisco, 1873).

BEADLE, J. H. "Life in Utah" (Philadelphia, 1873).

BELL, Major HORACE. "Reminiscences of a Ranger" (Los Angeles, 1881).

BRACE, CHARLES LORING. "The New West" (New York, 1869).

BURNETT, PETER H. "Recollections and Opinions of an Old Pioneer" (New York, 1880).

CHORPENNING, GEORGE. "Statement . . . of Claim" (pamphlet, 1889).

CLELAND, ROBERT GLASS. "A History of California" (New York, 1926); and "Transportation in California Before the Railroad" (annual publication of the Historical Society of Southern California, 1918).

CLEMENS, SAMUEL L. (MARK TWAIN). "Roughing It" (Chicago, 1872).

CODMAN, JOHN. "The Round Trip" (New York, 1879).

DICKENSON, LUELLA. "Reminiscenses" (San Francisco, 1904).

DOW, T. K. "A Tour in America" (Melbourne, Australia, 1884).

DOWNIE, WILLIAM. "Hunting for Gold" (San Francisco, 1893).

DUNBAR, SEYMOUR. "A History of Travel in America," four vols. (Indianapolis, 1915).

DUNN, J. D. "Massacres of the Mountains" (New York, 1886).

EARLE, ALICE MORSE. "Stage-Coach and Tavern Days" (New York, 1915).

EGAN, WILLIAM M. "Pioneers in the West, 1846 to 1878" (Richmond, Utah, 1917).

EVERETT, EDWARD. "Stage-Coach Travel Forty Years Ago" ("San Francisco Bulletin," June 22, 1859, quoting the New York "Ledger").

FARISH, THOMAS EDWIN. "The Gold Hunters of California" (Chicago, 1904); and "History of Arizona" (Phoenix, 1915).

FLETCHER, ROBERT HOWE. "A Trip in the Mountains" ("San Francisco Argonaut," September 9, 1889).

GREENBIE, SYDNEY and MARJORY. "Gold of Ophir" (New York, 1925).

HAFEN, LE ROY R. "The Overland Mail, 1849–1869" (Cleveland, 1926).

HASKINS, C. W. "The Argonauts of California" (New York, 1890).

INMAN, HENRY. "Great Salt Lake Trail" (Topeka, 1910), and "The Old Santa Fé Trail" (Topeka, 1910).

KNOWER, DAVID. "The Adventures of a Forty-niner" (Albany, 1894).

LITTLE, F. "Mail Service Across the Plains" (Salt Lake City, 1884; MS.).

McCLINTOCK, J. H. "Arizona, the Youngest State" (Chicago, 1916).

McILHANY, EDWARD. "Recollections of a Forty-niner" (Kansas City, Missouri, 1908).

MAJORS, ALEXANDER. "Seventy Years on the Frontier" (New York, 1893).

MAJORS, GREENE. "The Overland Pony Express" (Piedmont, California, 1926).

MARK TWAIN. (See CLEMENS).

MILLS, W. W. "Forty Years at El Paso, 1858–1898" (El Paso, 1901).

PAXON, FREDERICK LOGAN. "The Last American Frontier" (New York, 1911).

ROGERS, FAIRMAN. "A Manual of Coaching" (Philadelphia, 1901).

ROOT, FRANK A., and W. E. CONNELLEY. "The Overland Stage to California" (Topeka, 1901).

ROYCE, JOSIAH. "American Commonwealth: California" (Boston, 1886).

RUSLING, JAMES F. "Across America" (New York, 1875).

"San Francisco Argonaut" of September 1889, and of September 1890.

San José (California) "Pioneer," files 1877–81.

SHAY, JOHN C. "Twenty Years in the Backwoods of California" (Boston, 1923).

STEVENS, Mrs. F. S. Correspondence, 1927, 1928.

STEVENSON, ROBERT LOUIS. "The Silverado Squatters" (Boston, 1884).

STRAHORN, CARRIE ADELL. "Fifteen Thousand Miles by Stage" (New York, 1911).

STRATTON, EZRA M. "The World on Wheels" (New York, 1878).

STRAUS, RALPH. "Carriages and Coaches" (London, 1912).

TAYLOR, B. F. "Between the Gates" (Chicago, 1876).

TINKHAM, G. H. "A History of Stockton" (San Francisco, 1880).

TRISTRAM, W. OUTRAM. "Coaching Days and Coaching Ways" (London, 1914).

TRUMAN, BEN C. "Up with the Driver" ("Chicago Tribune," January 10, 1892).

TUCKER, J. C. "A Wild Ride" ("San Francisco Argonaut," September, 1890).

UNDERHILL, FRANCIS T. "Driving for Pleasure" (New York, 1897).

VIEUX, BARRON. "Sacramento in 1849" ("Sacramento Union," May 8, 1855).

VILLARD, HENRY. "Memoirs" (Boston and New York, 1904).

WALSH, RICHARD J. "The Making of Buffalo Bill" (Indianapolis, 1928).

WALLING, A. G. "History of Southern Oregon" (Portland, 1884).

WHETHAM, J. W. B. "Western Wanderings" (London, 1874).

WHITE, CHESTER LEE. "The Pacific Railroad" (Berkeley, California, 1927, MS.).

WILSON, VIOLET A. "The Coaching Era" (New York, 1922).

APPENDIX

The Pioneer stage route over the Sierra Nevada Mountains as traversed by the stage wagon of J. B. Crandall in 1857 followed roughly along the line of "The Sherman Day Survey" which had been made in compliance with California's State Wagon Road Act of April 28, 1855.[1] This line, coursing the South Fork of the American River, touched Slippery Ford, Johnson's Pass, Lake Bigler (Tahoe) Valley, Luther's Pass, Hope Valley, and Carson Cañon, the distance as surveyed to the State boundary—Cary's Mill—being 59½ miles. Allowing five miles for the necessary detours, the distance traversed by Crandall's stage to the same point was called 64½ miles. Later, after some road work had been done, "The Sacramento Union" (January 5, 1858) published the distances between points of the route as follows :

	Miles			Miles
Placerville	—	Smith's Ranch		4
Sportsman Hall	12	Old's "		4
Junction House	3	Cary's "		1
Brockless Bridge	2	Mott's "		½
Sugar Loaf	11	Corser's "		1
Cottage Rock	4	Daggett's "		½
Strawberry Valley	5	Vansycle's Hotel		½
Slippery Ford	2	Genoa		2½
Summit	6			—
Smith & Douglas	2			
Grass Lake	3	Total distance from Placerville,		
Hope Valley	3	California, to Genoa, Utah		
Cary's Mill (in Carson Valley)	6	(later Nevada)		73

[1] An act later found "unconstitutional."

391

APPENDIX B

THE SAN ANTONIO & SAN DIEGO MAIL ROUTE [1]

Miles between points.		Miles from San Antonio	Miles between points.		Miles from San Antonio
—	SAN ANTONIO	—	11	Hackleberry Pond	402
7	Leon River	7	32	Limpia Creek	434
18	Castroville	25	19	Fort Davis	453
25	D'Hanis (Saco River)	50	10	Point of Rock	463
9	Ranchero Creek	59	9	Baree Springs	472
4	Sabinal Creek	63	13	Deadman's Hole	485
5	Comanche Creek	68	33	Van Horn's Wells	518
8	Rio Frio	76	20	Eagle Springs	538
6	Uvalde	82	31	First Camp on Rio Grande	569
9	Nueces	91	35	Birchville	604
11	Turkey Creek	102	25	San Elizario	629
15	Elm Creek	117	6	Socorro	635
7	Fort Clarke (Moras River)	124	3	Ysleta	638
7	Piedra Pinto	131	14	EL PASO	652
9	Maveric Creek	140	22	Cottonwood	674
12	San Felipe	152	22	Fort Fillmore	696
10	First Crossing San Pedro River	162	6	La Mesilla	702
3	Painted Caves	165	65	Cook's Springs	767
16	Calf Springs	181	18	Rio Mimbres	785
2	Willow Springs	183	17	Ojo de la Vaca	802
16	Fort Hudson, second crossing San Pedro River	199	10	Ojo de Ynez	812
20	Head of San Pedro River	219	34	Peloncillo	846
44	Howard Springs	263	18	Rio Saur (San Domingo)	864
30	Live Oak Creek	293	23	Apache Springs	887
3	Fort Lancaster	296	9	Dos Cabesas	896
4	Pecos River Crossing	300	26	Dragoon	922
6	Pecos Springs	306	18	Mouth of Quercos Cañon	940
32	Point of leaving Pecos River	338	6	San Pedro Crossing	946
16	Aroyo Escondido	354	20	Cienga	966
9	Escondido Springs	363	13	Cienga Creek	979
19	Comanche Springs	382	20	Mission San Xavier	999
9	Leone Hole	391	8	TUSCON	1007
			30	Charcos de los Pimos	1037
			5	Picacho Mountain	1042

[1] Compiled from the Texas Almanac of 1859.

Miles between points.		Miles from San Antonio	Miles between points.		Miles from San Antonio
35	First Camp on Gila River	1077	7	Pilot Knob	1303
29	Maricopa Wells	1106	13	Cook's Wells	1316
40	Tezotal (across El Jornada)	1146	22	Alamo Mocho	1338
10	Ten-mile Camp	1156	21	Indian Wells	1359
8	Murderer's Grave	1164	32	Carrizo Creek	1391
15	Oatman Flat (Gila Crossing)	1179	18	Vallecito	1409
25	Second Crossing of Gila River	1204	17	Lassator's Ranch	1426
32	Peterman's Station	1236	7	Julian's	1433
20	Antelope Peak	1256	7	Williams's	1440
24	Little Corral	1280	14	Ames's	1454
16	FORT YUMA	1296	16	Mission San Diego	1470
			5	SAN DIEGO	1475

APPENDIX C

TABLE OF DISTANCES BETWEEN THE STATIONS OF

THE GREAT (SOUTHERN) OVERLAND MAIL [1]

FIRST DIVISION

	Miles		Miles
San Francisco	—	Whitmore's Ferry	17
Clark's	12	Cross Creek	12
San Mateo	9	Visalia	12
Redwood City	9	Packwood	12
Mountain View	12	Tule River	14
San José	11	Fountain Springs	14
Seventeen Mile House	17	Mountain House	12
Gilroy	13	Posey Creek	15
Pacheco Pass	18	Gordon's Ferry	10
St. Louis Ranch	17	Kern River Slough	12
Lone Willow	18	Sink of the Tejon	14
Temple's Ranch	13	Fort Tejon	15
Firebaugh's Ferry	15	Reed's	8
Fresno City	19	French John's	14
Elk Horn Springs	22	Widow Smith's	24

[1] Compiled from the Postmaster-General's Report of 1858; "The Alta California" (San Francisco) of November 19, and "The New York Times" of November 14, 1858.

	Miles		*Miles*
King's	10	Los Angeles	12
Hart's	12		
San Fernando Mission	8	Division Total	464
Cahuengo	12		

SECOND DIVISION

Los Angeles	—	Vallecito	18
The Monte	13	Palm Springs	9
San José	12	Carrizo Creek	9
Chino Ranch	12	Indian Wells	32
Temescal	20	Alamo Mocho	24
Laguna Grande	10	Cook's Wells	22
Temecula	21	Pilot Knob	18
Tejungo (or Awanga)	14	Fort Yuma	10
Oak Grove	12		
Warner's Ranch	10	Division total	282
San Felipe	16		

THIRD DIVISION

Fort Yuma	—	Gila Ranch	17
Swiveler's Ranch	20	Maricopa Wells	40
Fillibuster Camp	18	Sacaton	22
Peterman's	19	Picacho del Tucson	37
Griswell's	12	Pointer Mountain	22
Flapjack Ranch	15	Tucson	18
Oatman Flat	20		
Murderer's Grave	20	Division total	280

FOURTH DIVISION

Tucson	—	Mimbres River	16
Seneca (Cienga?) Springs	35	Cook's Springs	18
San Pedro River	24	Picacho	52
Dragoon Springs	23	Fort Fillmore	14
Apache Pass	40	Cottonwood	25
Stein's Peak	35	Franklin (El Paso)	22
Soldier's Farewell	42		
Ojo de la Vaca	14	Division total	360

FIFTH DIVISION

El Paso	—	Cornudas de los Alamos	36
Waco Tanks	30	Pinery	56

	Miles		*Miles*
Delaware Springs	24	Grape Creek	22
Pope's Camp (Pecos River)	40	Fort Chadbourne	30
Emigrant Crossing	65		
Horse Head Crossing	55	Division total	428
Head of Concho River	70		

SIXTH DIVISION

Fort Chadbourne	—	Earhart's	16
Valley Creek	12	Conolly's	16
Mountain Pass	16	Davidson's	24
Phantom Hill	30	Gainesville	17
Smith's	12	Diamond's	15
Clear Fork (of the Brazos)	26	Sherman	15
Franz's	13	Colbert's Ferry (Red River)	13½
Fort Belknap	22		
Murphy's	16	Division total	282½
Jackboro's	19		

SEVENTH DIVISION

Colbert's Ferry (Red River)	—	Riddell's	17
Fisher's	13	Holloway's	17
Wails' (or Nale's)	14	Trayon's	17
Boggy Depot	17	Walker's	16
Gary's	17	Fort Smith	15
Waddell's	15		
Blackburn's	17	Division total	282½
Pusley's	17		

EIGHTH DIVISION

Fort Smith	—	Smith's	11
Woosley's	16	Bolivar	11½
Brodie's	12	Yost's	16
Park's	20	Quincy	16
Fayetteville	14	Bailey's	10
Fitzgerald's	12	Warsaw	11
Callaghan's	22	Burns'	15
Harburn's	19	Mulholland's	20
Conch's	16	Shackelford's	13
Smith's	15	Tipton	7
Ashmore's	20		
Springfield	13	Division total	318½
Evan's	9		

NINTH DIVISION

By railroad from Tipton to St. Louis .... 160 **miles**
Total distance from San Francisco to St. Louis, 2,485 miles.

APPENDIX D

TABLE OF DISTANCES BETWEEN THE STATIONS OF

THE GREAT (CENTRAL) OVERLAND MAIL AND STAGE LINES [1]

Miles Between Stations		Miles From Atchison	Miles Between Stations		Miles From Atchison
—	ATCHISON	Kan. .... —	15	Gilman's	Neb. 333
10	Lancaster	" 10	17	Cottonwood Springs "	 350
14	Kennekuk	" 24	15	Cold Springs "	 365
12	Kickapoo	" 36	14	Frémont Springs "	 379
13	Log Chain	" 49	11	Elkhorn "	 390
11	Seneca	" 60	14	Alkali Lake "	 404
12	Laramie Creek	" 72	12	Sand Hill "	 416
12	Guittard's	" 84	11	Diamond Springs "	 427
10	Oketo	" 94	15	South Platte "	 442
11	Otoe	Neb. 105	14	Julesberg Col.	 456
11	Pawnee	" 116	12	Antelope "	 468
14	Grayson's	" 130	13	Spring Hill "	 481
10	Big Sandy	" 140	13	Dennison's "	 494
14	Thompson's	" 154	12	Valley Station "	 506
14	Kiowa	" 168	15	Kelly's "	 521
12	Little Blue	" 180	12	Beaver Creek "	 533
13	Liberty Farm	" 193	20	Bijou "	 553
15	Lone Tree	" 208	16	Frémont's Orchard "	 569
10	32-mile Creek	" 218	11	Eagle's Nest "	 580
12	Summit	" 230	12	Latham "	 592
13	Hook's	" 243	15	Big Bend "	 607
10	Fort Kearney	" 253	17	Fort Lupton "	 624
10	Platte Station	" 263	15	Pierson's "	 639
11	Craig	" 274	14	DENVER "	 653
15	Plumb Creek	" 289	11	Child's "	 664
15	Willow Island	" 304	12	Boon's "	 676
14	Midway	" 318	18	Little Thompson "	 694

[1] Taken, with the kind permission of George A. Root and the courtesy of William E. Connelley, from Root and Connelley's "Overland Stage to California" (Topeka, Kansas: 1901).

Miles Between Stations			Miles From Atchison	Miles Between Stations			Miles From Atchison
8	Big Thompson	Col.	 702	11	Kimball's	"	1226
16	Laporte	"	 718	15	Mountain Dell	Utah	1241
10	Boner	"	 728	14	SALT LAKE CITY	"	1255
12	Cherokee	"	 740	9	Travellers' Rest	"	1264
12	Virginia Dale	"	 752	11	Rockwell's	"	1275
15	Willow Springs	Wyo.	 767	9	Joe Dug Out	"	1284
15	Big Laramie	"	 782	10	Fort Crittenden	"	1294
14	Little Laramie	"	 796	10	No name	"	1304
17	Cooper Creek	"	 813	10	Rush Valley	"	1314
11	Rock Creek	"	 824	11	Point Lookout	"	1325
17	Medicine Bow	"	 841	15	Simpson's Springs	"	1340
8	Elk Mountain	"	 849	8	River Bed	"	1348
14	Pass Creek	"	 863	10	Dug Way	"	1358
16	North Platte	"	 889	12	Black Rock	"	1370
14	Sage Creek	"	 903	11	Fish Springs	"	1381
10	Pine Grove	"	 913	10	Boyd's	"	1391
9	Bridger's Pass	"	 922	10	Willow Springs	"	1401
10	Sulphur Springs	"	 932	15	Cañon Station	"	1416
11	Waskie	"	 943	12	Deep Creek	"	1428
13	Duck Lake	"	 956	8	Prairie Gate	Nev.	1436
12	Dug Springs	"	 968	18	Antelope Springs	"	1454
15	No name	"	 983	13	Spring Valley	"	1467
12	Big Pond	"	 995	12	Schnell Creek	"	1479
14	Black Buttes	"	1009	12	Gold Cañon	"	1491
14	Rock Point	"	1023	15	Butte	"	1506
14	Salt Wells	"	1037	11	Mountain Springs	"	1517
14	Rock Springs	"	1051	9	Ruby Valley	"	1526
15	Green River	"	1066	12	Jacob's Wells	"	1538
14	Lone Tree	"	1080	12	Diamond Springs	"	1550
18	Ham's Fork	"	1098	12	Sulphur Springs	"	1562
12	Church Buttes	"	1110	13	Robert's Creek	"	1575
8	Millersville	"	1118	13	Camp Station	"	1588
13	Fort Bridger	"	1131	15	Dry Creek	"	1603
12	Muddy	"	1143	10	Cape Horn	"	1613
10	Quaking Asp Springs	"	1153	11	Simpson's Park	"	1624
10	Bear River	"	1163	15	Reese River	"	1639
10	Needle Rock	Utah	1173	12	Mount Airey	"	1651
10	Echo Cañon	"	1183	14	Castle Rock	"	1665
10	Hanging Rock	"	1193	12	Edward's Creek	"	1677
10	Weber	"	1203	11	Cold Springs	"	1688
12	Daniel's	"	1215	16	Middle Gate	"	1698

Miles Between Stations		Miles From Atchison	Miles Between Stations		Miles From Atchison
15	Fair View	" 1713	14	Genoa	" 1832
13	Mountain Well	" 1726	11	Friday's	Nev. 1843
15	Still Water	Nev. 1741	10	Yank's	Cal. 1853
14	Old River	" 1755	12	Strawberry	" 1865
14	Bisby's	" 1769	12	Webster's	" 1877
11	Nevada City	" 1780	12	Moss	" 1889
12	Desert Wells	" 1792	12	Sportsman Hall	" 1901
13	Dayton	" 1805	12	PLACERVILLE	" 1913
13	Carson City	" 1818			

GLOSSARY

Among stagemen, the word *stage* was commonly used in the sense of vehicle; it was any coach, wagon, or sleigh used for staging purposes. The term *stage wagon* or *mud wagon* (see pp.147–148) was distinct in its meaning from "stage-coach" or "coach," the latter being improperly called "wagon." The term *thorough-brace*, like "stage," was also used in the sense of vehicle; it was any conveyance whose body was suspended by rockers upon leather straps or thorough-braces.

Stage, in its original and stricter meaning, was a section of road between relays of animals, and was, in the case of first-class lines, about ten miles in extent. A *drive,* which comprised generally a number of stages, was a section of road between the points or stations where drivers, and usually their vehicles, were changed—it was seldom more than 60 miles long. A *division* was a line unit of arbitrary length, comprising generally a number of "drives," in charge of an agent or a superintendent or both, and ranged in length between 150 and 450 miles. In some cases there were divisions made up of divisions, as, for example, on the Butterfield line, where the eastern division implied all divisions east, and the western all divisions west, of a named central point, these great divisions having each a superintendent in charge, the lesser division heads being subordinate.

Stations were either "home stations" or "swing stations."

Home stations, where often the station-master dwelt with his family, were also the dwellings of stage drivers and other line employees off duty, and were prepared to supply meals for passengers, and fresh teams for the stages as they arrived. *Swing stations,* where only several stock-tenders lived, were for purposes of relay only. A *stand* was, broadly, any station or relay post. But the word was used more often in connection with such points of the line as could scarcely be dignified by the name of "station." In the early days of the San Antonio & San Diego Mail, and of the overland routes of Chorpenning and Hockaday, most of the relay posts, for example, were "stands," boasting, as they did, only tents or mere brushwood inclosures for the shelter of stock-tenders.

A *conductor* was a traveling official (unknown to the later "shotgun messenger" days), who, usually as a ranking driver, was responsible for the welfare of passengers and cargo of a vehicle, or a train of vehicles, over long stretches of certain overland lines. In the earliest days of the San Antonio & San Diego Mail, one conductor conducted the whole "outfit" from one end of the line to the other, taking shifts with drivers where the length of the drive demanded. Later he traveled half-way in charge of a coach, or a train of coaches, and was then relieved by another conductor, who carried on. There were conductors also on the lines of Hockaday and Chorpenning, and even, in some instances over certain sections, on both the Great Southern and Central "overlands."

The word *coachman* does not exist properly in the West-American stage-coach world. It was used only by a few passengers, usually foreigners, who didn't know any better. A stage driver, though he could tolerate the affectionate or poetic expressions of "Jehu," "whip," "whipster," "Charlie," "knight of the ribbons," etc., could accept the appellation of coachman no more than he could accept a "tip."

He *might* accept a cigar, a box of cigars, a new hat (or, if over-tempted, even a ten dollar bill!), but the typical tip was as far beneath him as any coachman. Similarly the word *coaching* was not in his professional vocabulary—the operation was one of *staging*.

The spans of a six-horse team were named, in order from front to rear, *leaders, swings,* and *wheelers,* or *lead team, swing team,* and *wheel team*. The four-horse complement had only the leaders and wheelers. *Off* meant *right; near, left*. One spoke of the *off leader,* for example, meaning the right-hand leader as seen from the driver's box; or *near swing horse,* meaning the left-hand animal of the swing team as seen from the driver's box.

The whip, so much overused and unconsciously abused by pen drivers, was a very different thing to the driver of a stage. For practical purposes, the instrument was held with the butt resting in the palm of the right hand and the stock held in the region of, and parallel to, the lines —it was never held up, like a coachman's whip, but down where it could serve promptly its greatest function. That was to signal the wheelers, to encourage either one of them into the collar at the proper time, and often when there were no seconds to lose. The cracking of the whip, however, was a legitimate practice in the case of animals trained to answer that signal; and it offered the whipster an opportunity to show a skill which his passengers would be apt to appreciate. But the horse that actually required whipping did not belong on the line. Nor was it the practice to start the team with a crack of the whip, nor even to apply it shortly after starting; for to do so would ruin a team of any spirit—expecting the whip the animals could not be made to stand. The instrument itself comprised a hickory stock, five feet in length, and an eleven or twelve foot lash of buckskin—*it was not long enough to reach the leaders of a six-horse team.* Still, there were a few—a very few—drivers who used the "six-horse whip"; but the lash of it, being twenty-two feet long, was too unwieldy for the average driver, and generally unnecessary for the purposes of driving. Drivers were, of course, very proud of their whips—the symbols of their order. Off duty they hung them carefully; they never set them down, never wound the thong around the stock, nor lent the instrument to their most trusted friends. Silver ferules, or rings, set at intervals along the hickory, were common, but sometimes frowned upon, apt as they were to hinder the elasticity of the stock.

INDEX

Abbot-Downing stage-coach, 23-26, 36, 148, 158, 188, 190, 250, 311, 354, 358, 359

Abbot, Downing & Co., 13, 22-26, 358

Accidents, stage-coach, 32

Ackley & Maurison, 81

Ackley & Maurison's stage line, 22

Adams & Company, 246

Albuquerque, 171, 186

Alvord, E. S., 168, 259

Anderson, James, 276

Andrews, John, 98

Angel's Camp hold-up, 67

Apache Indians, 151-156

Apache Pass Station, 154

Atchinson, 241, 309

Atchinson and Salt Lake stage line, 241; see also Central Overland California & Pike's Peak Express, and Central "Overland Stage" line

Austin, 323

Balch, Ebenezer, 207

Bandits,
  Bill White, 59, 61
  "Dutch Kate," 70
  English Bob, 62
  Frank Williams, 307
  Jim Smith, 59, 61
  Joaquin Murietta, 56
  Juan Fernandez, 62, 65
  Monte Jack, 62
  Ned Connor, 61, 66

Smith Sutton, 61
Tom Bell, 57-67

Banditti, Tom Bell's organization, 59-61

Barlow, S. L. M., 349

Barlow & Sanderson, 352

Barnes, Demas, 315-332

Barrows, H. D., 157

Bartlett Springs, 84

Bascomb, Lieut., 151, 154

Bates, Mrs. D. B., 31

Baxter & Company, 44

Bell, Tom, bandit, 57-67

Bené, Jules, 260

Berford & Co.'s express and stage line, 21

Birch, James E., 8, 10, 11, 12, 13, 17, 18, 38, 39, 45, 46, 47, 75, 79, 91-96, 101, 111; death of, 98

Birchville, 117

Blair, Ned, 200

Blanchard, W. L., 268

Boots Hill cemetery, 259

Bordman, T. S., 279

Borthwick, J. D., 29

Bowles, Samuel, 280, 306, 314, 332

Brace, C. L., 332

Brady, Louis, 213

Brady & Company, 179, 213

Brakes, use of, 370-372

Bridger's Pass, 318

British coaching systems, 34

British mail coach, 357-359

Brockless Crossing, 84

Bromly, James, 274

403